A
DRINKING
LIFE

A
DRINKING
LIFE

A MEMOIR

Pete Hamill

Little, Brown and Company

BOSTON   NEW YORK   TORONTO   LONDON

First Edition

Permissions to quote from copyrighted material appear on page 266.

Library of Congress Cataloging-in-Publication Data
Hamill, Pete
    A drinking life : a memoir / Pete Hamill. — 1st ed.
        p.   cm.
    ISBN 0-316-34108-8
    1. Hamill, Pete, 1935–   — Biography.   2. Authors, American — 20th
century — Biography.   3. Irish Americans — Social life and customs.
4. Journalists — United States — Biography.   5. Alcoholics — United
States — Biography.   6. Drinking customs — United States.   I. Title.
PS3558.A423Z463   1994
818'.5409 — dc20
[B]   93-28629

                    10   9   8   7   6

                                    HC

Published simultaneously in Canada
by Little, Brown & Company (Canada) Limited

Printed in United States of America

For my sister, Kathleen

MOST of the people who helped make this book possible are mentioned in its pages; they also made my life possible. But in addition I would like to thank Bill Phillips of Little, Brown for his endless patience and superb editing; Lynn Nesbit, for helping make the book happen; my daughters, Adriene and Deirdre, for allowing me to invade their privacy; my secretary, Meri McCall, for holding off the demands of the world with good humor; and, of course, my wife, Fukiko Aoki, for reasons that are beyond listing.

— P.H.

INTRODUCTION

THIS IS A BOOK about my time in the drinking life. It tells the story of the way one human being became aware of alcohol, embraced it, struggled with it, was hurt by it, and finally left it behind. The tale has no hero.

The culture of drink endures because it offers so many rewards: confidence for the shy, clarity for the uncertain, solace to the wounded and lonely, and above all, the elusive promises of friendship and love. From almost the beginning of awareness, drinking was a part of my life; there is no way that I could tell the story of the drinking without telling the story of the life. Much of that story was wonderful. In the snug darkness of saloons, I learned much about being human and about mastering a craft. I had, as they say, a million laughs. But those grand times also caused great moral, physical, or psychological damage to myself and others. Some of that harm was probably permanent. There is little to be done now but take responsibility. No man's past can be changed; it's a fact, like red hair.

More than twenty years have gone by since I stopped drinking. My father died at eighty; my mother lives on. I'm happily married to a wonderful woman and work even harder than I did when young. But life doesn't get easier when you walk away from the culture of drink; you simply live it with greater lucidity.

I started writing this book when some of my friends from the drinking life began to die. They were decent, talented, generous, and humane. But as they approached the end, physically ruined by decades of drinking, I remembered more of their good times than they did. In a way, this book is about them too.

New York City
December 1993

I

DURING THE WAR

Little enough I know of your struggle,
although you come to me more and more,
free of that heavy body armour
you tried to dissolve with alcohol,
a pale face staring in dream light
like a fish's belly
           upward to life.

        — John Montague,
           "Stele for a Northern Republican"

1

AT THE BEGINNING of my remembering, I am four years old and we are living on the top floor of a brick building on a leafy street in Brooklyn, a half block from Prospect Park. Before that place and that age, there is nothing. But in those remembered rooms are my mother, my younger brother Tommy, and me. It is the winter of 1939. I remember the kitchen, with its intricately patterned blue-and-red linoleum floors, and windows that opened into a garden where an elm tree rose higher than the house. The kitchen light was beautiful: suffused with a lemony green in summer, dazzling when winter snow garnished the limbs of the elm tree. I remember the smell of pine when my mother mopped the floors. I remember her whistling when she was happy, which was most of the time. I remember how tall she seemed then, and how shiny her brown hair was after she had washed it in the sink. And I remember my brother Tommy, two years younger than I, small and curly-haired and gentle. I don't remember my father.

He was there, all right. Billy Hamill wasn't one of those Depression fathers who went for a loaf of bread at the corner store and never came back. He moved through those rooms. He slept in one of the beds. He shaved in the bathroom and bathed in the tub. But for me, he wasn't there. In some ways, it made no difference. On summer afternoons, I would sit outside the house, in a patch of earth near the curb, playing with a small red fire engine, telling myself stories.

Perhaps my father was in those stories. But he didn't take me on those long green walks through the endless meadows and dark woods of Prospect Park. My mother did. Nor did he take me to see my first movie. My mother did that too. It was *The Wizard of Oz*, and the streets were dark when we came out of the Sanders Theater and she took my hand and we skipped home together, singing *Off to see the Wizard, the wonderful Wizard of Oz, because because because because Because*. I have no memory of him bouncing me on his knee or looking at the drawings I made each day with my box of eight Crayolas. I remember sitting on the stoop, watching

Japanese beetles gnaw the ivy that covered the face of the brownstone next door and my mother teaching me a little song to be crooned to another insect neighbor: *Ladybug, Ladybug, fly away home. Your house is on fire, your child is alone. . . .* But I learned no songs from my father. Not then.

In large part, my father's absence was caused by his work. He left home before I awoke and returned after I was asleep. So in some ways, I didn't really miss him. He wasn't in my presence often enough to be physically missed. Besides, I was too busy learning the names of the world and even having small adventures. Once I went to Prospect Park with Billy Kelly, the boy who lived on the first floor. He was my first friend, a year older than I was, and his family owned 471 Fourteenth Street, the house where we lived on the top floor. Our adventure began in a very simple way. Billy said, Let's go to the park. And I said, Okay, let's go to the park.

And yet I knew that what we were doing was full of risk. Most important of all, it was the first time I'd ever gone anywhere without my mother and this act could lead to punishment. She might get cross. She might spank me. I went anyway, trusting Billy Kelly, certain we would be back before my mother noticed I was gone. I crossed the wide avenue called Prospect Park West, following the vastly more experienced Billy, watching for the trolley cars and the few big boxy black automobiles that moved through the streets in those days. We plunged into the park and wandered through that green world whose trees loomed high above us. Soon we were lost. We crossed streams, gazed at lakes, threw stones into the woods, but never could find the familiar playground and low stone wall beyond which lay home. I was filled with panic. I might never see my mother again or my brother Tommy or the kitchen at 471. We could end up in jail or someplace called the Orphanage, where they put kids without parents.

We were still in the park at dusk, when my mother found us. Her eyes were wide and angry, probably frantic. She did nothing to Billy Kelly; that was not her right. But she spanked me.

I've been looking *everywhere* for you, Peter, she said sharply. You had me worried *sick*.

I cried all the way home, full of remorse, and shocked too, because I had never before seen my mother angry, certainly not at me. And then we were at the house, going up the stoop in silence and into the vestibule and up the stairs to the top floor. Then, suddenly, quietly, she hugged me. And fed me. And put me to bed. The day had been the most turbulent of my short life; but from beginning to end, my father played no part in it at all.

In the summer of 1940, my mother started taking Tommy and me to visit my father where he worked.

You should be very proud of your daddy, my mother said. He only finished the eighth grade and he is working as a clerk. The reason is his beautiful handwriting.

She didn't explain what a clerk was, but she did show me his handwriting on some sheets of ruled paper. I was just learning to print the alphabet on the same kind of paper, and the shape and steadiness of my father's handwriting did seem very beautiful. He was working at the main office of a Brooklyn grocery chain called Thomas Roulston & Sons and brought home nineteen dollars a week. The Roulston company was housed in a redbrick factory building near the Gowanus Canal, more than a mile from where we lived. My mother would pack a lunch for him and put Tommy in a stroller and off we would go, first crossing along the parkside, then marching block after block, down the great slope. From Ninth Street, I could see all the way to the harbor, where there were ships on the water as small as toys. I loved arriving down near the canal, where the Smith and Ninth Street station of the Independent subway line rose high above us on a concrete trestle. On some days, a drawbridge would groan and squeal, rising slowly to allow some tough squat tugboat to plow through the canal's oily waters to the harbor. There was a mountain of coal on one of the banks and a machine for unloading it off barges and another for putting it on thin-wheeled trucks with odd sloped fronts like the points of steam irons. I'd wait beside the bridge with Tommy while my mother took her plump brown paper bag up to my father's office. He never once came down to the street to say hello to us.

But I do remember him sitting in the kitchen one bright Sunday afternoon in May. Suddenly among us there was a fat blond baby in a tiny crib. A white cake lay on the table and my father was there, bigger than he'd ever seemed before. He was celebrating his own birthday and the birth of my sister, Kathleen.

Through the door that afternoon came Uncle Tommy, gruff, friendly, my father's brother, and his wife, Aunt Louie, followed by another brother named Uncle David, tall and lean and grave, and his wife, Aunt Nellie, who was chubby and large and laughed a lot. Behind them came other men, great huge men with sour smells clinging to their jackets and enormous feet encased in shiny leather. They all wore hats and smoked cigarettes and laughed very loudly and drank beer from tall glasses and giant brown bottles. After a while, one of them began to sing, a sad mournful song. When he was finished my father rose and started singing too. His song was funny. His eyes danced, he smiled, he gestured with his hands to emphasize a point, used his eyebrows for other points, and when he was finished they all cheered. The baby cried. My mother picked her up and went into the other room while my father filled his glass with beer, took a long drink and started into another song. For a long time, I sat on the floor near the window, watching this magic show.

2

IN THE FALL, I started kindergarten at PS 107, down on the corner. We played with blocks. We learned songs. We made paintings and cut-outs. Then it was winter. Great piles of snow filled the schoolyard for weeks and once on a class trip to the park I took a great mound of pure fresh-fallen snow in my mittens and began to eat it. I didn't know exactly why; the snow was just so clean and white that I wanted it inside me. But the other kids laughed. I was mortified by their laughter and wanted to run home, but the teacher said, It's all right, young man; if you want to eat snow, there's no rule against it.

My mother had friends on the street: Mrs. Hogan directly across the street, Mrs. Fox, Mrs. Cottingham, who lived near the corner across from the schoolyard. Now I had another friend: a beautiful girl named Roberta Perrin, who had dark hair and lustrous eyes and inspired in me some vague desire; her mother and mine were also friends. Roberta was in my class at kindergarten, and I liked being with her more than with my friend Billy Kelly, who was now in first grade. After school, I found my way to her areaway, which was always dark under great thick-trunked trees, and we played together. When I ate snow, she didn't laugh. There was a grocery store on the corner, run by Syrians, but my mother didn't shop there; she went to a Roulston's branch a block away, loyal, as always, to my father. Except for those long journeys down to the canal, the world was a very small place.

Just before Christmas that year, we woke to the sight of a tree with shiny colored bulbs and tinfoil decorations my mother made from the lining of cigarette packs. We had no blinking lights. There must have

been Christmas trees in our house before then, but I don't remember them. This was a special Christmas. I was given some toys, some candy canes, and a copy of *A Child's Garden of Verses*, by Robert Louis Stevenson. My mother read from it to me, over and over, showing me the letters and the words. Then it was summer again and we were taking our long journeys to the Gowanus Canal. Now Tommy was walking and Kathleen was in the carriage. My father still didn't come down to see us. One sunny day I asked why.

Oh, he'd love to come down, my mother said. But the stairs are too hard on him. He works all the way up there.

She pointed to the top floor of the six-story building.

Then why can't we go up and see him? I said.

Because they don't let kids in the building.

Why?

Well, there must be two hundred men working for Roulston's. If every man had three kids visit him at lunchtime, there'd be a riot in there.

She laughed, told us she wouldn't be long, and hurried into the building. I stared at the top floor, wishing my father would come to a window and wave at us. He never did.

In the fall of 1941, I entered the first grade at Holy Name of Jesus elementary school. My mother took me by the hand to the schoolyard and then went away. A white brick school building rose like a fortress before me, three severe stories off the ground. At a right angle to the school was the back of the church, its bricks painted the color of dried blood. Those walls and the wire fence blocked any possibility of escape, and I was swiftly trapped in a wild sea of strangers. There were seventy-two boys in 1A that year, and a tall nun with creamy skin struggled to tame us. This was no easy task. On the first day, one frantic lank-haired boy danced on top of a desk. Others shouted encouragement, squealed in delight, whined, thumped each other, and slammed the desktops. I sat there, wishing I was home, alone on the stoop watching Japanese beetles or staring out the window into the safe stillness of the green garden. Somehow I got through the day. I was assigned a desk. I started writing letters of the alphabet in a composition book with a black-and-white cover. The boys calmed down. Sister asserted her command.

A few weeks later, there was great excitement everywhere: car horns blowing, bells ringing in a hundred church steeples, sirens screaming from firehouses. The Dodgers had won the pennant! I wasn't sure what a pennant was, but it must have been a glorious thing to win, for we were given the day off from school and my mother took us on another long walk, to Grand Army Plaza. There we stood, among thousands of joyful

strangers, on the new steps of the gleaming white Brooklyn Public Library and watched the Dodgers parade in triumph up Flatbush Avenue on their way to Ebbets Field. The ball players were huge tanned men with great smiles and enormous arms, sitting on the backs of convertibles, waving at us all. That night my father came home with two large bottles of beer and sitting alone in the kitchen (because my mother knew nothing of baseball) he celebrated the great triumph while listening to reports on the radio.

Just remember one thing, McGee, he said to me, in a grave voice. The Dodgers are the greatest thing on earth.

In school the next day, I told some of the other boys that the Dodgers were the greatest thing on earth. They all agreed with this, of course, and so did Sister, who had us pray for the Dodgers as they moved on to the World Series against the Yankees. But then a Dodger catcher named Mickey Owen dropped a third strike, the Yankees won the World Series, and we all had to wonder if God was a Yankee fan. That couldn't be possible. God was a Catholic, wasn't he? And since the Dodgers were from Brooklyn, they must be Catholics too. Or so we thought.

As young as we were, we were learning fast that year about the presence of calamity in the world. The Dodgers were only the beginning. On December 7, the Japanese attacked Pearl Harbor. I have no clear memory of that Sunday or of Franklin Roosevelt's famous speech on the following day. But I can still see my mother in the kitchen a few weeks later, cooking dinner and listening to music on the radio. Then an announcer interrupted to describe through veils of static the fall of Manila. He was telling us about explosions and gunfire and Japanese soldiers coming up the street when the broadcast abruptly stopped and another announcer, free of static, spoke softly about the war and this defeat. Suddenly, my mother was crying.

Those poor boys, she said, and hugged me. Those poor boys. . . .

She then explained to me that we were at war. I started to cry too. Not because of the war or the poor boys in Manila, wherever that was (the name itself provoked only an image of vanilla ice cream). I cried because I had never seen my mother cry before and I didn't like it. I could cry. Tommy could cry. Baby Kathleen could cry. We were kids. My mother wasn't supposed to cry.

That night, when my father came home, he bumped into something and woke me up. I got up and tiptoed toward the kitchen, stopping in the dark of the next room. His face looked different, his jaw hanging loose, his slick black hair disheveled and wild. He sat down hard at the

table and knocked over a glass of beer. My mother was no longer crying but she was what we kids called "cross."

Ach, Billy, she said, and started wiping up the beer with a dishcloth.

Don't say a thing! he said sharply. Just get me my bloody dinner.

She turned away and I thought she was going to cry again. Then he saw me.

What the hell are *you* looking at? he said to me. Get into bed.

Billy —

I saw how upset she was and I started to whimper.

You've got damn all to cry about! he said.

Leave him *alone*! she said. You're upsetting him! And you'll wake the baby.

He ignored her and pointed a finger at me.

Into bed! he said. Make it snappy!

I retreated into the darkness of the second room from the kitchen, and lay facedown on a bed beside Tommy and listened. I heard his voice, blurting and hard; then her voice; then his again; then silence. I heard water running and dishes clacking sharply against each other. Then silence again. I started back toward the kitchen. My mother was at the sink. My father's arm was straight out across the table, his head resting on it, a fork still in his hand, though his plate was gone. He was asleep.

3

IN SCHOOL that first year, I learned two things that began to give me some sense of self. One, I was Irish. At school, kids kept asking: What are you? I thought I was American, but in those days in Brooklyn, when you were asked what you were, you answered with a nationality other than your own. Since my parents were from Ireland, I was from a group called "Irish." There were other Irish in 1A, a lot of them, along with Italians and Germans and Poles. But because my name wasn't *obviously* Irish, like Kelly or Murphy or O'Connor, they kept on asking me. My mother had to explain it all to me.

She started with a book. For months, she had been buying an encyclopedia called the *Wonderland of Knowledge*, known to us simply as the

Blue Books. Every week there was a coupon in the *New York Post*; for the coupon and a dime the newspaper sent us a volume. We would soon have them all, and they truly were wonderful. My mother found the right volume and turned to some maps and showed me where Ireland was: a tiny spot off the coast of a huge multicolored mass called Europe. Then she tried to explain what it meant to be Irish.

I can't remember her exact words. But she had a strong sense of history and injustice, so I'm sure she told me that day (as she told me in so many ways in the years to come) that Ireland had been an independent country for more than a thousand years and then, about eight hundred years ago, the British had come with swords, horses, and treachery to take it for themselves. They destroyed the language of the Irish and made them speak English. They tried to destroy their religion too, particularly during the reign of the wicked Queen Elizabeth. But the Irish kept fighting, kept resisting, almost always losing, but struggling on, until in 1916, they rose in rebellion on Easter Sunday and drove the English out. Or at least drove them out of twenty-six of the nation's thirty-two counties. The way she told it, the story was thrilling.

What happened to the other counties? I asked.

They're still occupied by the British, she said. They kept six of them: the counties where *our* people are from. My parents, Daddy's parents. And there'll be no peace until they're free. Someday they'll finish the job they started in 1916.

She told me that 1916 was also the year her father died. His name was Peter Devlin and he was a seaman. He fell off a ship in a dry dock in Brooklyn and was crushed. So my mother, who was a little girl in 1916, went back to Ireland with her mother and her brother, Maurice. They lived there until 1929, when her mother died and she decided it was time to come back to America.

Those two dates always make me sad, she said, 1916 and 1929.

The room seemed to fill with sorrow as she tried, so carefully, to explain herself to me. Her mother and father were dead and she had come alone across that great expanse of blue on the map to live here in Brooklyn. I was happy she was here; who else could be my mother? But I felt sorry that she had no mother or father of her own. That was unfair. She had nobody except us. Even her brother, Uncle Maurice, was in Ireland, far across the ocean.

And where did you live in Ireland?

In Belfast, she said. Right here, see that dot?

She paused and her voice grew soft.

We lived on Madrid Street, she said. It was named after a city in Spain.

She showed me Madrid on the map, and I thought it was a wonderful thing to live on a street with a name like Madrid instead of a mere number, like ours. But she was unhappy as she told me about Belfast (on that day, and many others). The city was divided between Catholics like us and Protestants, who were a different kind of Christian. And though she knew some decent Protestants, in Belfast most of them were bigots. She was a little girl in Belfast when the Troubles started and the bigots formed into the Murder Gang and came into the Catholic neighborhoods to burn down houses and kill Catholics. The British army was there too, with armored cars and machine guns, terrible men who hated the Irish and hated the Catholics. All of that was in Belfast, where the bigots ran everything.

This was at once scary and thrilling, and I made her tell me the stories many times. I couldn't imagine myself on streets where gunmen shot rifles from the shadows, where soldiers came rolling upon you in iron trucks, where you could be beaten or killed because you were a Catholic. But my mother seemed to me to be an amazing woman, someone who had seen things when she was a little girl that were more terrible than any movie. And here she was. Smiling. Whistling when she was happy. Telling me that she loved America for its freedom.

Freedom is a lot more important than money, she said. Remember that. Here we're free. And you must never ever be a bigot.

What *is* a bigot anyway?

A bigot is a hater, she said. A bigot hates Catholics. A bigot hates Jews. A bigot hates colored people. It's no sin to be poor, she said. It *is* a sin to be a bigot. Don't ever be one of them.

No, Mommy, I said. I won't be one of them.

And imagined a bigot with yellow eyes and a tall black hat and fangs for teeth. I said I would watch for them and if a bigot came to our street I would tell her and she could use the telephone in Mr. Kelly's kitchen and call the police.

After I learned that I was Irish, I came to understand another big thing: my father was a cripple. That's what the kids in 1A said. He is not, I said (not knowing what they meant, thinking perhaps that it was something like being a bigot). He is too, they said. He's a cripple.

Yes, my mother said, he *is* a cripple. He lost his left leg in 1927. He was a soccer player. That's a game they play in Ireland, with a round ball that they kick. They also play it out in Bay Ridge, another part of Brooklyn, and in a lot of other countries. She took a tobacco-colored photograph from a drawer and showed it to me. My father was sitting with other members of a team, all of them wearing short pants.

See, she said. He has two legs in this picture. But he only has one leg now.

She explained how he had to wear a wooden leg. He had a stump above the knee that fit into the wooden leg and straps that went over his shoulders to hold it in place. That was why the stairs at Roulston's were hard on him. I hadn't known that. She told me more, about how he was playing soccer one Sunday, here in America, in Brooklyn, in Bay Ridge, and he was kicked very hard and his leg was broken and they left him on the sidelines while they waited for an ambulance. It was a long wait. When the ambulance finally came, it took him away to Kings County Hospital, but there were no doctors to treat him and by the next day gangrene had set in and they had to cut off his leg.

How did they do that?

With a saw, she said. They had to do it to save his life.

You mean he almost died?

That's what they said.

So that's what they meant in 1A when they said my father was a cripple. He only had one leg. Why did they yell that at me? It wasn't *his* fault. The ambulance was late. There were no doctors at the hospital. And besides, he had a *wooden* leg. You could look at him and not know the difference. And being a cripple wasn't as bad as being a bigot. It wasn't bad at all.

That's the way I reasoned to myself, but I'm sure I said nothing to the kids at school. After a while, boredom must have set in, and they stopped tormenting me about my father's leg. But I looked more closely at my father after that and asked to see again the picture of him in his football uniform with two legs sticking out of his shorts. Sometimes when it was dark, the word "gangrene" would seep through me, and I would see my father in a hospital bed, turning green. His skin was green and rotting and his eyes were green and his hands were green and there was a man at the door with a saw.

4

THAT WINTER, after the war started in the Pacific, we moved out of 471, leaving behind the elm tree, Roberta Perrin, and the ivied walls next door. The Kellys had six children of their own, and after Kathleen was born there were simply too many kids for one three-story house. Mrs. Kelly wanted the rooms for a nice mild bachelor. Without warning, we packed everything into cardboard boxes and moved to the first floor right at 435 Thirteenth Street. The colors of the world instantly changed.

The new house was only one block away but it butted up against the dirty redbrick bulk of the old Ansonia Clock Factory, built in 1879 and for a while the largest industrial building in New York. The dark blue shadow of the Factory (as everyone called it) fell upon the stoop and across the backyard. Nothing grew in that bald, forlorn yard; it was made of tightly packed orange clay that cleaved as neatly as ice cream when you drove a shovel into it. To get to the backyard, we could climb out the kitchen window, or go down into a damp cellar and up a flight of slippery stone stairs. Usually we went out the window. Once, I planted watermelon seeds in the orange clay and was astonished when a tiny green plant shot up a few days later. The plant didn't last; everything withered in the hostile clay and permanent darkness of that yard. It looked beautiful only when packed with fresh snow.

There were some advantages, of course. The rooms were larger and wider. More important, the apartment was on the first floor and my father did not have to haul his wooden leg up flights of stairs one step at a time. And the rent was twenty-six dollars a month, including steam heat.

Within days, I knew that life would now be different, and the principal reason was small, glossy-backed, and dark brown: the cockroach. I saw them moving along the hot water pipes, scurrying in corners of the kitchen, darting around the tin breadbox, rising from the drain in the bathtub, hiding in nests under the edge of the linoleum. They were everywhere. At night, I was afraid to sleep, certain that one of them would enter my ears and begin gnawing at my brain. We hit them with newspapers, stomped them, threw shoes at them. We learned what millions of New Yorkers learned: cockroaches were invincible.

Within months, we were settled. I convinced my mother that I could make my way to Holy Name without her beside me (fearful, as were all the others, of being called a momma's boy). But the first few times I walked past our old house at 471 Fourteenth Street, looking up as I passed *our* stoop, walking under the familiar leafy canopy of *our* trees, seeing Mrs. Hogan or Mrs. Fox or Mrs. Cottingham, seeing Roberta Perrin with new friends, hurrying through that place that was once the center of my existence, the essence of my dailiness, then reaching the corner and turning right under the marquee of the Sanders, I was filled with a chaotic sadness. I couldn't name what I felt. But for the first time, I sensed that there was such a thing as the past.

So I changed my route, using Fifteenth Street, where great boxy trolley cars rattled on steel tracks in two directions and the neighborhood's only black man worked as a super in a large apartment house on the corner. There were no trees here either, but that street had one virtue: it did not make me sad.

In the roachy new house on Thirteenth Street, there were some compensations. I discovered that a boy from my class lived on the top floor. His name was Ronnie Zellins. He was my first friend on the new street. I did homework with him and went to the park with him and his mother, who seemed to me to be the most beautiful woman in the world. Best of all, Ronnie Zellins introduced me to comic books. He had a collection but he couldn't read them yet, so he just followed the pictures. I could read them from the very beginning, explaining to him what was in the balloons and how the words helped make the pictures more exciting. When it was cold, we sat in the vestibule just inside the door, reading book after book and then reading them again. Other kids had collections too and would come to the door and shout: Wanna trade? And then we would go through an elaborate process, the most refined bargain being a decision to trade two ten-cent comics without covers for one copy of *World's Finest*, which was thicker than the others and cost fifteen cents.

In the spring and summer, we were out on the stoop, which had only three deep slablike steps (unlike the narrower steps of the high stoop on Fourteenth Street). We played card games. We fiddled with some kind of punchboard that you pushed with a wooden match to find tiny printed messages on compacted paper. We went roller skating. The girls skipped rope or played potsy, and sometimes we joined them. Other times, Ronnie and I and my brother Tommy wandered down the street to look at the Alley, a wide noisy cobblestoned warren of ancient trucks and escaping steam and iron-barred windows. The Alley ran from Thirteenth Street to Twelfth Street, splitting the Factory into two unequal sections, and in the years of the war, it seemed always jammed with men at work. I would stand at the Thirteenth Street end, sometimes with Ronnie

Zellins, sometimes alone, and stare into the sweaty turbulence. My mother told me to stay out of the Alley because I might get hurt, and I knew that disobedience was a sin. But after many months, I found the courage to dash through to the other side. When I confessed this to a priest in the confessional box at Holy Name, I was sure I heard him laugh.

Now too I started to see more of my father. After we moved, he left Roulston's and took a job with the Arma Corporation in a place called Bush Terminal. The leg, his age, and his family combined to keep him out of the war, but he was doing war work anyway. He started working nights, earning the unbelievable salary of eighty dollars a week, four times what he made as a clerk. But because he was there through the night, my mother couldn't bring him lunch anymore; she packed it into a black metal lunchbox that contained a thermos for tea or soup. I loved staring into the thermos, where glass seemed laid upon glass, layer upon fluid layer, in an impossibly perfect form.

My father slept during the days, so we had to be quiet in the afternoons. I didn't mind. He was helping the war effort. More important, he was there. I could see him, feel his rough beard, stare at the wooden leg. He never stripped his trousers from the leg; it stood in a corner beside the bed, with the tops of his trousers stuffed into the socket. Most days, he would rise late in the afternoon, pull on the leg, shave and dress, eat quickly, listening to the radio, smoke some Camels, drink a few cups of tea with milk and sugar, and then go out to the stoop, where some other men would pick him up in a car. He seemed to have two faces then: one long, the other round. He wore the long face when he woke up with his hair all black and spiky and wild. Then after he came out of the bathroom, his hair was tightly combed to his skull and his face was suddenly round. He shaved with a small heavy razor and used a bristle brush and a mug. Sometimes after he left for work I would use the brush to foam up the soapy block in the mug and cover my face with lather and try to scare my brother Tommy. He always laughed.

On Sundays, after I came home from the nine o'clock Mass at Holy Name, my father was usually in the bathtub. He was a man of routine. Bathed and shaved, he would go into a bedroom and return all dressed up. We had no washing machine, and the first launderettes didn't open until after the war. So while my mother washed his work clothes by hand, or prepared his breakfast, he would look at the sports pages of the *Daily News*. He ate breakfast and talked to my mother. Sometimes there would be a pale blue one-page onionskin letter from Ireland, slipped into the mailbox on the second delivery on Saturday afternoon, after he'd gone off to Arma, held for my father's inspection on Sunday morning. The letter was usually from his twin brother, Frank, and my mother would read part of it aloud, and he'd look at it carefully when she was through reading. They were always happy to hear from Belfast and always a bit anxious. After all, the Germans had bombed the Belfast shipyards; they might come back and bomb civilians, particularly on the Falls Road, where the Catholics lived. Whenever a letter arrived on a weekday, my mother's face was a tight mask until she'd opened the envelope. On Sundays, she wrote letters back to Ireland; for all the beauty of his handwriting, I never saw my father write a letter.

After that late Sunday breakfast, after the talk, after the reading of the Irish letter, my father would go out, down the dark linoleum-covered hallway, into the street. He'd turn left outside the areaway, and walk up the block, saying hello to people. Sometimes I'd watch him from the stoop. He'd step hard on the good right leg and swing the wooden left leg behind him, and I thought that being a cripple wasn't such a terrible thing; he walked in his own special way, and that made him different from the other men. Along the way, most of the Sunday people smiled at him. He was off to Mass. Or so he said.

And then one Sunday when I was almost eight, he said to me, Come on, McGee. I walked with him up to the corner and for the first time entered the tight, dark, amber-colored, wool-smelling world of a saloon. This one was called Gallagher's.

In I went behind him, to stand among the stools and the gigantic men, overwhelmed at first by the sour smell of dried beer, then inhaling tobacco smells, the toilet smell, the smell of men. The place had been a speakeasy during Prohibition, and the men still entered through the back door. There was a front entrance too, opening into a large dim room with booths and tables; it was supposed to be a restaurant, but the kitchen was dusty and dark and nobody was ever there, except a few quiet women, who could not get service in the barroom proper. In that room, the men were jammed together at a high three-sided bar, talking, smoking, singing, laughing, and drinking. They drank beer. They drank whiskey. There was no television then, so they made their own entertainments.

Hey, Billy, give us a song! someone yelled. And then he started.

Mister Patrick McGinty,
An Irishman of note,
He fell into a fortune
And bought himself a goat.

A goat's milk, said Paddy,
Of that I'll have me fill,
But when he got the nanny home
He found it was a bill . . . .

Laughter and cheers and off he went, verse after verse, even one about Hitler, added to help the war effort. Then everyone in the bar joined him for the song's final lines:

And we'll leave the rest to Providence —
And Paddy McGinty's Goat!

They cheered and hooted and asked for another, and my father raised his glass to his lips, beaming, delighted with himself, took a long drink, and gave them what they wanted. From where I was huddled against the wall, he was the star of the place, ignoring the stools that the other men used, standing almost defiantly with one hand on the lip of the bar for balance, his face all curves, clearly the center of attention. Even the portrait of Franklin Delano Roosevelt, hanging in the dim light above the cash register, seemed to approve.

This is where men go, I thought; this is what men do. When he was finished, they bought him drinks and then someone else began to sing and then Bing Crosby was singing on the jukebox. One of my father's friends slipped me a nickel, another gave me a dime, and Dick the Bartender, a mysterious shiny-faced fat man in a starched collar, passed me some saltine crackers in cellophane and a ginger ale with a cherry in it. Strangers rubbed my blond head. They told me I was getting bigger. And then my father said, Go on now, go along home.

5

I WAS ALWAYS GLAD to leave Gallagher's. I loved seeing my father in his special place, but I hated the sour smells of the bar and the cigarette smoke. Besides, the coins in my hands seemed to be burning. I had discovered money and what you could do with it. Darting out the side door of Gallagher's, a fortune in my hand, I would go down three steps and hurry across the street into Foppiano's candy store. The glass cases and boxes on the counter held amazing treasures: hard caramels, Houton's (small chocolate bars that were sweeter and cheaper than the products of Mr. Hershey), gummy Mexican sombreros, chocolate-dipped twists of nougat, strips of paper with small dots of candy stuck to them, Black Crows and Dots, Clark bars and Sky Bars, Kits and Jelly Royals, Mary Janes and Winter Greens. I would buy what I wanted, and then go down the block, looking for my brother Tommy so we could share the sweet treasures.

But after the first great rush of chocolate days, when I was gorged on this junk (my body suddenly light and my blood tingling), I began to spend my fortune on more substantial treasures: comic books. Comics I could own, instead of borrowing from Ronnie Zellins. Comics I could read over and over again. Comics I could trade with others. These were the first great wartime comic books, thick plump sixty-four-page extravaganzas, all in color, for a dime: *Superman*, *Captain Marvel* and *Batman*, the *Human Torch* and the *Sub-Mariner*. The heroes were all masked or caped and far more powerful than any seven- or eight-year-old could ever hope to be.

More important, many of their secret powers came from laboratory accidents or the ingestion of secret formulas. There was the Blue Beetle, with a scaly chain mail costume, a thin black mask, and strength that came from the amazing vitamin ZX. In *Police Comics*, there was Plastic Man, the only superhero with a sense of humor, able to shrink or elongate or compact himself into any shape, thanks to his own secret formula. More baroque, muscular, and explosive was the great Captain America. Cap' (as he was called) was really a mild fellow named Steve Rogers who before the war was just another skinny 4F, like the guy in the Charles Atlas ads on the back covers. Then he too drank a secret serum. Within seconds, he was transformed into a pile of muscles. The scientist who invented the serum was then killed by Nazi agents, the formula lost forever. No longer 4F, Rogers went into the army, designed his Captain America costume, and teamed up with Bucky Barnes, a teenager who was allowed to hang around the army post. For most of the war, these two were in steady pursuit of a ferocious Nazi saboteur named the Red Skull.

I was very worried about the Red Skull, who was always blowing up factories like the one where my father worked nights. One evening, I told my father to be careful when he went to work because the Red Skull might be around, lurking somewhere in the dark.

Who? he said. The red who?

The Red Skull.

What the hell are you talking about? he said.

I showed him a copy of *Captain America*. He laughed out loud.

You idjit! he said. That's a goddamned comic book!

I know, Daddy, but —

It's not *real*, he said. It's a *lie*.

I never showed him another comic book. Somehow, I knew that he was right: they were all lies. If we had all these caped people on our side, if we had all those secret serums and magic formulas, the war could be ended in about twenty minutes. But they were lies as irresistible as candy or ice cream. They certainly couldn't be the kinds of lies that were called sins in the catechism I was studying at Holy Name. To start with, they were patriotic lies. And *I* wasn't telling the lies. The stories of Cap' and Bucky were told by the men who wrote their names on the crowded, bursting first pages of each episode: Joe Simon and Jack Kirby. They must be the liars. Still, I couldn't understand how their lies could be bad, if they were on our side, just like Joe Louis and God.

Until I learned the names of Simon and Kirby, around 1943, I didn't know that men actually sat down to write and draw comics. That knowledge would change my life. But when we lived on Thirteenth Street, the *content* of the comics was driving deep into me. They filled me with secret and lurid narratives, a notion of the hero, a sense of the existence of evil. They showed me the uses of the mask, insisting that heroism was possible only when you fashioned an elaborate disguise. Most important was the lesson of the magic potion. The comics taught me, and millions of other kids, that even the weakest human being could take a drink and be magically transformed into someone smarter, bigger, braver. All you needed was the right drink.

Up at Holy Name, I went into the next grade, and the next, and the ones after that; listened to Miss Doheny and then Mrs. Hubbard and then Miss Smith, as they sketched the contours of the world and supplied the platitudes by which I must live: *Birds of a feather flock together* or *Show me your friends and I'll tell you what you are*. I learned to write compositions and do arithmetic. But at night, when my father was gone to work, I would lie in the dark and drive away the fear of roaches and Nazis by imagining myself mixing secret liquids in a glass beaker.

6

ONE DAY my mother took us to New York on the subway. We came out in a place of immense buildings, and she started walking in her rushed, breathless way, all the way to the river. Here were the great piers for the ships I saw in the harbor. There were soldiers with guns guarding the entrances to the piers and high fences with barbed wire at the top and warnings about staying out and not using cameras. We could see giant cranes loading crates into the ships, and shirtless men heaving on ropes, and men with hooks in their belts showing passes to the soldiers. Seagulls careened around the sky. Deep throaty horns blew as one ship eased away from a pier out into the flowing waters of the Hudson.

Did your father work here? I said.

I'm sure he did, my mother said. But he didn't do this kind of work. He was an engineer.

What is that?

He helped put in the refrigeration system, the air conditioning, she said. He worked for United Fruit, you see, and they had to keep the bananas from spoiling. That was his job. He was an officer.

Was he in the First World War?

No, she said. He was killed *during* the war, but he wasn't *in* the war.

Then up ahead we saw a lot of people staring at something we couldn't see. There were sailors in leggings holding rifles, Marines with .45s on their hips, New York policemen, all keeping people back; I paused, wanting to look at these men with guns, among the first I had seen in life. My mother walked faster, and then we saw what the crowd was looking at: the S.S. *Normandie*. The great French liner was lying on its side, wedged into the mud beneath the water, like a fat woman killed in a bathtub. The hull was scorched and tendrils of smoke still leaked from open portholes. I had never seen anything like it, even in the comics.

That's the *Normandie*, my mother said. She was a great passenger ship before the war. A French ship. Then they were converting her for troops and she went on fire.

Wow, I said.

Wow, Tommy said.

They think it was sabotage, she said.

Wow!

I don't know how long we stayed there but it must have been hours. All through the war, we would pester her to go back. Let's see the *Normandie*, Let's go back to Pier 88 and see the *Normandie*. And she took us there again and again, to gaze at the parched hull, more than a thousand feet long, its giant propellers high out of the water. In my memory, the ruined liner looks humiliated, like a drunk who has fallen down in public. But at the time, the *Normandie* represented something else to me: proof that not all the tales in the comics were lies. Maybe the Red Skull didn't do the job, but *somebody* did.

7

ONE SUNDAY afternoon on Thirteenth Street, I looked up from the stoop, where I was playing with Ronnie Zellins and some other kids, and saw my father coming down the street. There was another man with him, taller, holding my father's left elbow, while my father used his other hand to grip the picket fences of the areaways. I got up and hurried to him, certain he was hurt.

I looked up at him. His eyes were unfocused, his jaw slack.

Daddy, I said, are you all right?

He looked at me as if I were a stranger.

Zallright, the other man said. Just drunk as a skunk.

They went past me, and turned into 435 and my father wheeled, as if to fall. The other man grabbed him roughly and held him up. But all the kids laughed. One of the other kids was Brother Foppiano, the son of the owner of the candy store.

Hey, hey, your old man's drunk, he said, in a singsong teasing voice.

Shut up, I said.

Your old man's an Irish drunk! Your old man's an Irish drunk!

As my father and his friend disappeared into the hallway, I had my first fight. I had never hit anyone before and had never been hit. But I threw myself in a rage upon Brother Foppiano. He hit me and hurt me and hit me again. My face went numb. Blood spurted from my nose. And I turned in tears and ran inside, full of shame. Behind me, everyone was laughing. Even my friend, Ronnie Zellins.

My mother was out with Tommy and Kathleen, so I went into the bathroom and saw the blood on my hands and shirt, then watched it drip into the sink. I turned on the taps and the water made the blood thin and pale, forming a rosy whirlpool before vanishing down the drain. I held a cold washcloth to my nose. The inside of my mouth was slippery and sticky, and I lurched aside and threw up into the toilet bowl, feeling as if my insides were coming out through my mouth. The stench was disgusting. I looked at the water pipes and saw cockroaches moving in steady lines, their long hairy feelers out in front of them. I flushed the toilet and closed the door behind me.

My father was facedown on a bed, his wooden leg hanging off the bed in an awkward position. He smelled like vomit too.

For a long time after the fight with Brother Foppiano, I didn't play with the other kids, not even Ronnie Zellins. I had cried and run away from a fight, and that was a humiliation. So I went to school, I came home, I passed them on the stoop and retreated into homework, the *Wonderland of Knowledge*, and my comics. No book revealed the ingredients of any magic potion. I could not emerge from my room in mask and cape to avenge myself upon Brother Foppiano. I could not, like Billy Batson, the orphaned newsboy, say the word *Shazam!* and be transformed into Captain Marvel. My mother said nothing that I can remember, but she must have known that something awful had happened to me. Winter came. The yard filled with snow, and I would stand at the window and gaze at the blue shadows of the piled snow and the redbrick walls of the Factory and remember the light and the trees of the lost window on Fourteenth Street.

Around this time, I also started reading Big Little Books, squat thick bricks of text and pictures that were sold at the five-and-ten-cent stores. The text was on the left-hand page, the illustrations on the right. Their heroes were different from the great baroque four-color visions of Simon and Kirby, or from Captain Marvel pursuing the mad scientist Dr. Sivana. Here were Dick Tracy, Dan Dunn, Tailspin Tommy, Smilin' Jack, Don Winslow of the Navy, all neatly contained in square black-and-white panels. They were more mundane heroes, men without masks or capes or occult powers, but I liked reading the text and glancing at the pages to see if the drawings matched the images in my mind. My mother looked at them and explained that these were comics that first appeared in newspapers.

This is my favorite, she told me, pointing at a comic strip across the top of a page in the *Daily News*. It was called *Terry and the Pirates*. The

drawing was beautiful, full of realistic detail, oiled guns, perfect airplanes, skies or mountains brushed in with great rich blacks. But the
balloons were dense with dialogue that I didn't really understand. *Terry*
was definitely made for grown-ups. Still, I was thrilled that my mother
could also care for a comic strip. She didn't say, This is my favorite *lie*.
And because of her, I started looking at the newspaper comics.

One day I ran into Brother Foppiano again. He was nastier now, because
he had bloodied me and made me cry and run. *Your old man's an Irish
drunk, your old man . . .* I realized I was being watched by other kids,
including my former friend Ronnie Zellins, and I knew that this time I
couldn't run. So I piled into Brother, frantic, afraid, but determined not
to cry, not to "give up." He hit me and hit me, but I held on to him,
tripped him, fell upon him, hit him, then felt his hard wiry arms lock
around my neck. I struggled. I jerked. But I couldn't get free.

So I whispered the word: *Shazam.*

Nothing happened. Brother Foppiano tightened his grip and I tightened mine on him.

We might be locked in that violent embrace to this day if Ronnie
Zellins's beautiful mother hadn't come along and ordered us to stop.
I watched Brother walk away, his green striped shirt as dirty as mine.
There was a sneer on his face, but he didn't say anything; he didn't speak
badly about my father. I felt better for another reason: the humiliation of
public crying and loss was erased. Then Ronnie Zellins came over to me.

Want to go down the Alley? he said.

No.

What about comics? Want to go trading?

No, I said. I don't want to do anything with you.

One Sunday afternoon, a week after my second fight with Brother
Foppiano, my father ordered me out of Gallagher's. His face was loose
and bleary again, the way it had been the day I first saw him drunk. I
imagined him leaving the saloon, helped by one of the men, staggering
down the street to our house, and Brother Foppiano emerging from hiding to start his cruel chant. I asked him to come home. Maybe I whined.
Maybe I was annoying. I know I was holding on to his coat. He jerked
the coat out of my grip, looked down at me, and ordered me in a harsh
voice to go home to my mother. Hurt and angry, I ran outside.

But I didn't go home. I went directly to Foppiano's candy store. I was
desperate now, even willing to fight Brother again to be sure that he
wouldn't see my father drunk. I could punch him. I could tease him. Or
I could talk to him, argue with him, maybe even try to make friends with

him. I just didn't want him to see my father being helped down the block. But Brother wasn't around, not behind the counter, not in the back room. His father sat there, reading a newspaper and smoking a cigarette. And with a sense of relief, I looked at the comic book racks near the door. I had read most of the new comics and was not interested in the books about funny animals or high school girls. Then I found the very first issue of Master Comics. I began to read the story of Captain Marvel, Jr., and was lifted out of Brooklyn.

Hey, Mister Foppiano said, ya gonna read or ya gonna buy?

I handed him a dime and rushed home, clutching my copy of Master Comics. Back at 435, I read this issue over and over, watching a crippled boy named Freddy Freeman hobble on his crutches. Suddenly he said *his* magic word — "Captain Marvel," the name of his hero — and was transformed into a lithe, strong hero in a sleek blue gold-trimmed costume. After my fight with Brother, I knew that "Shazam" didn't work for me; it probably was just a lie. But maybe it could work for others. Maybe words, like potions, were also capable of magic. And I wished that my father had a secret word too. He would come home from Gallagher's and sit in the kitchen and whisper . . . *Captain Marvel.* A lightning bolt would split the sky and there he would be: two legs, young, whole, like the man in that old photograph, his eyes sharply focused. He would smile at me and reach over and hug me and off we would go together to play ball.

That never happened.

After two years in the first floor right, we moved again.

8

THE NEW FLAT was only a few blocks away, but it was another descent, into a harder, poorer world.

Seventh Avenue was a wide avenue with trolley cars of the 67 line moving in both directions. The steel wheels of those sleek green-and-silver "streamlined" cars ran on steel tracks, and we would hear their squealing clattering sounds through the night; some of us heard those trolleys for the rest of our lives. The power lines were hidden in steel poles that made a deep bonging sound when you hit them with bats or pipes; from the tops of these poles cables fed the lines that ran above the trolley tracks. Those poles and lines and the steel tracks gave the avenue the look of an artist's exercise in perspective, with diminishing lines flowing away into infinity, or its equal: Flatbush Avenue at one end of the avenue, Greenwood Cemetery at the other. In the mind of an eight-year-old, both were as far away as Madrid.

Our building was 378, a tenement rising four ominous stories above the street. It was in the middle of the block, between Eleventh and Twelfth Streets, with a butcher shop on one side of the doorway and a fruit and vegetable store called Teddy's to the right. That first day, it was a place in another country.

I stood on the sidewalk with my mother and Tommy and Kathleen, who was bundled in a red snowsuit in a stroller and bawling. My mother moved the stroller back and forth, shushing Kathleen, while I gazed around at this new piece of geography. There was a barbershop across the street, with a red, white, and blue pole turning slowly outside. On one side of the barbershop was a dry cleaner's, the windows opaque with steam, then a notions shop, a variety store, a fish store, and a diner. To the left, filling the corner of Eleventh Street, was Rattigan's Bar & Grill, dark inside, with men going and coming through the front door. Nobody used the side door.

Across the street, on a diagonal from Rattigan's, there was one glimmer of the familiar: the red, white, and blue sign of still another Roulston's store. But otherwise I felt like a stranger as we waited outside for the large men from Gallagher's to arrive in a truck with our furniture and our stuffed cardboard boxes. My mother said, You'll like it here. But I looked up and saw fire escapes climbing the brick face of the building, as if drawn with rulers, and a strange canopy hanging over the edge of the roof, and a flock of pigeons circling against the hard sky. I shivered in the cold, and my mother told me to wait in the hallway. But I was afraid to go through that door. I didn't think I would like it here at all. I wanted to go back to 471 Fourteenth Street, my real home.

Do they have roaches here? I said.

My mother laughed. I hope not, she said.

I don't want to live here if they have roaches, I said.

Well, she said without much hope, let's wait and see.

Then the truck arrived and my father eased out of the cab, smoking a cigarette, while the large men unloaded the furniture and started moving us into 378. Groups of nameless kids were gathering at the corners, watching us with a mixture of curiosity and hostility; some of them were my age, and all were wearing long pants while I still wore knickers and knee socks. Faces appeared at the windows of Rattigan's. Someone wiped a peephole in the steam of the dry cleaner's. Maybe they had come to see the cripple. Or maybe they had heard about the Irish drunk. Or a crippled Irish drunk. Or maybe they just wanted to look at the kid who still wore knickers.

When the truck arrived, my mother took us into the warmth of a candy store, two doors away, and I felt better. Nobody could watch us in here. The place was called Sanew's (we pronounced it Sen-you). Immediately inside the door, atop a glass-topped counter, nickel candies were arrayed on a stepped rack, like a sugary stoop. Beside it, a small change dish, advertising Dentyne gum, sat on top of a pebbled rubber mat, with the cash register next to it. There were racks of cigarettes on the wall behind the counter, including my father's beloved Camels. That was good. He could walk next door to get his cigarettes, even in the snow.

Most of the good things of Sanew's were on the right as you walked in, including a soda fountain with four swivel-topped stools. Behind the marble counter, spouts poured soda, seltzer, a variety of syrups in endless combinations (egg creams and lime rickeys and cherry Cokes), and below the counter were silver-covered hidden places filled with tubs of ice cream. That first day, Mrs. Sanew mixed soda for us kids and made tea for my mother, looking distracted in a way that would soon become familiar to all of us. Mrs. Sanew had gray-streaked black hair pulled into a tight bun, thick eyeglasses wedged on a longish nose, a pinched sour mouth. She always wore thick-heeled sensible shoes and a wine-colored wool sweater that buttoned in the front. The sweater had two pockets, and sometimes, when distracted, she would jingle coins in those pockets, her eyes seeing something that was a long way from Brooklyn. Behind that counter, seven days a week, from seven in the morning until ten at night, Mrs. Sanew made egg creams, or filled dishes with ice cream, or prepared tea, or poured coffee. She sold cigarettes, cigars, candies, and newspapers; she rang up purchases on the cash register; she made change. There was simply no time for joy or laughter. There also might have been some darker cause for her permanent air of distraction, some fierce Catholic denial of self, some permanent act of mortification or penance. In all the years we lived there, I never saw her eat or drink even one of the treats she made for others; it was as if that would be some sign of weakness, some surrender to illicit pleasures or desires she held in contempt. That first day, as she served my mother, her face was locked into a sad or angry mask.

There was one other ornament of Sanew's: a rack on the wall to the left of the door. The top row was filled with movie magazines or copies of *Collier's, Liberty, Life*. The next was thick with pulps, with their garish, disturbing covers. But the two bottom racks were full of comic books. Comics with titles I didn't know, covers I'd never seen, comics that could have been from another country. *Blue Bolt. Sheena, Queen of the Jungle. The Spirit*. They were completely different from the comics at Foppiano's and I must have stared at them with something like passion and desire, because I remember my mother saying to me: "Well, you'll be happy *here*."

Then we walked back to 378, entering through the street door for the first time. There were brass mailboxes on the left of the vestibule, white octagonal tiles on the floor, then a second door, filled with a panel of frosted glass, leading into the hallway. For a moment, I was scared; the hallway space was high, narrow, murky; the dark air was stained by strange odors, as if something was rotting. On the left a passageway led into the back of the hall, where I could see three battered garbage cans. On the right were the narrow stairs, with strips of ridged metal tacked to the lip of each step, to protect the linoleum from the assault of thousands of footsteps. My mother lifted Kathleen from the baby carriage and parked it against the wall on the left and started leading us up the stairs, into a deeper darkness. The rough plaster walls were shiny with paint, dark brown from the floor to the height of my mother's shoulder, then a paler ocher to the ceiling. I could smell meat cooking. I could hear radios: music on one floor, announcers talking on another. On the second landing, dogs barked from behind a door. On each landing there was a small bare yellowish light bulb, which heightened the feeling of deep rich earth-colored darkness.

We went up three flights, to the top floor right, where a door was open to the kitchen. This was where we were now going to live. I paused in the hall, unable to move. Maybe if I just stood there, they would change their minds and we would put everything in the truck and drive away, skipping 435 Thirteenth Street, going all the way back to Fourteenth Street. My father and some of the large men were standing there, drinking beer from quart bottles, laughing and smoking cigarettes, using saucers for ashtrays.

Don't stand there like an idjit, my father said. Come in.

The large men laughed.

Come on, my father said. Give us a hand.

So I went in and the large men shook my hand and said to my father, We shoulda brung some soda for the kid, Bill.

And my father said, We'll bring some back.

And one of the men said, Hell, he's big enough for a beer, ain't he, Bill?

My father smiled, and turned away, lifting silverware and glasses from a Campbell's soup box, discarding the newspapers that wrapped them, then laying them in the sink. It was as if I'd disappeared.

For a long time, the large men shifted furniture, grunting, sweating, while my mother asked them to move a chair here, a couch there. I wandered through the rooms of the railroad flat. There was a small bedroom off the kitchen, then a larger bedroom, then the living room, with two windows looking down at Seventh Avenue. The new building was only one story higher than the flat on Fourteenth Street, but after two long years on the ground floor at Thirteenth Street, the height here amazed me. I could see the roofs of trolley cars, the tops of the black steel poles that supplied their power, the bobbing hats and shoulders of passing strangers. Unlike Fourteenth Street, there were no trees to break a fall, no branches or tree trunks to supply direction to the eye or the illusion of safety. If I fell from this window, I would die. It was like coming to the edge of the cliff I saw in the advertising on the back of the comics, all about the Rosicrucians, whatever they were, and the secrets of life.

To the right of the living room, facing the avenue, there was a small room with a window that led to the fire escape. We called this the Little Room and it was unique: it had a door. From the Little Room's window, I could see across the avenue into the apartments of strangers, turrets and chimneys on the rooftops, and away off, the distant ridge of Prospect Park. I thought: This must be what it's like to be a giant.

In a rush of excitement, I ran back into the kitchen. This wasn't so bad, maybe. Up here in the top floor right, the world was bright again after the darkness of the hall. The kitchen windows looked down a long slope toward the harbor, and I could even see the concrete railway trestle where the subway went over the Gowanus Canal. That astonished me. I had been *under* that trestle many times, waiting for my mother when she brought my father his lunch; now, I was *above* the trestle, up here at the top of the long slope. From this back window, I could see the receding rectangles of a thousand rooftops and the skeletal shapes of ten thousand winter trees and the steeples of a hundred churches rising above the houses. There were ships moving in the distant harbor, sailing away to fight Hitler, and my mother came over and pointed out the Statue of Liberty, green and tiny, and the skyline of Manhattan, naming some of the buildings. But there was something missing.

Where's the backyard? I said.

Well, my mother said, that's a wee bit of a problem. There's no backyard.

I looked straight down from the window and saw fenced-off yards filled with the scrawny shapes of stunted trees and patches of blackened snow. But those yards belonged to the smaller houses on the side streets. The tenements on the avenue had no yards. This was hard to imagine: a house without a backyard. And I wished I still had the backyard on Fourteenth Street or even the bald shadowed clay of Thirteenth Street. After all, if there was no backyard, where would I play on summer afternoons?

Suddenly the moving job was finished and my father and the large men started to go out.

Will you bring me a soda, Daddy?

Sure, he said.

Hell, Billy, one of the large men said. He's gettin' pretty big, the kid. Whyn't you bring him over the bar?

Yeah, my father said, not meaning it.

But you gotta get him outta them knickers, another man said. Ya can't go drinkin' in knickers, kid.

Yeah, one of these days, my father said.

And they went out. My mother then turned to look at the boxes and bags, the mounds of clothes, the cluttered table, the dishes in the sink. She sighed.

Mommy, I want long pants, I said.

You'll have long pants soon enough, she said.

I hate knickers, I said.

We'll talk about it later, she said. Let's get moved in first.

And so we moved in. All that afternoon, we began to explore this new place high above everything. The kitchen was to become the center of almost everything we did; we ate there, talked there, listened to the radio there, did homework there. I can remember every inch of it, with the table of much-painted pine in the center under a ceiling light whose cord bobbed in the air. There were four chairs around the table, with a sugar bowl in the middle beside my father's ashtray (my mother didn't smoke or drink). Just inside the door was a shallow corner closet shaped like a triangle. It had no door, only a drape hanging from a rod. Sometimes on rainy days, when we kids played hide and seek, I would huddle in there under piles of clothes and sheets, burrowed into a cave, wishing that I'd never be discovered.

On that first day at 378, my father came home hours later, bleary with drink. My mother tried to get him to eat some sandwiches and soup. He couldn't do it. He tried to sing but the words stopped coming, choked in a phlegmy cough. Finally, he rose from the kitchen table. I was in the first room in a narrow bed that fit tightly against the wall. As he went by I said, Hello, Daddy. He didn't hear me. From the next room, I heard him removing his trousers, change jingling in the pockets, then the straps and the leg being slammed against the wall before he fell heavily into bed. Then there was silence from my mother in our brand-new kitchen. Except for her sad breathing.

9

WE LIVED to the rhythms of the war. Years later, we even marked time in a special way: Before the War, During the War, After the War. There were other wars, Korea and Vietnam, and American invasions of too many other places, but for people my age there was only one War. That war was in our comics, our movies, our dreams. The radio was filled with it. Every evening, my mother listened to Edward R. Murrow and Gabriel Heatter, and in school we followed the war on maps. There was North Africa. And Tobruk. And somewhere in all that yellow emptiness, El Alamein.

At Holy Name, I heard about the war from new teachers every year, each of them rolling down the maps and showing us the places that were in the newspapers and on the radio. There was much excitement when the Allies landed in Sicily because the parents of most of the Italian kids were from that island. They wanted the Americans to win. They had brothers in our army and some of the brothers died in those first battles. All of them said their parents were worried. I got an aunt there, said Vito Pinto. My grandmother is there, said Michael Tempesta. I got an uncle over there, said George Poli. The war went on and on.

I'd like to give that Hitler a boot in the ass, my father said one night.

Billy, my mother said. The children . . .

I would, he said. I mean it. Let him walk into Rattigan's and drop one on his chin.

That struck me as a wonderful idea. Hitler goose-stepping down Seventh Avenue, with Göring and Goebbels and Himmler behind him (for we knew each of their names), all of them marching into Rattigan's, and my father walking over and punching Hitler right in the mout'. Then my father's friends could mop up the rest of them, the way Captain America went after the Red Skull. That would be that. No more war.

But the war went on. We learned its common and proper nouns: bomb, rifle, pillbox, Guadalcanal and grenade, camouflage and convoy, submarine and torpedo, Salerno and Monte Cassino, Rommel and Montgomery, infantry and air force, destroyers, PT boats, cruisers and carriers, casualties and conning towers, depth charges and bomb bays, antiaircraft, bazookas and howitzers, wounded, ambulances, shrapnel and flak, generals, colonels, majors, lieutenants, sergeants, corporals, privates, along with admirals, commanders, captains and seamen, WACS and WAVES, 1A and 4F, Tojo and Mussolini, .45s and .88s, tanks and jeeps, occupation and refugee and resistance. And in comics and radio serials, in movies and schoolyards, we heard the words Secret Weapon. Hitler might have one; we had to get one.

In the windows of the neighborhood now you saw small flags bearing a star for each son who had gone to serve the country. Some flags had as many as four. And after the invasion of North Africa, some of the stars were gold, telling us that a son had died. There were more after Sicily and many more after Anzio.

Up on Eighth Avenue and Thirteenth Street, a sandlot football team called the Arrows erected a sign on the wall beside Foppiano's, listing the names of all the men who were away in the service. Even after we moved to Seventh Avenue, I passed it every day on my way to Holy Name. The lettering was small and neat, but before the war was over, the sign was completely filled and many of the young men were dead. The sign was there for years After the War, battered by weather, the names bleached by sun and washed by rain, then repainted, then washed away again, until the names were gone for good and nobody was left in the neighborhood who could remember the living or the dead.

Like other families, we experienced the war in small ways. In addition to the vocabulary of the war itself, I learned the word "shortage" and the phrase "black market." There was a shortage of sugar. There was a shortage of meat. Butter was rare and there were no more bananas because of the German submarines in the Caribbean. The Germans were sinking all of the ships that used to come to New York Before the War.

Ships like the ones your father worked on? I asked my mother one night.

Yes, she said. Exactly like the ones he worked on. He was all over South America, you know. He used to write letters to my mother from all those places. He was even at the Panama Canal when they were building it.

In the Blue Books, we found maps of the Caribbean and Central America and located the Panama Canal. She showed me a deck of playing cards adorned with scenes of the canal's construction, cards sent to her mother long ago, and all the while, I was trying to imagine my mother when she still had a father. He certainly existed, because she had a photograph of him, in a dark suit, taken in New Orleans. And she told me that I was named after him. Or I was named after my father *and* her father: William Peter. But they called me Peter anyway. So I had some connection to that lost grandfather who had died. But when I asked her to tell me about him, she always got busy doing something else, and became very quiet.

When she talked about the black market, I imagined some terrible place down near the Gowanus Canal, a huge building painted black and filled with men in black suits and black masks.

No, she said, it's not like that.

A bunch of terrible people she called reprobates cheated the government by hiding things that were part of the shortages. If you knew the right people, you could get all the sugar you wanted, all the meat. You just needed to know the black market people, the reprobates. Why didn't *we* know them?

Because they're bad people, she said. They love money more than they love their country.

Are they bigots? I asked.

Probably, she said. For sure, they are gangsters.

At some point, my mother received ration books and tokens. When she went to buy meat or butter, she needed to hand over the ration stamps or dime-sized cardboard tokens. She saved bacon fat in tin cans, and when she turned in the bacon fat at Semke's butcher shop, she was given more tokens in exchange. Once a month, she said, the government picked up all the cans of bacon fat. One day, I asked my father why the army needed bacon fat.

To grease the guns, he said. And for the soldiers to put on their boots to keep out water.

I tried to imagine this. Wouldn't the Nazis smell *breakfast* when the Americans tried to sneak up on them in a raid?

There were some questions that could never be answered, particularly about the war.

10

FOR THE CHRISTMAS of 1943, my mother bought me a pair of roller skates. They were strong and tough, with clamps over the front of your shoes that were tightened with a skate key. The wheels were shiny; they would never wear out, filling with those ruinous holes we called skellies. They had probably cost her a lot of money, at least three dollars. But on a frigid Saturday a week later, there was a huge scrap metal drive, men in trucks moving slowly along the avenue, shouting to everybody to haul out their old metal and iron so we could turn the stuff into bombs and bullets. People came out with beaten-up old metal chairs and lengths of pipe and broken bicycles. I thought it was my duty to make the ultimate sacrifice. I threw in my skates.

But as I watched the truck pull away, I began to cry. I wanted those skates back. And then felt as if I were a traitor, a regular Benedict Arnold. I stopped crying. I walked around the block. A cold wind was blowing off the harbor. I went home and lay down on my bed and started to read a *Newsboy Legion* comic to restore my sense of patriotism. Yes: I had made a sacrifice. But it was worth it. Somehow, my skates would help beat Hitler and the Japs. Then my mother came in and asked me what was the matter.

Nothing, I lied.

Come on, something's the matter.

Nothing's the matter.

What happened?

I was quiet for a moment and then I whispered: I gave my skates to the scrap metal drive.

Mother of God.

She looked upset and I said, I'm sorry, Mommy.

Oh, she said, this damned war.

Then she went into the kitchen and started cooking in silence. But that wasn't the end of it.

An hour later, my father came home drunk. We sat down to eat dinner. And he learned about the skates.

What? he said. *What?* You gave away your *skates?*

I didn't give them away, I said. I gave them to the scrap metal drive, you know, the war effort.

You bloody *idjit*, he said.

And he reached over and slapped my face.

My head seemed to explode. I went off the chair and got up and ran into the other room, my face stinging, my ear ringing.

Billy! my mother shouted. For the love of *God*, he's only a boy!

Tommy was crying, and that set off Kathleen.

I had to *work* for those goddamned skates! my father shouted. And he gave them *away?*

Billy, he's a *boy.* He wanted to help with the war! He meant nothing bad, he —

I covered my head with a pillow. I didn't want to hear any more of it. I was full of shame, a real idjit. My father had worked at Arma all night and paid for the skates and I gave them away. Skates I loved. The first real pair of skates I ever had. An idjit, an idjit.

Then my brother Tommy was beside me. He put a hand on my head.

Don't cry, Peter. Please don't cry.

I took a deep breath and stopped. My face was still stinging.

Come on, Tommy whispered. We'll go in the Little Room and read comics.

And so we did.

11

IN THOSE FIRST YEARS at 378, the roof became our backyard. It was directly above our heads, reached by a flight of stairs. A small tar-papered building sheltered the staircase, rising off the roof itself like a second house with its own skylight. When we first moved to 378, there was a wooden deck running the length of the roof, with structures like goalposts at each end and clotheslines strung between them. On sweltering August afternoons, nothing was more pleasurable than walking in shorts through the cold wet wash. But in winter, the clothes froze and if you hit them you would hurt your hands; when it was that cold, my mother hung clothes on a line in the kitchen.

From the roof of the little house above the stairs, we could see forever. In one direction, facing the harbor, we saw the hills of Staten Island and the distant smudge of New Jersey and the Narrows opening out to the Atlantic. The harbor traffic never stopped; every day, ships moved out

through the Narrows, going to the war, while others arrived in lines as
steady as the trolley cars on Seventh Avenue. To the right, we could see
the towers of the Brooklyn, Manhattan, and Williamsburg bridges, the
giant building ways of the Navy Yard, the Empire State Building and
the Chrysler. We could not see the piers where the *Normandie* lay in water
and mud.

The New York sky was crowded with birds then, and I would stare
at some brave and lonesome hawk as he caught an air current and
careened away, heading for the skyline until he vanished, and I would
have dreams that night about flying: magically possessed of the secret
powers of my heroes, weightless and strong, high above Brooklyn, soar-
ing to the towers of Manhattan.

One afternoon on that little roof, as I lay reading in the sun, there was
a deep churning sound in the distance, growing steadily louder. My
brother Tommy suddenly burst through the door below me, looking at
the empty sky. I reached down and pulled him up. Then, above us, came
a flight of B-17s. Ten of them, twenty, then more and more, *hundreds*,
and we were frozen, suddenly jumping, as the sky darkened with airplanes, the two of us yelling without words, trying to roar with them,
waving triumphant fists at the Flying Fortresses as they flew over us,
heading for the Narrows, heading out over the Atlantic, going to get
Hitler.

When my father woke up, we started telling him about the airplanes,
the words coming in a rush, and he told us that out at Arma, they made
bombsights for those Flying Fortresses. We got very excited. This was
war information. The Red Skull would kill us to know this; he would
kidnap my father and threaten to drop him into a pool of sharks if he
didn't give him the plans to the bombsight.

Now don't *tell* anyone, he said, going in to shave. Remember, he said:
Loose lips sink ships.

Loose lips sink ships. That was one of the mantras of the war. I was sure
that loose lips had sunk the *Normandie*. But that night, I didn't want to
talk about the *Normandie*. I wanted to tell everyone about the bombsights,
and how my father might be a cripple, he might not be a soldier, he might
be a drunk, he might be *a crippled Irish drunk*, but he was helping beat
Hitler too! He was doing it every night, going out to Arma, out there in
Bush Terminal, and making bombsights that would help our men blow
up Nazi shipyards and Nazi bases and Nazi tanks. And I remember
thinking, up on the roof one day, that maybe that's why he was a drunk.
Maybe it was very hard to carry that secret around, to have that inside

him, knowing that he could be captured. Maybe he thought that if he was drunk he wouldn't be able to talk. His loose lips would not sink ships.

Yeah, I thought. Maybe that was it.

When I left our cramped rooms for the roof, I always felt free. The sky was limitless, the turmoil of the street far below. The tenements and their roofs were all connected and I explored every inch of that open terrain: roofs with white or black pebbles, others with plain tar paper, some with clotheslines, others with rough planked decks where people sat on summer evenings. There were metal chimneys on some rooftops, brick on others; the buildings without hot water had no chimneys at all. A few tenements were higher than the rest, and between several of them there were air shafts.

One air shaft was wider, deeper, more foreboding than the others. I sometimes stared into it, holding tightly to the ledge beside it, and could barely see the black distant bottom, which was a rubble of broken bottles, rusting cans, old clothes. I dropped a pebble down the shaft; it took a long time to hit bottom. Tommy and I called the shaft the Bottomless Pit.

Then one afternoon, I was on the roof with Tommy and two kids, Billy Rossiter and Billy Delaney. We wandered to the edge of the Bottomless Pit. Rossiter, tall and skinny, suddenly pushed me, then grabbed me before I could fall, and laughed at the fear on my face. My heart thumped.

I dare you to jump across, Rossiter said.

Nah, I said, still full of fear.

I can do it, Delaney said.

What for? I said.

A dare is a dare, he said.

Then he backed up the width of one rooftop, took a deep breath, started to run, leaped, and hit the ledge on the far side of the Bottomless Pit. He didn't make it! He was holding on to the edge, dangling, grunting, the darkness below him. Rossiter looked frightened, and then he and I and Tommy were scrambling around to the other side to save Delaney from falling.

But he held on and pulled himself up over the ledge without our help and rolled over on his back. He laughed at us.

Okay, he said, now it's your turn.

Rossiter smiled thinly. He had made the dare. Billy Delaney had accepted it. Now Rossiter had to do it. That was only fair.

He backed up, the way the shorter Delaney had, a wan look on his face. He shook his hands loosely and then started to run on his long thin legs. He jumped. And landed cleanly on his feet on the other side. He laughed like a loon, jumped up and down, raised clenched fists to the sky.

Now it was my turn. Tommy was too small. I had to be the last to leap across the Bottomless Pit.

Tommy whispered, Let's go home, Pete. Come on . . .

I remembered my shame after Brother Foppiano made me cry. I imagined Rossiter and Delaney laughing at me down on the street, telling all the other kids. I had to do it. Maybe I would die, but I had no choice. A dare was a dare.

I backed up the way the others had, not looking at them, not looking at the air shaft. I imagined Robin Hood leaping across the parapets of castles. I saw Gene Autry on his horse Champion, jumping across canyons. Then in my mind my father was on that roof. At my age. With two legs. He would do it. I must do it. Even if I fell to my death in the Bottomless Pit.

I ran in a burst, my legs pumping, head down, came to the lip of the shaft, closed my eyes and made a roaring sound as I jumped.

I hit the other side and rolled. When I opened my eyes, I saw the sky. And Tommy's face. He looked terrified.

I got up and hugged him and then Rossiter and Delaney were there, laughing and excited. Rossiter said, That was *beautiful*, wasn't it? Whatta ya say we do it again?

No, I said, let's get something to drink.

We turned away from the Bottomless Pit and went down to Sanew's to share an icy bottle of Mission Bell grape soda.

On hot summer days, we went to the roof in bathing suits. So did other people on the endless expanse of rooftops that we later called Tar Beach. One humid August afternoon I was alone on the roof and saw Billy Rossiter's sister in a bathing suit, lying out on the rooftop. His sister was much older than Billy, maybe twenty, and she lay there alone, not knowing she was being watched. She lathered suntan oil on her bright pink body, rubbed some on the tops of her breasts, then lay back with her eyes closed and her abundant black hair spilling onto a large white towel. I didn't know why but that made me feel funny. I turned away and went down to the street. I did not tell my mother about this.

Projecting upward from the edge of the roof, out over Seventh Avenue, was a sloping tin canopy, its peak two feet higher than the roof itself. It must have been designed to dress up the building from the avenue side and to keep kids like us from falling to our deaths. Sometimes I'd lie back against the canopy, watching the clouds form horses or lions against the sky. Other times, I'd lie with my head over the canopy's edge, staring down at the life of the street, or into the apartments across the avenue. When winter ended, people laid pillows on the windowsills and watched the street for entertainment. Usually, the watchers were women, looking for their children or their husbands or any signs of danger. My father never gazed out the windows, but neither did my mother. She was always too busy.

But on the top floor above Rattigan's, there was an entire family of Syrians who took their places in the windows, all day long: a grand-mother, a mother, a middle-aged son, three daughters. They watched everything and talked back and forth from window to window. My mother called them the Gapers Club.

On our roof, with just my head showing over the edge of the canopy, I'd gape at the Gapers Club, trying to make them nervous. Once I even succeeded. Fixed in my stare, the grandmother heaved herself inside. And that afternoon, down on the avenue, the mother complained to my mother that I was a Peeping Tom. I didn't know what this meant when she told me about it at dinner. Did it have something to do with brother Tommy?

A Peeping Tom is someone who looks at women in their homes, she said carefully.

But the Gapers Club looks at us *every day*, I said. Even at night sometimes.

A Peeping Tom, my father said, wants to see women take off their clothes.

That scared me; I didn't mention looking at Billy Rossiter's sister. I couldn't be a Peeping Tom. After all, I couldn't see into her *house*.

Anyway, my father said, a Peeping Tom's worse than a masher.

A potato masher?

No, no, he said. It's different.

Billy, my mother said, you're confusing him.

Well, he's got to learn, sooner or later.

I said, Is Tommy a Peeping Tom?

My father laughed and said, I've got to go to work.

I looked at my mother. She was laughing too.

12

O N DAYS of heavy rain, I sat inside the roof door, watching little rivers carve their way through the glistening black pebbles to the drain that emptied into the backyards. Sometimes the water flowed in torrents. The rain came in driving gray sheets off the harbor. And I felt safe and sheltered, like Bomba the Jungle Boy in a cave in the jungle.

I found my first Bomba book in a dingy little store on Sixth Avenue near Tenth Street. The store sold old comics and loose cigarettes (two cents each, two for three cents, just like the pretzels in Sanew's). But on a shelf I saw a book called *Bomba the Jungle Boy at the Moving Mountain*. The ocher cover showed a line drawing of a boy wearing an animal skin that went over his right shoulder. He was holding a bow in his left hand, while a mysterious animal — either a monkey or a small jaguar — peered from the jungle. The book cost six cents. I had a nickel in my hand. I asked the old man at the door if he could trust me for the penny.

Are you kiddin'? he said. Dat's a *hard-cover book!*

I went home and told my mother about the Bomba book and she gave me a milk bottle and told me to bring it to Roulston's and get the deposit. I took the bottle to the grocer, was given two cents, and ran to Sixth Avenue, my heart pounding with fear that someone else might buy the Bomba book.

It was still there. I paid my six cents, held it in my hand, smelled the paper. I hurried home and went to the roof. The first sentence reached out and grabbed me: "As silently as a panther, Bomba climbed the great dolado tree, the giant of the forest. . . ." I soon learned that Bomba was about fourteen and lived in a cabin deep in the jungles of the Amazon, wearing the skin of Geluk the Puma, armed only with a machete and a bow and arrows. With him was a white-haired old naturalist named Cody Casson, who gave Bomba some education but was evasive about the boy's origins. The old man was frail and had lost most of his senses in an accident; he was really in the care of the boy.

That first book, and all the others in the series, were driven by Bomba's search for his lost parents, and therefore a solution to the riddle of his own identity. The entire series was a classic quest.

Once, when my father shouted at me, I ran to Prospect Park and crawled into Devil's Cave, which was hidden beside a stream that fed the Swan Lake. In times of peril, Bomba almost always took refuge in a cave. Mine was low, narrow, extending about six feet into the hill. I sat there alone, wishing for a thunderous Amazonian storm, fierce lightning, the stream transformed into a swollen river. Instead, a parkie came over and said, Hey, kid, you better beat it. It's gettin' dark.

When I went home that evening, my father was gone. I took down a Bomba book and retreated into the jungles of South America, moving through the swamp of death, wary of anacondas, using a pole to test for quicksand, the rubber trees so tall that there was no light. In a way, I hoped Bomba would never find his father. He might be sorry.

13

AT NIGHT FROM the kitchen windows, we could not see New York. There were wartime blackouts, every light in the city extinguished so that German bombers could never find us and so that German submarines couldn't see the freighters and navy ships as they left New York Harbor. Mayor La Guardia was in charge of all this, talking in his thin squeaky voice over the radio, asking all New Yorkers to cooperate. Everybody did, because almost everybody loved Mayor La Guardia, except one of my aunts, who lost her job when Jimmy Walker lost his. To keep out the light, people began buying blackout shades, which were, of course, black, and on some nights there would be air raid drills, with sirens blaring from the firehouse up the block and air raid wardens walking around in the dark streets shouting orders at the deaf, the careless, or the indifferent.

On summer nights, these drills were exciting. Everybody would be out in the street, sitting on chairs or stoops or the front steps of the stores. Some of us even sat on Sanew's newsstand. If it was hot, the big people drank hot tea, which was supposed to make you cooler. Most of the time they talked and joked and made fun of the air raid wardens, whose helmets for some reason were white, making them perfect targets for roaming Messerschmitts.

On one such evening, a warden started shouting into Rattigan's. Someone shouted back. Then the warden went into the saloon. Then he came hurtling out of the saloon and landed on his back, the helmet skittering away into the gutter. A group of men came outside behind him. One of them was my father.

The warden stood up, shouting. On our side of the street, everybody was standing now, moving down to the corner. The argument got louder, the words still not clear. Then my mother started across the street. I followed her.

Billy, she said, come on home.

Stay out of this! he shouted.

What's the matter?

This bum called Eddie Malloy a draft dodger!

Draft dodger! The worst words in the English language. Draft dodgers were rich guys. Draft dodgers were cowards. Some draft dodgers even wanted the Nazis to win.

Yiz are all a bunch of draft dodgers! the warden said, standing now, adjusting his white helmet, trying through his anger to look dignified.

Then a big suety guy with a flushed face came forward. This was Eddie Malloy.

You say dat again, you bum, I put you down the sewer! I got t'ree kids in de army. I got one kid in da navy. I went down an' volunteered da day after Poirl Harba! *Dey* toirned me down on accounta as'ma. An' because I'm too old. I tried da navy. I tried da Marines. Don't call me no draft dodger, you bastid.

Then suddenly a police car with its lights out came around the corner of Twelfth Street and another one hurried along the avenue from Ninth Street.

Come on home, Billy, my mother said, taking my father's arm as I watched from the doorway of the Gapers Club.

You go home, he said, shaking off her hand. This is none of your god-damned business, woman.

She backed away, shocked and hurt. Then the cops were piling out of the patrol cars, shouting, What the hell's going on? The air raid warden pointed at the crowd.

They assaulted me while I was doing my duty! he said.

That's a load of bullshit, my father said. He came in looking for trouble and he got it. Eddie Malloy was smoking a cigarette at the bar and when this idjit told him to put it out, Eddie laughed. Then he called Eddie a draft dodger.

The biggest cop said, You're Mister Malloy? I went to Holy Family with your son Jackie. How is he?

Inna Sout' Pacific, killin' them Japs.

The big cop turned to the crowd and said, Okay, let's everybody go home now.

Then he said to the air raid warden, Relax, pal. Go check out who's smoking on Thirteenth Street.

Then to Eddie Malloy, Go inside now, and for Chrissakes, don't smoke 'til the drill is over.

The warden strode away in a fury. The cops got into their cars and left. The men were laughing and slapping each other on the back and then started inside. My father's face was beaming. He'd told them, yeah. He'd told them. Then, as if remembering something, he separated from the others and came over to my mother.

I'm sorry, Annie, he said. Come in, we'll have a drink in the back.

You can drink alone, she said, and took my hand and walked quickly back across the street.

14

THE WAR was always with us. On the radio, we heard about the men who were building Liberty Ships in two weeks and how, at the great plant in Willow Run, a complete bomber was coming off the assembly line every hour, twenty-four hours a day, seven days a week. But in the summer at Coney Island, we saw lumpy blobs of congealed oil on the beaches and were told they came from sunken ships. It was true: *Loose lips sink ships, loose lips sink ships . . .* We were losing; we were winning; everyone must play a part. At one point, we were told to roll up toothpaste tubes while we used them and were forced to turn them in before we could get another; my mother started buying tooth powder, which was cheaper, the canister made with cardboard; but after a while there was none of that left either, and we brushed our teeth with bicarbonate of soda or didn't brush them at all.

On the radio now, they were singing *Don't sit under the apple tree with anyone else but me* and *I got spurs that jingle jangle jingle*, and every morning, on a show called "Rambling with Gambling," we heard *Oh what a beautiful morning, Oh what a beautiful day* from a Broadway show called *Oklahoma*.

I'd love to see that show, my mother said one day. I love those songs.

Why don't you go and see it? I said.

It's over on Broadway, she said, as if explaining it was in Madrid. It's much too dear.

She said this as if ending the discussion. I was persistent.

Why can't Daddy take you? He has money for Rattigan's. Why can't he save up and take you over to Broadway?

Well . . . maybe after the war is over.

I'd like to see Broadway too, I said.

She smiled and said, After the war . . .

During the second year of the war, my father started giving me an allowance of a dime a week, and with a few more cents (again, deposits on those bottles) I began to go to the movies with other kids. Almost always, on a Saturday morning, our destination was the Minerva, which was one large malodorous room, with two aisles and about twenty rows noisy with kids. There were usually three features, a serial (which we called the "chapter"), a cartoon, a newsreel, and coming attractions; all for twelve cents if we got there before noon. We never knew what time a movie started; we just went to the Show. And sitting there in the noisy dark, I was transported to other worlds.

I loved the Tarzan movies, with their lush scenes of jungles, tree houses, Johnny Weissmuller swinging on vines and bellowing his great triumphant calls. I also discovered the glories of the American West, vistas of amazing beauty, of deserts and mesas and mountains. Sitting in the dark of the Minerva, I could smell the leather saddles, the beans cooking in skillets on sagebrush fires, the dirty smoke billowing from an Iron Horse as it raced across the prairie. At the movies, I dove into mountain streams. I survived raging snowstorms and stampeding cattle. I faced down Indians, black hats, rustlers, desperadoes. I was pursued by posses and escaped into Mexico.

In those westerns, in the gangster movies, in the war movies, and even the love movies, the men were always drinking. They shot each other in saloons and nightclubs. They got drunk on leave and got into wild, hilarious fights in waterfront bars. Some of the movie drunks were comical, some mean. With the exception of a few cowboys, even the heroes drank whiskey. They never got drunk.

In the third year of the war, the Kilroy signs started appearing everywhere, brought home to America from Europe. They showed a long-nosed cartoon figure, his nose hanging over a fence, and the slogan: Kilroy Was Here. Nobody knew who Kilroy was. But he was everywhere (they said on the radio), he was every GI, he was every American fighting overseas. I mastered the head and nose of Kilroy hanging over the fence and chalked it on a hundred walls and fences. That year, Kilroy even made it to Brooklyn.

On the radio there were stories about zoot suit riots in Los Angeles, on the other side of the country; sailors were chasing the zoot suiters, most of whom were Mexicans, stripping off their clothes, shaving their heads, and then beating them to a pulp. Almost everybody seemed to think this was a good thing. A riot broke out in Detroit, blacks against whites, and people were killed by the police. Then there was a riot closer to home: in Harlem, over in Manhattan, where the Negroes lived. I saw pictures in the *Daily News* of black men with bloodied heads and tough cops with faces like slabs standing in front of them.

They oughtta kill *all* them niggers, a kid named Tommy Moore said, standing outside Sanew's, as we looked at the headlines about the riot.

Why?

Why? We're fightin' Hitler and the Japs, and the niggers are rioting! Whose side are they on?

Maybe they got a good reason. The paper says they won't let them in the army with whites.

Of course not! said Tommy Moore. They're *niggers!* They won't fight!

But they're fighting in Harlem!

That's different! You can't fight the Nazis wit' a knife!

This was a puzzlement. There were no black people in our part of Brooklyn except for one tall man in overalls, who worked as a super in an apartment house on Fifteenth Street. Nobody seemed to bother him; certainly he didn't bother anybody. When we traveled with my mother on the subway, we saw blacks, but they behaved like everybody else: dozing or reading newspapers or talking to each other. Joe Louis sure could fight; but when I thought about blacks in the movies I understood what Tommy Moore was saying. In the movies, blacks were always wide-eyed and comical, full of fear, running from ghosts or bad guys or their own shadows. If they saw Nazis with guns, would they say, as so many did in movies, *Feets, get movin'?*

As always, I brought this to the kitchen table. My mother was rushing around, ladling out food. My father had gone to work.

How come niggers won't fight? I said.

What? she said. What did you say?

The niggers, you know, from Harlem? How come —

Don't use that word in this house, my mother said. They are called colored people. Or Negroes.

Everybody calls them —

Only bigots call them niggers, she said. And what does a bigot know about fighting? Bigots are cowards and bullies.

She knew everything.

When the rioting ended, we were back to news of distant battles. And other matters. A gangster named Lepke went to the chair, and everybody talked proudly about how he wouldn't squeal on anyone, right up to the end, because he was from Brooklyn and if you're from Brooklyn, you don't squeal, ever. Jimmy Durante started saying "umbriago" on the radio, and though nobody knew what this meant, in school we said umbriago as if it were another version of Shazam: a magic word, a curse, a mystery. There were stories about strikes, and people cursed John L. Lewis, who was keeping the coal from reaching the cities. My father wondered how Lewis could be a union leader, anyway. He was a god-damned *Republican*.

Then one wartime winter, there were no cigarettes. My father was always irritated, smoking strange brands, like Wings and Fatima (because the GIs were now using up the entire supply of Camels); the black market had them, he said, and they were holding them back to drive up the prices. Paper matches suddenly disappeared too, so my father started using wooden kitchen matches, snapping the sulfur heads into flame with his thumbnail. Alone in the kitchen I tried to do this many times, and always failed.

The war went on and on.

15

AT 378, Big Jack McEvoy was the super. He lived on the first floor right, with his wife, Mae, his son, Jackie, and his daughter, Marilyn. Everybody in the building thought they were strange people. For one thing, Big Jack was a Giant fan. We never knew another Giant fan, though there was a rumor that a Yankee fan lived on Ninth Street and Eighth Avenue. Both breeds were as rare as Republicans. Big Jack was probably a Republican too.

He's a strange bird, my father said one Sunday morning.

Why? my mother said in an irritated way. Because he doesn't spend hours in Rattigan's?

My father gave her a hard look.

He's making good money at the shipyards but he still works as a super, saving every dime, he said. He's a cheapskate. He comes into the bar and never says a word and takes his pail home. I never trust a man that drinks alone.

In spite of the father who drank his beer from a pail at home, I became friendly with his son, Jackie. He was lean, taut, black-haired, and a great stickball player. We didn't mind that he was a Giant fan too. He could play. Jackie was three or four years older than I was and he had a terrible temper, which was why the boys his own age wouldn't play with him, even though he was a great hitter. But he seemed to like me. In the hall one day, a few weeks before Christmas, I asked him if he wanted to trade comics. Sure, he said, come to my house after dinner.

The McEvoy flat amazed me. Most of the living room was filled with a green-topped table upon which an entire model railroad line was operating in a perfect miniature world. There were mountains, a farm with cows and horses, a lake, streams, trees, stations, water towers, with the Lionel trains racing through them all.

My father built it for me, Jackie said casually, showing me how he operated switches, how he could make the trains move from one track to another, how they could even go backwards.

My father can build anything, Jackie said.

I said nothing in reply, thinking of my father calling Big Jack a cheapskate before heading for Rattigan's.

I was awed by the McEvoy living room. In a corner of the room, an immense fat Christmas tree stood bright with bulbs, blinking electric lights, silver strands draped along the branches. Against one wall, a piano was covered with Christmas cards. Our own living room was barren in comparison; we wouldn't have a tree until a few days before Christmas, when the prices came down, and we could never afford a real piano. Then Jackie showed me his collection of comics, great stacks of them. And added something else: comics he had drawn himself.

He had about seven of them, all in composition books, the pages broken up into panels like real comic books. Jackie's hero was Smilin' Jack, and the stories were all about his pursuit across the Pacific of a villain called the Red Bat. The panels were full of ships and airplanes, desert islands and dying Japanese soldiers. At the end of each book, he wrote the ominous words: To Be Continued.

Pretty good, huh? he said.

Yeah, yeah, I said. They're great, Jackie.

That night, back in our house, I started drawing my own comic books. I had one blank composition book and used a number 2 pencil to make my drawings. I asked my mother for a story and she said I should just make one up. So I did, sending Smilin' Jack after the same Red Bat created by Jackie McEvoy. But in my story I made them roam the jungles of South America, using places from the Bomba books. The airplanes were hard to draw, so I looked at some comics, and tried to copy them. They didn't come out well. The page grew rough and dirty from erasing, but when I was finished, they did look like airplanes.

When I finished my first book, I took it to show Jackie McEvoy and he said it was lousy. I thought, Well, maybe it is, but let me try again. I started filling book after book with my own comics, all about Smilin' Jack, then adding other characters, then changing my hero's name to Bob Sterling, Secret Agent. My mother loved these books. She would actually read them and laugh. Once more, she showed me the comics in the newspapers, in particular *Terry and the Pirates*, by Milton Caniff. I still didn't quite connect with this strip, but I liked Terry Lee, who was blond and in the air force, and his commander, Flip Corkin, and his friend, Pat Ryan. I just didn't understand the talk.

But on other pages in the *Daily News*, I found *Smilin' Jack*, who didn't look anything like Jackie McEvoy's version of the character. In the newspaper, he was a handsome guy with a mustache, who flew all over the Pacific, fighting the Japanese. He met beautiful women everywhere and had two friends: Fat Stuff, a black guy whose buttons kept popping off his enormous belly, and Downwind Jaxon, who was always seen in three-quarters view from the rear so that his face remained a mystery. The airplanes were great. But I could never draw Smilin' Jack the way he really looked. That's why I invented Bob Sterling, who was a kind of flying G-man, chasing Nazis through Brazil, where they had taken over a lost city in the jungles. Naturally, they had a secret weapon too, the incredible Death Bomb.

That summer I showed some of my later books to Jackie McEvoy. This time, he didn't dismiss me with contempt. He got furious.

What are you doing? he shouted at me. Stealing my idea? *I* write comic books, not *you*!

I never showed him another one.

In a way, I didn't care. Jackie McEvoy's approval didn't matter all that much to me; on the street, even the big guys didn't want to hang around with him. Besides, I had begun to think that I could draw better than he could. After a year of practice, I could make a credible Dick Tracy or

Flattop without looking at the *Daily News*. I could even turn out a pretty fair Smilin' Jack. I couldn't draw women at all. But I would sit at the kitchen table after dinner, filling pages with airplanes, jungles, submarines, and heroes, packing balloons with talk, ignoring the heat or the cold, the cockroaches or the radio. The truth was, I only wanted the approval of one person.

But when my mother showed him my hand-drawn comic books one night, he stared at them, riffled through the pages, nodded, said Nice, and reached for his cigarettes and the quart bottle of Trommer's.

16

UP TWELFTH STREET, in one of the buildings across from the Factory, there was a woman with flaming red hair who was called Betty the Whore (we pronounced the word *who*-uh). We would see her in the late afternoons, coming down the street in very high heels, short skirt, and jacket with padded shoulders. She changed her hairstyle all the time, letting it flow out, piling it on top of her head, flattening it under a pillbox hat. She was also the first woman in the neighborhood to wear slacks, which caused people to stare at her just as much as that tangerine hair. Most afternoons, when she started her walk, men would slowly step out of the bars, just to look at her, and they'd yell at her and she'd yell back and then she'd get on a trolley car and go off toward Flatbush Avenue. The men would all laugh and nudge each other and then go back into the bars.

I remember asking my mother about her: what the word "who-uh" meant and why the woman wore slacks and why the men yelled at her. She smiled and then shook her head.

She's just a poor unfortunate, my mother said. Her husband's in the army and she's all alone.

Why do the men shout at her?

Because they are horse's asses, she snapped. If they had any pity in them, they'd pray for her.

Do you pray for her?

I will. And you should too.

That night I prayed for Betty the Whore and the night after that, and then I forgot about her. There were so many people in the world to pray for that I just didn't have time for the Poor Unfortunate with the rolling hips and flaming red hair.

17

THEN one June afternoon, I came home from Holy Name and saw everyone rushing around, waving newspapers, shouting, pumping clenched fists in the air. D day! We had invaded France! Radios blared from hundreds of windows, telling about landings in Normandy and heavy fighting as the troops moved into France. My mother was happy, listening carefully as my father shaved.

Well, maybe it'll be over soon, she said.

How soon? I said.

They say it might be Christmas.

I thought she was going to cry, but she didn't. My father came out of the bathroom and I was proud of him. The radio said that men were fighting on the beaches near Cherbourg and flights of bombers were smashing the Ruhr, which I knew was in Germany; they must have been using his bombsights. He didn't say anything for a long time, just listened to the news reports.

Good, he said at last. They can hang old Hitler from a telephone pole.

Off he went to work, and after a while I heard people coming up the stairs. Mae McEvoy and her daughter, from the first floor; Mrs. Halloran and Carrie Woods from the second floor. They had sandwiches and soda bottles and pails of beer and were heading for the roof. Across the hall lived the Caputos, who were wonderful people. Mike Caputo had a tough face and wore a tough longshoreman's cap but he always smiled at us and remembered our names. Mrs. Caputo taught my mother how to make sauce for spaghetti, which we immediately wanted to eat every night instead of barley soup and stew. They had three sons, Sonny, Babe, and Junior, and they were always friendly. Then their door opened and all of them started for the roof too.

Let's go, Mommy. Come on! Everybody's going up to the roof.

She said, Okay, but be careful. It's almost dark.

The roof was as packed as the street during an air raid drill. I saw people from every building on the avenue, and men from the bars, and they were all looking out at the harbor. Mr. Caputo asked me how I was doing in school and I said, Okay, vacation's soon, and he said, Great, you can get a job f' the summer. But I wasn't thinking about a job. I was nine. Who would hire me at nine? The sun was now setting into New Jersey, the sky all red and purple, the skyline beginning to disappear into the darkness. We could hear the foghorns of dozens of ships. And then the sun set, the sky turned mauve and then black. The skyline disappeared as it did every night during the war. For a long time, people murmured to each other in hushed expectant voices.

What's going to happen? I asked. Why is everyone here?

Just wait, my mother said. Watch the skyline.

And then, without warning, the entire skyline of New York erupted into glorious light: dazzling, glittering, throbbing in triumph. And the crowds on the rooftops roared. They were roaring on roofs all over Brooklyn, on streets, on bridges, the whole city roaring for light. There it was, gigantic and brilliant, the way they said it used to be: the skyline of New York. Back again. On D day, at the command of Mayor La Guardia. And it wasn't just the skyline. Over on the left was the Statue of Liberty, glowing green from dozens of light beams, a bright red torch held high over her head. The skyline and the statue: in all those years of the war, in all the nights of my *life*, I had never seen either of them at night. I stood there in the roar, transfixed. And then softly, her voice trembling with emotion, my mother began to sing:

> *There'll be bluebirds over*
> *The white cliffs of Dover*
> *Tomorrow, when the world is free . . .*

And the others joined in, most of them women, some of whom had men in the army, fighting or dying out beyond the Narrows, their voices now joined, singing hard and loud, some crying, all gazing at that blaze of light.

> *There'll be love and laughter*
> *And peace ever after*
> *Tomorrow — just you wait and see . . .*

The war wasn't over by Christmas. There was a lot more killing and a lot more dying. Across the summer, I played ball in the street, learning the mysteries of stickball. But the fall was very cold and the winter was brutal. The radio was on almost all the time. I read and drew more comics, and started drawing in sketchbooks. At the same time, I searched for Bomba books, pushing out beyond the edges of the Neighborhood to find little bookshops. I got good grades in school. In 4B, I was given the religion prize, a book about Thomas Aquinas, illustrated with silhouettes. I copied the silhouettes and then made some of my own.

Roosevelt died in April. Flags were lowered to half mast at the firehouse and the post office, schools were closed, and my mother prayed for Roosevelt's departed soul. His picture remained on the kitchen wall. Truman became president. My mother didn't like him but my father said, At least he's a Democrat. Then on May 8, there was another collective roar in Brooklyn, and when I came home from school, people were out on the street, cheering and dancing while others banged pots from their windows and hung American flags on the fire escapes. The war was over in Europe! This was V-E Day. Hitler was dead, the Nazis had quit. Seventh Avenue was having a block party.

Patty Rattigan set up a keg of free beer on the sidewalk. Mrs. Caputo burst out of 378 with a huge pot of spaghetti. Other people brought down platters piled with sandwiches. My mother cooked a rhubarb pie. Even the Gapers Club abandoned the windows and came down to the street to gape at the food and drink. Radios appeared on fire escapes, loud with patriotic music and news from Washington. There was wild dancing, with grown-ups doing the Lindy Hop. Everybody was singing and drinking. My father was still asleep and he went to work that night without saying good-bye.

But V-E Day didn't end the war. The fighting was still going on in the Pacific, getting more brutal as it came closer to Japan. In the *Daily News* maps I found Tarawa and Iwo Jima and Okinawa, showing them to Tommy, talking about them in the street. I added "kamikaze" and "flame thrower" to the nomenclature of war. And then on a still, thick day in August, Tommy Moore came bursting from his house with the news about the atom bomb.

We got a friggin' secret weapon, he said. It blew up a whole friggin' city!

I ran upstairs and turned on the radio. It was true. The American secret weapon had blown the entire city of Hiroshima to pieces. I ran downstairs again. To the kids in the street, this was great news. The Japs had bombed Pearl Harbor and now they were paying for it. Now the war would end. The secret weapon that was part of the plot in so many comic books was called the atomic bomb. And we had it.

But that night my mother was upset by the news, and for me that was confusing.

Those poor people, she said.

What poor people? my father said. They're Japs!

They're just people like us, she snapped back. Women and children and working people. They didn't start the war. Some old politician did. But now thousands of them are dead.

They had it coming, my father said.

They did not.

What the hell do you know about it? he said in a hard voice. You're not the president!

I know they're just people, she said, holding her own.

He shut up then and finished his dinner and went to work. When he was gone, my mother hugged me.

Pray for the poor Japanese, she said. And I did.

Three days later, Nagasaki was bombed. And now my mother was more angry than sorrowful.

That old Truman, she said. He picked the one city in Japan where the Catholics lived.

How do you know? my father said. I never heard of a Jap that was Catholic.

It was on the *radio*, she said.

I don't believe it, he said. Japs aren't Catholics.

They are so, she said. Some of them. The Jesuits were in Nagasaki, the French and the Portuguese. My *father* was in Nagasaki.

With that, he went quiet. But I was in awe. Peter Devlin had been in South America. He had seen real jungles. He had refrigerated bananas. He had watched the building of the Panama Canal. And now I learned that he had even crossed the Pacific! He had been in Japan! In *Nagasaki!*

I ate fast and went down to tell everybody this news. Nobody believed me; what could an Irishman be doing in friggin' Nagasaki? On the way home again, I met Jackie McEvoy coming down the stairs. I told him all about my grandfather and the Pacific and Nagasaki.

You're such a goddamned *kid*, he said, and went past me to the street.

18

THEN THE WAR ended for good. And on Seventh Avenue, V-J Day was celebrated with the biggest, noisiest block party of them all. Strangers kissed each other. Georgie Loftus, the bartender, kissed Pat

Mulroney, the taxi driver. Mrs. Irwin from the second floor even kissed a cop. Carrie Woods fell down the stairs, skinned her knees, and made Cliff bring her another whiskey. A wild young guy named Paulie McAleer vomited on a parked car and then smashed his fist through the window of the Kent cleaners. Teddy from the fruit store gave away free watermelon. My father took the night off from work and joined the crowd in front of Rattigan's, where five kegs of free beer were lined up on the sidewalk. The firemen all got drunk. A firehouse dog bit a priest. Betty the Whore danced with three sanitation men. The trolley cars kept ding-dinging for passage but the avenue was so packed that the drivers opened the doors and let everyone take free rides. For that long day and into the night, everyone you saw was happy. This was the fabulous tomorrow from the song, the day when there would be joy and laughter and peace ever after. This was tomorrow. The world was free.

Going upstairs that night, gorged with watermelon, spaghetti, candy, and soda, I felt that I was about to begin my life. The next day, at last, would begin the time called After the War. The ballplayers would come home. My mother would see *Oklahoma!* All shortages would end. We'd be happy. Every one of us.

But on the second landing, I found my father asleep on the stairs. I woke him up and he looked at me with dazed, watery eyes, his jaw slack, saliva drying in the corners of his mouth.

What's the problem? he said.

Come on, I said. The war is over.

Yeah, he said. The war is over.

I helped him up the stairs, like Bomba taking Cody Casson back to the cabin.

II

AFTER THE WAR

A father's no shield
for his child.
We are like a lot of wild
spiders crying together,
but without tears.

— Robert Lowell, "Fall 1961"

The happy leave no clues.

— John Hewitt, "The Happy Man"

1

AND SO the pattern had begun, the template was cut. There was a celebration and you got drunk. There was a victory and you got drunk. It didn't matter if other people saw you; they were doing the same thing. So if you were a man, there was nothing to hide. Part of being a man was to drink. I was ten years old that summer of the end of the war, but I was learning the ways of the world.

In the lot on Twelfth Street, we still played war games, using shovels to dig foxholes and trenches. We mowed down Japanese holdouts with rifles made from broom handles or guns shaped from the corners of orange crates. We stuffed tin cans with stones and used them as hand grenades, usually aimed at cats. We even played a game called concentration camp, made up of jailers and the pursued, sprinkling our talk with German words learned from comic books and movies: *Achtung!* and *Schweinhund!*

I played these games with all the other kids, but then one rainy Sunday afternoon I went to the RKO Prospect to catch a double bill and saw for the first time the newsreels from Buchenwald. Grizzled American soldiers were at the edge of the camp, some of them weeping. And just past them, beyond the barbed wire, were men and women and children in striped pajamas, unable to move, full of fear, staring with eyes that couldn't be seen. Some were lying on tiers of bunks, too close to death to ask for help, their long skeletal hands limply hanging to the floor. Their arms were tattooed with numbers. Their heads were shaven. They looked like zombies I'd seen in a movie at the Minerva. This was what Hitler had left behind after killing himself in the bunker: these silvery gray images of European horror, these bony heaps that had once been human. I tried to get someone to answer my questions: *How did this happen? Who did this?* But my father only said, That son of a bitch Hitler. And my mother said, That terrible bigot. And in school, there was no answer at all.

For weeks, I read the newspaper stories about the camps and stared at the photographs in *Life* that I found on the racks in Sanew's candy store, and there were no answers. I dreamed of the camps, of slush-eyed men in black SS uniforms herding us from boxcars into barracks and finally to showers where gas hissed from the nozzles on the ceiling. In one repeated dream, I was fighting, struggling, pushing at the skeletal men, trying to get out of the packed showers, trying to reach the door, to get to Brooklyn, to safety, to my mother and father, and at least once I woke up screaming. My mother came in and asked what the matter was, and I cried and talked about the concentration camps and the gas and the barbed wire, and she crooned to me, *Don't worry, now, don't worry anymore, don't worry, Peter, the war is over.*

After that trip to the Prospect, I never played concentration camp again.

During this time, I began to look more closely at the grown-ups who inhabited the world of Seventh Avenue. Around the corner on Twelfth Street, the men wore overalls or army surplus and heavy steel-tipped boots. They always needed a shave. Their hands were filthy. Most evenings, they lurched home drunk from the bars on the avenue. The other kids made fun of them, but I was almost always silent. In one way, they made me see my father the way others might see him. He didn't dress like them; his lost leg made heavy manual labor impossible. He did drink the way they did. So the drunks were also consoling figures. They told me that my father was not unique.

Once, I saw a man named Dix, rawboned and scary-eyed, fight his wife, who was also drunk. They drew a huge crowd. The wife, small and thick in what we called a housedress, kept coming in a frantic rage, while Mr. Dix stepped back and jabbed her, breaking up her face, making blood flow from her mouth and nose, smirking until his cap fell off, and then enraged, bending her over a fence and hammering her until two of the other women stepped in and broke it up. The men in the crowd did nothing to stop the fight. Most of them laughed and cheered at the end, and I heard one of them say: Never marry a woman you can't knock out with one punch. But a few feet from me, under the lamppost, the smallest of the many Dix kids was sobbing, holding on to his mother as the blood ran down between her heaving breasts.

You *fuck!* she shouted after her husband, as he moved off to the bar. You big *fuck!*

He turned, looking ominous.

Get inside, he said, or I'll break your fucking neck, woman.

Make me! she screamed. *Make* me, you bum! Hit a woman! You fuckin' *bum!*

The other women surrounded her, putting their bodies between her and her husband, and took her into the house, the sobbing kid behind them. Then Mr. Dix turned to us.

What are you little cocksuckers looking at? he said.

We walked away. The fight was sickening. I hated the way he kept punishing her after he had made her bleed. I hated the other men cheering.

But in some secret way, it made me feel better. My father would never do that to my mother. He might speak harshly to her, as he did the night of the blackout. He might tell her she didn't know what she was talking about; he did that often. He might get drunk and miss meals or sleep in the halls. But *hit* her? Curse her? Make her bleed in front of a hundred people and her own kids? Never. When I compared him to Mr. Dix, my father made me proud.

That afternoon, I retreated from the drunken melodramas of Twelfth Street to the comparative serenity of Eleventh Street, where the men wore suits to work and always looked sober. First I went upstairs and found a Bomba book, then I drifted around the corner to lie on the slanted wooden cellarboard beside the Kent dry cleaning store, whose windows had been smashed on V-J Day and were now whole again.

I was reading there alone when I looked up and saw a soldier moving slowly along Seventh Avenue. That was not unusual. The soldiers were all coming home now. Troopships arrived each day in the harbor, and there were pictures in the newspapers of women rushing to kiss husbands and sweethearts. Every morning, I'd see new signs in neighborhood doorways: Welcome Home, Jimmy, and God Bless You, Eddie. But this soldier was different. He was alone. And he was on crutches. One trouser leg was pinned up. Obviously, he'd lost a leg.

And then I saw my father coming out of Rattigan's. He stood alone on the corner, watching the soldier from another angle. He hesitated, then started across the street, swinging his wooden leg behind him. I stood up. My father reached the younger man in front of Kent's.

Hey, soldier, he said.

The soldier stopped, his eyes wary.

Yeah? he said.

You lost a leg, my father said.

Yeah.

So did I, my father said.

Well —

Don't let it get to you, my father said. You can still have a life.

The soldier shrugged as if he didn't believe this at all.

Come on, my father said. We'll have a drink.

Without discussion, they started back across the avenue to Rattigan's, the soldier swinging on the crutches, my father leading the way.

I loved him very much that day.

2

ON THE STREETS I learned the limits of the Neighborhood. This was our hamlet, marked by clear boundaries. Sometimes we moved beyond those boundaries: to visit aunts and uncles out in Bay Ridge; to gaze at the *Normandie;* and on one wondrous fog-choked Saturday in July, to stare up at the Empire State Building after a twin-engined B-25 crashed into its north side between the seventy-eighth and seventy-ninth floors, killing fourteen people and hurting many others. But it was to the Neighborhood that we always returned. Other neighborhoods were not simply strange; they were probably unknowable.

I was like everybody else. In the Neighborhood I always knew where I was; it provided my center of gravity. And on its streets I learned certain secrets that were shared by the others. The fight between Mr. Dix and his wife was one secret. I learned who the gangsters were in the Neighborhood and the name of the bookmaker. Their presence created other rules, none of them written on paper. I heard tales of police informers who disappeared in the night and others who were slashed with a knife, from the corner of the mouth to the upper point of the cheek, the mouth gashed into a grotesque elongation like the face of the grinning man at Steeplechase Park in Coney Island: the awful Mark of the Squealer. Such people were called stool pigeons or rats.

There is no person worse in this world, my father said, *than a goddamned informer.*

I learned too about what they called in religion class "infidelity." I didn't know anything of the mechanics of sex, but I did understand that if a father left a mother for another woman, the family would be destroyed. I couldn't imagine my father leaving my mother for anyone else; but sometimes, when he lay drunk in bed, I was terrified that she might leave him. Sometimes I heard her say, *Bill, I'm fed up.* And wondered if she would get so fed up she would pack a bag, like women in the movies did, and just go away.

In the Neighborhood, there were many women during the war whose husbands were off at the fighting, and on summer evenings, as the grown-ups sat around outside, and one of these women went by, I heard whispers and giggles. They weren't just about Betty the Whore. I heard about the woman who lived across the street from the Minerva and welcomed men visitors at night while her husband worked in the Navy Yard. And the woman from Sixth Avenue who had a baby fifteen months after her husband left for the South Pacific. None of this was absolutely clear to me, but I knew they were talking about sin. In some way, all sin had the same weight, so I also knew the names of those who refused to go to Mass; those who were forced to make general confessions after years away from the Church; and, of course, the names of the drunks.

All of these people were citizens of the Neighborhood, a small state bound together by rivers — rivers of alcohol. On weekends, my father moved on those rivers. Sometimes I would follow him, desperate to know what he did and why. On a few sunny Sunday afternoons, he would take me with him, the way he took me to Gallagher's when we lived on Thirteenth Street. He said little; but I soon had charted the map of his world.

In the center, of course, was Rattigan's, directly across the street, packed and smoky, the men discreetly hidden from view by carefully hung café curtains. After the war, the men of Rattigan's started the Doghouse Club — as in "I'm in the doghouse wit' the little woman" — and behind the bar there were rows of small white doghouses each with the name of a member lettered on the front. Inside the doghouses were bar tabs or messages, tickets for racetracks or ballparks left by local politicians.

They give you a racetrack ticket, my father explained, and you give them a vote. It's a good deal.

There were stools at the bar and booths in the back room, but most of the men preferred to stand. So did my father. In those years, there was no jukebox or television set. As they did in Gallagher's, the men entertained themselves. As in Gallagher's, my father was a star performer.

Presiding over the place was a huge man named Patty Rattigan, round-faced and balding, like a pink version of the Jolly Green Giant. He had a generous heart, a thick brogue, a job in the borough president's office, and proud membership in the Democratic party. Patty wasn't simply a saloonkeeper. He helped find jobs for customers or their sons. He loaned them money. He threw out the crazy people. He loved singing and food and men drinking on summer afternoons. My father loved him and loved his bar.

If anything ever happens to me, my father said one day, Patty Rattigan will take care of the lot of you.

What about Mommy?

He'll take care of her too.

He sipped his beer, and then started to sing "Galway Bay." I left, unable to bear the idea of something happening to him, even if Patty Rattigan would take care of everything.

But on weekends, he went on small excursions beyond Rattigan's and I discovered other fueling stations on those ceaseless rivers. Prospect Park meant nothing to my father; what good were summer meadows if you couldn't play ball? But on Bartel-Pritchard Square, across from the entrance to the park, he often stopped in two saloons: Langton's, and the bar attached to Lewnes' restaurant. The first was dark, odorous, and the only saloon in the Neighborhood that served women at the bar. Lewnes' (pronounced Looney's) was full of heavy-set men crowded against the bar in their Sunday best. My father knew many people in both places but never stayed long.

Usually he was heading up the street, where Prospect Park West became Ninth Avenue, to the bar that he kept returning to until the end of his life: Farrell's. A lot of Belfast men were always there, short and wiry like my father, and they would talk about the old country while I listened and watched. The place was always packed, the men three deep at the long polished wooden bar, served by two bartenders in starched white shirts and neat ties. In the men's room there were two huge curved ceramic urinals, as high as my head, and I loved pissing on the blocks of ice that lay at the bottom, melting little gullies and caves. At that bar, where the men made jokes, drank beer and whiskey, placed bets on horses, and put cigarettes out on the tile floors, I felt at home. I was, after all, Billy Hamill's son.

There were other bars on my father's map. He still went to Gallagher's, of course, but on weekend afternoons, when the weather was good, he would patrol along Seventh Avenue, where there were bars on almost every corner. There was McAuley's on Eighth Street, Diamond's and Denny's on opposite corners of Ninth Street, Fitzgerald's on Tenth Street. I'd see him go in, and faces turn, and smiles break out. If he walked in the other direction, he'd visit Unbeatable Joe's on Twelfth Street, Quigley's on Thirteenth Street, Connolly's on Fifteenth Street. In a neighborhood of cliques, Billy Hamill was welcomed by all of them. Occasionally there were wider forays: down to Loftus's on Fifth Avenue, where the ironworkers did their drinking; the Blue Eagle on Third Street, named after one of the symbols of the New Deal, where a friend from Belfast tended bar; a nameless place on Sixth Avenue and Ninth Street next to the Knights of Columbus. He was known everywhere, for his singing, his laughter, his Irish blarney. When he took me with him, he was always greeted with slaps on the back and glasses of beer. But there was another side to him: on the days when I followed at a distance, he often seemed lonesome and sad, heaving the wooden leg behind him, lost in some abyss of memory right up to the second that he opened the doors.

3

THAT WINTER, Betty the Whore's husband came home. He was a gaunt, hollow-eyed man who had been a German prisoner for two years. But when he went into the building there were no Welcome Home signs and no Betty either. We all heard about the way he reacted. He went into Unbeatable Joe's and got very drunk. Then he started throwing glasses and ashtrays and punched out the mirror in the men's room. The other men were very gentle. They took him home and put him to bed.

The next day, he left the Neighborhood and never came back.

4

IN THE FALL of the year the war ended, we were suddenly poor. The ferocious winter came howling into New York, and so did a new kind of fear, replacing the old fear of Nazis and Japanese. One afternoon, my father came home to announce that he had lost his job at Arma. They were laying off thousands, he said, now that the war was won. So instead of a sense of triumph, we were filled with uncertainty and doubt. My father had always worked, even in the Depression that everyone still talked about in tones of horror; now he was out of work, and on some of the radio shows they were talking about the possibility of a return of the Depression and how this one might even be worse.

If Roosevelt hadn't died, we wouldn't have this problem, my mother said. *Truman is just some damned haberdasher.* . . .

In the other rooms, while my mother and father talked about the lay-offs, the bills, and the rent, Tommy and I whispered in the dark about what would become of us. We wondered if they'd have to put us in an orphanage, like Oliver Twist, who was on the back of the HO Oats box, begging the cook for more gruel. Tommy wondered if we'd be evicted, like the Murphy family, who ended up sitting on the furniture in the rain down on Twelfth Street, bawling in shame while the street kids jeered.

Don't worry, I told Tommy, Patty Rattigan will take care of us.

And what if *he* loses his job?

He won't lose his job, I said confidently. He owns a bar.

My father did lose his job. Now he was home every day. He no longer slept in the afternoons and went off to work through the night. He was here, waking late, going out to look for a new job, often coming home drunk and sour.

My mother wasted no time with either blame or consolation; she started working as a nurse's aide at Methodist Hospital, leaving at three in the afternoon, coming home around eleven. Sometimes Tommy and I walked her to work, passing the bars of my father's world, and watched her vanish into the hospital. On the way back, we often saw him through the windows, head lifted in song. If he was afraid, he didn't show his fear to his friends. But I'd wonder: If there is no money in the house, if we are so poor that Mommy must go to work, then how can he afford to drink? He is having fun while Mommy works. When he *was* working, he couldn't save enough money to take her to Broadway. Now the war is over, he has no money at all, and he still can go to Rattigan's. My longing for him, my desperate need to know him, was turning into anger.

We had an account at Roulston's, where the cost of food was entered in a composition book behind the counter, to be settled later when my mother was paid. When she went off to work, she left lists of groceries for me to pick up, and I learned to say "on the book" with confidence. My father never shopped. Nor did he cook. My mother left cooked food in pots: lamb stew and barley soup, mixtures of potatoes and carrots, potatoes and peas, potatoes and turnips. These were to be heated up at dinnertime. And so, while my mother helped feed patients at the hospital, Tommy and I did what we called "the cooking." There was never any beef, of course. And that winter there was no butter. The war might be over, but the shortages were not. Into our kitchen came margarine. My mother told us the butter people wouldn't allow margarine to be pre-mixed, so we'd place the white waxy blocks in a bowl, sprinkle them with a yellow powder, and churn and mix and mix and churn until the results looked vaguely like butter. My father never did this job either; it was, he said, woman's work. But after Tommy and I did the work, he refused to use margarine on his toast; if he couldn't have butter, then he would have nothing. My anger was building.

The rationing of shoes ended, then of meat and finally of butter. But the shortages were not over. There was a shortage of coal, and when the winter of 1946–47 arrived in full force, we sat in the kitchen in sweaters — and on some frigid nights wore coats, mackinaws, and mittens — while listening to Jack Benny and Jimmy Durante or Commissioner Lewis B. Valentine on "Gangbusters." I was finished with knickers now, wearing long pants to school, but I was always cold and wore knee socks to bed. My father never seemed cold; he slept his deep phlegmy sleep, insulated by drink.

In the living room, (or as we called it, "the front room"), we saved money by using the kerosene stove only a few hours in the evening, to burn off the chill. But when the stove burned down and went out, the windows grew frosted and I would draw faces in the frost with my fingernails. When we talked, steam came in small puffs from our mouths. Overnight, shirts, underwear, and towels froze stiff on the kitchen clothesline. The drainpipes of the 14th Regiment Armory exploded from the cold, and great elaborate ice sculptures bloomed from the broken places. Almost every night, the fire engines woke us as they screamed to another disaster caused by kerosene stoves that burst into fire. The wind off the harbor howled through the night, and in the mornings the trees in the yards were glazed with ice. I've never again seen such a winter.

On the radio they were talking about starvation in Europe and Japan. My mother used this information whenever she served something like kelp. What did I mean, I didn't like kelp? *Don't you know they're starving in Europe?* Yes (I thought, but did not say): Yes, I know that, I know they're starving; but we're not doing too good in Brooklyn either. On those bitter nights when there wasn't enough food, I devised a mental trick: I conjured up pictures from the concentration camps, saying the words "Buchenwald" and "Auschwitz," reciting the rosary of horror. I made emaciated men in striped pajamas walk through the top floor right at 378 Seventh Avenue, all of them barefoot, their eyes mere dots in black holes, their cheekbones sharp and bare, their arms like dowels, their mouths slack; and I'd say to myself, *You have it good, you have a bed, you have food to heat up at night, you have pancakes, you have a kerosene stove, you are not from Buchenwald, you are not being buried by a tractor, fatherless, motherless, brotherless, sisterless, you are not a Jew.* Almost always, that cured my hunger and my cold and beat down my self-pity. And I would lie in the dark, thinking that no matter what I would be when I grew up, I would do nothing that sent men into camps to die.

And then I would fall into the gray nightmare, fighting my way through the skeletons of the gas chamber.

That winter refused to end. After school, every other afternoon, I went down to Fifteenth Street, my head bent into the wind off the harbor, and bought cheap day-old bread in a bakery next to the Globe movie house. Scabs of black snow were everywhere. My shoes wore out and my mother lined them with cardboard. At school, my number 2 Eberhard Faber pencils wore down to stubs, and some kids had no pencils at all. I drew my cartoons on wrapping paper, and sometimes it was too cold to draw.

One freezing afternoon, in a hallway on Twelfth Street, I heard from a friend about relief. If you were poor, he said, you went to the government and they gave you money that they called relief. There were many people on relief now, my friend said, just like the Depression. He named the families. And that night, after my mother came home, I asked her why she didn't get relief.

Never, she snapped.

Why?

Because we're proud people. We'll take nothing from them. We'll work.

In the spring, I went to work too.

5

THE *BROOKLYN EAGLE* was a handsome broadsheet that sold 300,000 copies a day and was read by four times that number. It was an afternoon paper and most of its circulation was home delivered. One afternoon, as I was walking to school at Holy Name, I saw Danno Kelly, one of the older brothers of the Kelly family from 471 Fourteenth Street, and said hello. He asked about my father and mother and then asked me what I was doing. Nothing, I said. Then he told me that if I wanted to work after school, he could give me a job helping him deliver the *Eagle*.

I started the next day.

After school, I met Danno at the *Eagle* storefront on Sixth Avenue, where dozens of boys were "boxing" papers in a triple fold and sliding them into delivery bags. I was very nervous. All of the boys were older than I was and they shouted and kidded and worked with amazing speed.

Here, Danno Kelly said, help me box these and put them in the bags.

I did, ineptly and clumsily, until I filled a bag. He was filling two others.

Now, Danno said, put the bag over your shoulder and let's go.

We set out together, to the route (always rhymed with "out") that Danno had on Fourth and Fifth streets, tree-lined streets of brownstones and white sandstone apartment houses. The arrangement was simple: Danno worked for the *Eagle* and I worked for Danno. I was discovering the rudiments of capitalism.

Danno's blocks were not part of the Neighborhood; the comfortable people lived here, people even better off than those on Eleventh Street. There were no fire escapes on these blocks, no stores or bars, and every house had a backyard. Peering through windows I saw another world, made of polished tables, muted lamps, elaborate wallpaper, rugs on wood floors. The men and women seemed always dressed up; there was nobody like Mr. Dix. The men were formal and sober, the women grave. But they took a lot of newspapers, paying for them once a week. Danno showed me how to throw a paper into a basement doorway, how to wedge it between cut glass doorknobs or into the grills of iron gates beneath the stoops. At the beginning of the route, I wobbled under the weight of the bag. But as I moved on, delivering the papers, the load got lighter, and toward the end, with only a few papers left, I felt stronger and light-headed and even powerful. I was delivering a *newspaper*.

At the end of the route, my shoulder was sore and I was wet with sweat inside my mackinaw but I felt as if I'd grown six inches in one afternoon. Danno put an arm on my shoulder and handed me a free copy of the paper.

Good job, he said. You're a little slow, but you'll get faster. Meet me tomorrow at the *Eagle* office.

I ran home. I took the stairs two and three at a time and burst into the kitchen, giddy with excitement. Nobody was home. There was the usual note from my mother, explaining that the big pot contained the soup, the saucepan the peas. No matter. I sat at the table and read the *Eagle*. I looked at the comics. I read the sports pages. I looked at all the other pages. And then I went back and read through it again. I worked for a newspaper now. The *Brooklyn Eagle. My* newspaper. My skin pebbled with awareness; I was now a member of the real Newsboy Legion.

When my father came home, I told him about the job. He smiled and rubbed my hair and laughed.

Great, he said. Great.

He took the *Eagle* and turned to the want ads. Then looked up and said, What's for dinner?

I worked every day after that for Danno Kelly, earning a dollar fifty a week. That was more than I'd ever had in my hand at one time. Because we were poor now, I gave the money to my mother, and she hugged me, and gave me fifty cents back. That was still a lot of money, and I used it in pursuit of Bomba books and the great new comics and some of the lost old ones. I also read the *Eagle* every day. The comics were an odd collection, from *Steve Roper* (which used to be called *Big Chief Wahoo*) to a dog strip named *Bo* and a terrific strip about a woman who could press a nerve in her wrist and vanish from sight: *Invisible Scarlet O'Neill*. I thought that would be a terrific power to have. But more important than the comics, I was reading the sports pages, where the columnists were Tommy Holmes and Harold C. Burr, and where there was only one real story: the Brooklyn Dodgers.

And the Dodgers brought me closer to my father.

6

A FEW WEEKS before Christmas, 1945, there was a sudden delivery of coal, carried into the house by a burly man with a blackened face. And on the day before Christmas, another man arrived with a turkey. I asked who the men were and was told by my father, the party. What party? The *Democratic* party. Said in the tone of: Are you an idiot? But I was still puzzled. This wasn't relief, was it? Of course not. Well, if they give you a turkey and coal, what do you have to give them in return?

Loyalty, he said. Always remember the most important thing in life: Vote the straight ticket.

On the street, someone pointed out a person called the district leader to me and explained that he worked out of Jimmy Mangano's Democratic

Club on Union Street. The man was tall and bald and cheerful, and he worked the same piece of the world as my father, moving from bar to bar. He was very close to Patty Rattigan, who also worked for the party. They were important people, I was told. They were Big Shots.

In the spring of 1946, a few weeks after I became an *Eagle* boy, I realized what a Big Shot could do when my father finally went back to work. One of the Big Shots had arranged for a job, right across the street in the Factory. On Thirteenth Street, we had lived in its cold shadow; now the Factory would give my father a living. He was going to work for the Globe Lighting Company, which made the new fluorescent lights in the building on our side of the Alley. He would work on an assembly line in a vast loft on the second floor, wiring fixtures all day long. I remember his mood when he came home one Saturday with news of the job.

Well, Annie, he said, the bad times are over.

That's wonderful, Billy, she said. I prayed and prayed, you know. I did a dozen rosaries.

You can buy that living room set now.

Well, maybe, she said. We'd better wait a bit and see.

He was drunk that night and drunk on Sunday too but he started on Monday, walking across the avenue, carrying his thermos, joining the stream of men coming up from the subways. Even with his wooden leg, he walked in a different way when he had a job.

That night, he came home late, looking tired. I heated up some stew and started talking about the Dodgers, rehashing a column from the *Eagle*. The team was on its way north and would soon begin the season at Ebbets Field.

This year, they'll go all the way, he said. Mark what I'm saying. All the way.

So I had discovered one of his passions. I would understand later that baseball was what truly made him an American; the sports pages were more crucial documents than the Constitution. He loved Leo Durocher, who was the manager all through the war, and Eddie Stanky, the grizzled little second baseman. But now the war was over and here they were coming back to the ballfields: Pete Reiser and Pee Wee Reese and Carl Furillo and hundreds of others. The Dodger war veterans were joining the players who were Dodgers through the war years, Augie Galan and Ducky Mcdwick and Dixie Walker. The pitchers were Kirby Higbe, Ralph Branca, Joe Hatten, Hank Behrman, Hugh Casey, Vic Lombardi. But Mickey Owen, who dropped the third strike in 1941, would not be back; he had run off to the Mexican League, like all those movie desperadoes who crossed the Mexican border ahead of the posse. It didn't matter. *He's just a bad memory*, my father said of Owen. I kept asking about Reiser, the outfielder they called Pistol Pete, the brilliant centerfielder who led the league in almost everything in 1941 but got hurt in 1942, crashing into the Ebbets Field wall, before going off to the navy. The *Eagle* was full of stories about him, his speed, his eye, his power, his immense heart.

He's a great ballplayer, my father said. You'll see.

Will the Dodgers win the pennant?

This is the year, he said. The pennant and then the World Series. That Mickey Owen's gone and good riddance. This year, we win.

The Dodgers started winning from opening day, and all over the Neighborhood that spring, you could hear Red Barber on the radio, announcing the games. I heard them from the buildings with fire escapes; I heard them while delivering the *Eagle* to the comfortable people. The games lived in our heads with a gorgeous reality. The *Eagle* covered the Dodgers in encyclopedic detail and even carried long reports on the Dodger farm teams in Montreal and St. Paul; in addition, my father started bringing home *The Sporting News*, a tabloid published in distant St. Louis, home of the fearsome Cardinals; it was jammed with information about every team in both leagues, and all the minor league teams too. And I learned that in 1946 up at Montreal, the Dodgers had one spectacular rookie. He was tearing up the league. His name was John Roosevelt Robinson. He was a Negro.

Ya can't have a nigger on a major league team, Tommy Moore said on Twelfth Street.

He can hit, I said. He can run. He can steal bases. Who cares if he's colored?

He'll never make it, Tommy Moore said.

We'll see.

I listened to Red Barber and talked to my father and read the newspapers (not simply the *Eagle*, but the *Daily News*, *Daily Mirror*, and *Journal-American* too) and learned to hate the Giants and fear the Cardinals of Musial and Slaughter. Baseball was only happening in my imagination; we simply couldn't afford to go to Ebbets Field, where tickets cost fifty cents. I fell into an afternoon routine: rushing home from school, delivering the *Eagle*, running home to listen to the serials and Stan Lomax, with the day's doings in the world of sports. And while I tried to concentrate on homework, on the Louisiana Purchase and the Dred Scott decision, on the differences between the predicate nominative and

the predicate adjective, as I diagrammed sentences and divided fractions, my head teemed with the Dodgers, with statistics, names, plays, and the distant figure of Jackie Robinson.

Then one evening, my father came home from work with a great smile on his face.

How'd you like to go to a ball game? he said.

That Sunday, in a big old Packard crowded with his friends from Rattigan's, I went for the first time to Ebbets Field. They had been given tickets by some Big Shot. We parked on a street near the ballpark, and I waited outside while they all went into a bar that was packed with fans. I didn't mind waiting. I watched thousands of people walking to the great ballpark, which seemed to rise heroically from the ground. People carried radios, stopped for hot dogs, even bought *my newspaper*, the *Eagle*. Music was playing. Traffic was jammed. I was jittery with excitement.

After a while, the men came out of the bar and we walked together to the ballpark, the other men pausing from time to time to let my father catch up. One of the men had the tickets, and we waited on line and then passed through the narrow gate into the rotunda. *Ebbets Field*. Hot dogs, music, shouts back and forth, thousands of fans: and we were going up a ramp, turning, climbing on another ramp, and then walking through a dark passage into the light.

And there it was: green and verdant and more beautiful than any place I had ever seen. Until that moment, the Dodgers were frozen black-and-white figures on the back pages of the *Daily News* under a headline saying FLOCK NIPS JINTS IN 11. But here they were, the color of human beings, running, throwing, hitting, lounging around, the white uniforms and blue caps gleaming in the sun. Down on the field, the Dodgers were taking batting practice, and one of the men handed me a program and showed me where the uniform numbers were listed. I knew most of them by heart, but now I could see them. There was Higbe. There was Furillo. That was Reese, slapping balls into the outfield. And there was Dixie Walker. The People's Cherce, they called him. And hey, shagging flies, running across the grass: Pete Reiser!

What do you think? my father said.

I love it, I whispered.

He smiled and nodded his head and said: Yeah. I love it too.

Then it was time to play the game. The Dodgers took the field to a gigantic roar. They were playing the Pirates. All through the game, the men kept ordering beer. They bought me two hot dogs and a Coke and an Eskimo Pie. A band called the Brooklyn Sym-phony played music.

The crowd cheered Durocher. They all stood and booed the umpires after a close play at second. They roared when Reiser doubled. They roared when Walker singled him home. The Dodgers won. It was the happiest day of my life.

That day, coming home in the crowded car from Ebbets Field, I was sure that now my father and I would be like fathers and sons in the movies and the magazines. He would teach me things about life. He would take me to places I had never seen. He would hug me when I did something right. We would be joined together, father and son. I was sure the Dodgers would win the pennant too.

7

ON MAY 8, 1946, my brother Brian was born in Methodist Hospital. I have no memory of my mother being pregnant; I still didn't understand the way children were conceived and born. She certainly never said anything to me, and my head was full of so many other things: comics, Bomba books, the Dodgers, school, the *Eagle*, and the sudden, mysterious appearance of erections in my life. The last had begun to happen on an almost daily basis and without any means of control: when I woke up; at school when I said the morning prayer with the rest of the class, pushed up against the back of a desk in a kneeling position; while gazing at Burma or the Dragon Lady in *Terry and the Pirates*; while falling asleep. I had no idea why this was happening and had nobody to ask.

But I remember the abrupt change at 378 Seventh Avenue in the first week of May. My mother was gone for a few days and then I came home from school and Brian was in a tiny crib in the kitchen, his head covered with black hair, his features all squinched up.

What's this? I said.

That's your new brother, my mother said, obviously blissful. His name is Brian.

Another brother. I was so used to the three of us kids, and now there was a fourth. Tiny. A baby. Everything was changed again. I touched Brian as he slept, his hair silky, and then my mother let me hold him. I was afraid I would drop him, but she stood there and smiled. She showed

me how she changed his diaper, washing him, using baby oil so his skin wouldn't get sore, then pinning up the diapers with large safety pins.

You have to be careful, she said. You don't want to stick him with the pin. He's such a wee thing.

Again, as there was for Kathleen's christening, we had a family party. The christening took place on a Saturday afternoon in the marble gloom of a long narrow church called St. Stanislaus, which was five blocks closer to us than Holy Name. Brian screamed when the priest poured water across his skull, and then everyone looked happy and posed with the baby for photographs and we walked home. The apartment soon filled up with everyone from 378 except the McEvoys. The aunts and uncles arrived, and my various cousins, along with the regulars from Rattigan's and Patty Rattigan himself. Someone brought in a vat full of ice cubes. Everyone else arrived with bottles and gifts for the baby. Soon there were songs and sandwiches and beer, more singing and more beer, and then just beer. Gallons of it.

Now I was in the grip of the curiosity that had ruined Adam. Everybody was drinking, except my mother, who never drank and was on this day too busy laying out sandwiches and finding clean glasses for the new arrivals. They all seemed so happy. And I wanted to taste the apparent source of their happiness: the beer. I knew it could harm people. I had seen it turn my father into a shambling wreck. But I wanted to know for myself.

When no one was looking, I lifted a half-full glass off the kitchen table and retreated through the rooms. There were people in all the rooms, but they didn't notice me. I went into the Little Room and locked the eye hook on the door. I stared at the glass, overwhelmed by the sense of the forbidden. But I needed to move into this unknown place, to cross this line, to see the back of this grown-up cave. I took a sip.

The taste repelled me. It was sour, even bitter. The smell was vile as the glass passed under my nose when I sipped. But this couldn't be all there was to drinking beer. If it was, why did anyone do it? I took another sip, then a third, expecting some powerful charge, some magical transformation, like the changes wrought by magical potions in the comic books. But nothing happened. Someone knocked on the door.

Who's in there? someone said; the voice sounded like that of my cousin Billy.

Me, I said. I'll be right out.

I finished the glass in one long gulp, belched, waited, hid the glass beside the bed, and left the Little Room. Nothing seemed different. The party roared on. But as I moved through the rooms, I did feel a kind of tingle. It was probably not from the drink. But I was sure that with one action I had changed. I had taken my first drink of beer. And I had done something that I could not reveal to my mother.

Back in the kitchen, nobody realized I'd been gone. My cousin Billy was down in the street with his sister Marie; so were Tommy and Kathleen. The singing got louder. Then, at one point, my father almost dropped Brian. My mother took the baby and handed him to me.

Don't let your father have him, she said. Not while he's drinking.

At dusk that Saturday, I sat in a big chair in the living room with Brian in my arms while my father once more delivered "Paddy McGinty's Goat." As always, the whole crowd joined in the last lines about leaving it all to Providence and Paddy McGinty's goat. But I gazed out the window, thinking about the waterfront dives I'd seen in movies and ports along the Amazon and lost cities in Yucatan, and I imagined myself coming to those places, standing at the bar in some forsaken outpost and ordering drinks like a man. Someday I'd do that. Someday.

8

AT THE END of June, a few days after my eleventh birthday, school ended and so did my job with the *Eagle*. Danno told me that people were canceling their subscriptions because of the Depression (for that's what everybody called it now in the Neighborhood). To make things worse, some of the other readers, the ones with a lot of money, were going off on summer vacations. In the fall, he said, he could hire me again. If the Depression ended. He would even recommend that I be given my own route.

Thanks, kid, said Danno Kelly, and I'll see you after Labor Day.

I was heartbroken. It wasn't just that I would no longer be earning money, but after four long months, I had grown used to the routine, hauling my *Eagle* bag over my shoulder each day and walking alone up the hill, delivering newspapers. That job gave me an identity; I wasn't just an American, an Irish Catholic, a student, a son, a brother; I was an *Eagle* boy. Now that identity was gone. For those months, I had given my all to the *Brooklyn Eagle*, my work and my loyalty, and now it had rejected me. Without that job, I understood how my father must have felt when they laid him off at Arma.

But I had little time to mourn. My mother told me that she had enrolled me for summer camp. The camp was sponsored by the Police Athletic League out of the 72nd Precinct, and it was up in the Adirondacks in the north of New York State. I'd be gone for three weeks.

This was fabulous news: an adventure, a trip into the unknown, far from Brooklyn. One morning, my mother took me to a Trailways bus station in New York, where I joined a group of other kids for the journey north. She kissed me good-bye, telling me to write. But as the bus pulled out, and I saw her waving at me from the platform, she seemed sad, even tearful. And I wanted to get up, rush to the front, get off the bus, and hurry back to Brooklyn.

But it was too late. The bus groaned and turned a corner, its engines making a gassy gargling sound, and my mother and the bus station vanished from view. I settled back, tense, guarded, looking at no one, thinking: At last, I am off on an adventure. I am leaving home to see the world.

The camp was nestled in a green valley between mountains. We lived in tents large enough for eight cots. The floors were wooden platforms. In the center of the tents was the main building, made of logs, where the kitchen was and where the counselors lived. Along one side of the camp, a cold clear stream moved swiftly over a bed of smooth stones. On the other side, deep piney woods climbed abruptly into the foothills. From a distance, the place seemed like paradise.

Up close, Fox Lair Camp was much more complicated than any paradise. I met poor boys from the great city beyond the borders of the Neighborhood: Italians from Red Hook and Bensonhurst; blacks from distant Harlem and mysterious Bedford-Stuyvesant; Jews out of Brownsville and the Lower East Side; "Spanish" kids from East Harlem and the Bronx. It was like one of those scenes from a desert movie, where the Red Shadow sends out his call and from all points of the horizon, groups of fighting men rally to his summons. Nobody had summoned these kids, of course, but they all told wild tales of fighting and robbing, knifing and shooting. They knew about all the great gangsters, from Lepke Buchalter to Al Capone. They'd seen blood and bodies. Or so they said. I thought Twelfth Street was pretty tough, but these kids made me feel like some sheltered boy.

On the first day, as I unpacked my small cloth bag and shoved it under my mattress, I was forced to fight. It was like a scene in a dozen movies. A kid named Cappy came over to me.

Whatta you? he said.

Whatta you mean, what am I?

You a Jewboy? A Mick? A guinea like me? What *are* you?

American, I said.

You a fucking wise guy or what? I ast you what the fuck you are.

American, I said. Irish American.

I shoulda figured dat, he said. A fuckin' Mick. 'Ey, who cut your fuckin' hair, Mick? Tonto?

I tried to ignore him, afraid of him, afraid of a fight, and he stepped between me and the cot.

I'm tawkin' to you, he said.

For a moment, I was riddled with fear. This was like the first day in 1A, mixed up with Brother Foppiano, who was also Italian American. Worse, I thought I saw something cold and heartless in Cappy's glistening brown eyes. Then, I knew that if I let him beat me up, the three weeks in Fox Lair Camp would be a long humiliation.

I don't want to talk to you, I said.

Zat so?

He pushed me and I fell back a few feet and then lunged at him. I punched him and kicked him and punched him again, and he careened out through the tent opening onto the dirt path. And then the counselor was there. He was tall, tanned, thick-bodied, with hairy arms and the attitude of a cop.

Hey, come on, what is this? he said, getting between us.

Nothing, I said.

Cappy was up now. He had a surprised look on his face.

We wuz just foolin' around, he said.

Yeah, I said. Just kidding.

Kid around some other way, the counselor said. I'm in charge of this tent and I don't want any fighting. Got me?

Cappy shrugged.

Now shake hands, the counselor said. The voice of authority.

Cappy held back. So did I. I had a strange feeling, as if I were part of this scene but also watching it from outside.

I gotta tell you *twice?* the counselor said. Shake *hands!*

So we shook hands. And when the counselor was gone, Cappy asked me my name and told me his and we went together to dinner. He made me laugh, with his rowdy talk and thick Brooklyn accent, and when the conversation turned to comics, and he talked on and on about Captain America and the Red Skull and Dr. Sivana and Hawkman, we became friends.

After that, we fell into the rhythms of the days in camp: softball, where I learned I could hit; footraces; nature walks; swimming and fishing in the stream. I loved the early mornings before breakfast, when the grass sparkled with dew. The nights were rowdier. There were assemblies around a roaring campfire, with sparks rising into the air to die in the dark, and songs made popular by the Sons of the Pioneers. "Cool Water" and "The Streets of Laredo." While the city boys shouted, cursed, whispered, and fought, while they squirmed and scratched and slapped at mosquitoes, while they bragged about the many beers they'd drunk back home and the gangsters they knew and the women they'd "boffed" or "humped," the poor counselors tried to get them to sit still for *The Song of Hiawatha.*

But I loved those campfires, the primitive sense they gave me of having a center, combined with the eerie feeling that I'd been there before, on an ancient battlefield or in Indian camp or on the edge of some lost city. Most of all, I was thrilled to be part of the crowd, sitting in the dark among the rough tribes of New York. Thrilled. And envious. And a little afraid.

The fear grew more specific when I came to know a black kid from our tent. His name was Arnold and he was from Bed-Stuy. He was small, taut, with skin the color of tea with milk, and hazel eyes that made him look both feminine and sinister.

Arnold was a steady presence at Fox Lair Camp, though he seemed also capable of vanishing as swiftly as Invisible Scarlet O'Neill. I don't remember him playing ball, fishing, swimming, hiking along mountain trails. But there he was at breakfast, using the word "motherfucker" in every other sentence, explaining "cocksucker," making detailed diagrams on writing paper of the mechanics of sex. As he walked across the field between the tents and the commissary, words like "cunt" and "pussy" would fall from his lips, followed by "muff diver" and "cunt lapper." Even Cappy was both enthralled and mystified.

At dusk one day, Arnold motioned us into the woods. We disappeared behind a screen of bushes and Arnold reached into a hole burrowed in the roots of a tree. He removed a dirty quart bottle of red wine.

Where'd you get that? I asked.

Found it.

Where?

In the kitchen.

He looked at us with those eyes, a sly smile on his face, and removed the cork. He took a sip and handed it to Cappy. Without a word, Cappy took a swig. Then it was my turn. I didn't want wine. I wanted to sit beside the campfire and watch the sparks merge with the stars. But this was a kind of dare, like that time on the roof with the Bottomless Pit. If I didn't take a swig, they'd think I was a kid, a scaredy cat, a momma's boy, a sissy.

So I took a drink, holding the wine in my mouth as I passed the bottle to Arnold. I hoped I could spit it out while the other two weren't looking. But Arnold was staring at me, judging me. I swallowed the wine. Arnold grinned. Cappy whispered: Not bad. Arnold took another sip. Cappy talked about how his grandfather from Italy made his own wine, putting all the grapes in a big vat and jumping on them with his bare feet.

Arnold said: The motherfuckin' wine must taste like fuckin' feet.

Cappy said: No, no, it tastes fuckin' great. I had some at my cousin's wedding.

Arnold took a third swallow and passed the bottle to Cappy. My mouth felt sticky.

Cappy said: Not bad, Arnold, not motherfuckin' bad.

They giggled. The bottle came to me again. I took my swig, swallowed, handed the bottle to Arnold. The sense of the forbidden flooded through me again. My father had once said to me, *The wino is the lowest form of man, except for an informer.* Would I become a wino if I kept drinking? Was drinking wine a mortal or a venial sin? And how could it be a sin at all? At every Mass, the priests drank wine. The blood of Jesus, they told us. How could it be a sin in the woods and a virtue on an altar? The bottle came around again and I drank once more of the blood of Jesus.

Then Arnold produced a cigarette. A Camel. My father's brand. He lit it with a wooden match, snapping off the head just the way my father did during the match shortage, the way I never could. Arnold took a drag, handed it to Cappy, who did the same and passed it to me. I was listening for the sounds of counselors or other kids, afraid of being discovered.

Don't slob it, Cappy said as I took the cigarette. Don't get it wet wit' spit.

I took a tense drag. The smoke made my head balloon. I started to cough, and Arnold looked around toward the camp, alarmed. But I didn't slob the cigarette. I handed it to Arnold and said with confidence: Pass me the wine.

I took a slug, the cough stopped, but I never had another sip. Someone was crashing through the woods. Arnold capped the bottle, slipped it under the roots, then tamped out the cigarette.

Anybody in there? a grown-up voice said.

Yeah, Arnold replied. We looking for snakes.

Do that some other time. We're roasting marshmallows.

So off we went to the marshmallow roast, looking, I suppose, like kids off a brotherhood poster.

In the first few days that followed the night of the wine, I found reasons to avoid the hideout in the woods. I was playing softball. I was swimming. I was picking wild strawberries. Arnold just stared at me with a thin smile on his face, as if he knew how much I wanted to return to the wine and the cigarettes, to the forbidden, to the secret life of the outlaw. I was desperate now for things to read, starved for the alternate lives of fantasy and imagination that had become part of my days; there were no books or newspapers in the camp.

But Arnold was weaving another world of fantasy for all of us in the tent. Sometimes he bragged about the number of times he had been drunk and how many times he'd smoked reefer, a kind of cigarette that made you feel *real* good. He described the taste of rum, of whiskey, of bourbon, beer, and wine. He described roaring parties, wild music, amazing adventures in the nights of motherfucking Brooklyn. One evening, he smuggled another bottle of wine into the tent and we all took swigs. It tasted better this time, like thick grape juice.

And when he wasn't describing his greatness as a drinker, Arnold's subject was sex. He told us that he fucked lots of women, all over his neighborhood. Fat ones, skinny ones, girls with big asses and tits. He even fucked his older sister once when she was drunk. That was the best way to fuck a woman. Get her drunk first. Wine and kisses. That was the way.

Arnold also led the way to one of the great astonishments of Fox Lair Camp: masturbation. I wasn't the only boy in that tent who was ignorant of the practice. Once again, the devil's agent was Arnold, age eleven. One night, after lights out, as we all shifted in our cots to find comfortable positions, Arnold spoke from the darkness.

Hey, why don't we have a circle jerk?

Cappy said: A what?

Arnold said: We get in a circle and jerk off.

One kid said: Wuz dat?

A couple of kids laughed in a knowing way. But Arnold was a determined pedagogue. He got up, dropped his shorts (which all of us wore to bed), and stood before the boy in the dim shimmer of leaking moonlight. Arnold held his small penis in his hand.

Watch me now, he said, and started playing with himself. Almost immediately, his penis got larger and harder.

Now *you* do it, Arnold said.

The boy did.

Now you go up and down like this, Arnold said.

The boy moved his hand up and down on his erection. Everybody else was silent.

Now, Arnold said, you think about some woman . . . you know, like Betty Grable or Rita Haywort'. She got big tits. She gotta big ass. And you on top of her, you stickin' it *in* her, you in her big wet hairy pussy, you in her motherfuckin' *ass!*

Arnold groaned and ejaculated on the floor. The boy ejaculated on himself, moaning and whimpering. Some of the boys giggled. Then Arnold sneaked outside, felt under the floorboards of the tent platform, came back with a bottle of wine.

Here, drink this, he said, handing the bottle to the boy. Make you feel sweet and good and ready to do it again.

The boy took a sip, Arnold a long swallow.

Who wants some juice? he said.

Cappy took a swallow, then passed it to me. I swallowed a long swig, then turned away to sleep. Arnold went back outside. He came back and stood before the other boy, holding his penis.

Wanna do it again? Arnold said.

Nah, I'm too tired. Maybe tomorrow.

Arnold went back to bed and then the tent was very still. Boys shifted in their cots. Then one boy moaned. And another. Arnold laughed. Away off in the mountains, coyotes howled. The night breeze made the tent flaps billow and sigh. Under the army blanket I reached down and touched my hard penis and thought about the Dragon Lady.

I learned to talk the way the others did, using "fuck" and "shit" and "prick" for punctuation and rhythm, saying "dis" and "dat" instead of "this" and "that," dropping my *g*'s, removing *t*'s from other words ("bottle," for example). I practiced walking like the tough guys, in a rolling way, putting the weight on one foot while the other dragged behind. I stopped saying "excuse me." I spit a lot.

Twice more, Cappy and I sneaked away to drink wine with Arnold in the woods, but I did this more to show that I could be as bad as anyone rather than for any real desire for wine. To me, the taste of wine was as sickly sweet as the taste of beer was sour; I wished I had a bottle of Frank's Orange. And though I felt a tingle in my head from the wine, and an odd thickness in my hands, I felt no ache to have a bottle all to myself. I much preferred hitting a softball past the third baseman.

Then one night near the end of the second week, I was awakened from a deep sleep. Arnold was beside me in my bed, his hard prick up against my rectum.

Hey, I said. What —

Come on, baby, Arnold whispered. Open up your sweet white ass.

I turned. His penis was against my hip now. His breath had a stale sweet smell, like dried wine.

Get the fuck outta here, Arnold, I said.

Come on, baby, he purred. Make Arnold happy.

I pushed him away, but then his voice changed and he locked an arm around my neck.

Do what I say, he whispered coldly. I got a knife and I'll cut your motherfuckin' white throat.

I panicked at the mention of the knife, and shoved him hard, kicking at him as he fell on the floor, and then Cappy was awake, followed by the other kids. I kept punching and kicking at Arnold as if my life depended on it. Cappy looked astonished. But my fury must have convinced him about who was right, so he kicked at Arnold too and stomped on his knees. And then the lights came on. The counselor stood there in his underwear. His hair was mussed, his face rumpled and irritated.

Okay, he said, what's going on in here?

Arnold stood up slowly, his hazel eyes wide in righteous anger. I couldn't see any knife.

This fuckin' white boy is a *faggot!* he screamed.

His nose was bleeding, his lower lip split. He pointed at me, spitting out the words: I'uz sleepin' real peaceful and he gets in bed with me, tries to fuck me inny ass!

That's a lie! I said, rushing at him again. The counselor grabbed me and spun me around. I was crazy with rage. He's *lying!* He's a motherfuckin' *liar!*

All right, watch your language . . .

Then Arnold looked at me from those eyes, a sneer on his face, and made a slicing sign across his neck with a finger. The counselor must have seen this too. He turned to the other kids and asked them if they'd seen what happened. There was a long silence. Nobody wanted to be an informer. Arnold smirked. And then one boy spoke. It was the boy who learned to masturbate from Arnold.

He tried to do it to me, too, he said.

Who did?

Arnold.

Then another kid cleared his throat and whispered: Me too.

The counselor looked around at us, studying our faces, and then turned to Arnold.

Pack up, Arnold, he said. And come with me.

They went off to the main building, Arnold limping on the leg hurt by Cappy's stomping. He looked as if he were under arrest. But as he vanished into the dark, carrying his small cloth bag, I felt neither relief nor triumph. Instead, I lay awake in the dark for a long time. I felt like a rat. A stool pigeon. A creature even lower than a wino. It didn't matter that Arnold had lied about me and I had answered him back. I had collaborated with the enemy.

The next day, Arnold was gone from Fox Lair Camp.

9

WHEN I CAME HOME from Fox Lair Camp, I was a changed boy. I felt tougher, older, suddenly conscious that I was moving toward becoming a man. After all, I had traveled hundreds of miles to the distant Adirondacks, far beyond the frontiers of the Neighborhood, an immense distance from New York itself, and I had made that journey without the protection of my mother or father. In the great mountain gathering of the New York tribes, I had survived. I thought I knew about sex now, that immense blurred mystery. I had drunk wine. And fought off Arnold. Softball and wild strawberries were marginal to the journey; I had learned to walk in the world, with no help from anyone. It didn't matter that I could not explain much of this to my mother. These were three weeks in *my* life, not hers, and certainly not weeks in the life of my father; that journey belonged to me alone.

In some ways, the trip to Fox Lair Camp was my first true opening to consciousness. And drinking was a crucial part of it. Drinking wine in the woods wasn't simply another sensual pleasure, like eating ice cream; it was an act of rebellion, a declaration of self. The camp had rules and I was breaking them. It was also an act of communion, with Arnold, with Cappy. Both states of consciousness would remain with me through years of drinking. Through the agency of Arnold, I also discovered Evil. I don't mean that *sex* was evil. That, and drinking, were only part of a generalized negation that flowed from Arnold with a dark steady force. He made me afraid. The fear he inspired wasn't physical; it was deeper and darker than that. Arnold lived by his own rules, not the rules I was learning. Nothing could persuade him from his desires except force.

That summer, I was converted to the creed of machismo, although I would not hear that word for another decade. On the street when I was back from camp, I began to talk tough, sprinkling my language with "fuck" and "cocksucker" and "prick." I could be as tough as the other kids on Twelfth Street; from the start, language was part of the pose. At home, my mother corrected my slide into "dis" and "dat," "dem" and "dose," but I reverted to them when I hit the street, wearing the Brooklyn accent like armor. I walked in the rolling gait I'd picked up from the bad boys at camp. I talked about girls and asses and tits. Much of this was a mask, but I was quickly making myself comfortable behind it. And of course I wasn't alone; in that neighborhood, looking like a hard guy was part of the deal.

On the roof next door to ours, Mr. Sicker and Mr. De Saro built a pigeon coop that summer, talking with passion to anyone who'd listen about "tiplets" and "homers" and the intricacies of flight and habit and instinct. They spent hours on the roof, watching their flocks gliding in tight formation around the sky, as happy in their intensity as I was with my books and comics. Their passion impressed me, but as hard as I tried, I couldn't share it; there was something disturbing to me about the gurgling, swallowing sounds of the pigeons. Besides, if you could fly like a homer, why would you ever come home?

A few buildings away from ours, I met Mr. Dexter, a change clerk in the subway. He went to work before the morning rush hour and came home in early afternoon. Every afternoon in the good weather, he appeared on his roof to lift weights. Mr. Dexter was small and wore glasses, but his upper torso was ropy with muscle. I asked him if I could try lifting the barbell and he said sure. I was stronger than I thought I was. He showed me how to do curls and presses, how to adjust the bells with a small wrench, how to create daily routines of "reps," the same exercise repeated dozens of times. Soon, I added weight lifting to the rhythm of my days.

At some point, I started going to the Police Athletic League gym on Eighth Street to watch the amateur fighters. Again, I saw how important repetition was to learning; on the floor, the fighters repeated the same punch over and over again, while time was chopped into three-minute segments by an automatic bell; then the punches were joined to others in combinations, with the flat-nosed paunchy trainer shouting his instructions: Jab, *bend!* Double the jab, *bend!* Now *punch* outta da bend! I was still too young for the boxing team, and too shy to insist (and afraid of getting hurt). But back home, alone on the roof, or crouched in front of the bedroom mirror, I would practice jabs and hooks and right hands. I would bend at the knees after the jab. I would double the jab and throw the right hand. All the while breathing hard through my nose, my mouth clamped shut into a hard mask.

On the street, boxing was as much a part of our talk as baseball. In the summer of 1946 everybody in New York was talking about Rocky Graziano, who was knocking out all comers. Rocky, the tough middleweight from the East Side, Rocky, who talked like a lot of the kids from Fox Lair Camp. But my father didn't care much for Graziano. He fights little guys, he said. He's the best middleweight in the welterweight division. Or put another way, he never fights anyone his own size. My father's favorite was Willie Pep, a featherweight like himself, fast, fresh, audacious, a champion of the world. I was sure that if my father had legs, he'd box like Willie Pep.

But even Willie Pep wasn't the best. One day, my father showed me a picture of a black fighter in the *Daily News*, handsome and slick and lean. *That's Sugar Ray Robinson*, he said. *He's the greatest fighter who ever lived.* There were no qualifications; he described Robinson in the same flat way he would use to describe Mount Everest as the highest mountain in the world.

How would he do against Graziano? I asked.

He would knock Graziano out in four rounds, he said flatly.

When they did fight years later, Robinson knocked out Graziano in three.

In the streets, we still played the now forgotten games of the New York summers. Stickball was the supreme game, a kind of tabloid version of baseball, played with a broom handle as a bat and a pink rubber ball manufactured by the A. G. Spalding Co. In every street in New York, this ball was called a spaldeen. The spaldeens had vanished during the war and the game was played for a while with hairy tennis balls, until even they had disappeared. But coming home from Fox Lair Camp, I felt a special excitement spreading through the neighborhood: *Spaldeens are back!*

From out of Unbeatable Joe's and Rattigan's and the other bars, the men and the veterans came piling into the streets again, taking our bats, once more playing the city's greatest game, whacking spaldeens past trolley cars and over rooftops, running bases on heat-softened tar, making impossible catches, dodging trolley cars and trucks, almost delirious with joy. The war was over. The fucking war was finally over.

Stickball ruled us. On Saturday mornings, the older guys played big games against visitors from other neighborhoods or went off themselves to play beyond our frontiers. *Money game!* someone would shout, and suddenly we were all moving to the appointed court and the great noisy fiesta of the stickball morning. The players drank beer from cardboard containers on the sidelines and ate hero sandwiches and smoked cigarettes. They were cheered by neighbors, girlfriends, wives, and kids. And standing on the sidelines during those first games were the veterans, holding the spaldeens, bouncing them, smelling them in an almost sacramental way.

The men played on summer weekends; we kids played every day. There were still very few cars on the streets in that year after the war, so the "court" was always perfectly drawn, with sewer plates marking home and second base, while first and third were chalked against the curbs. The rules were settled before each game: one strike and you were out; off the factory wall or off a passing trolley car was a "hindoo" — which meant the play didn't count. The great hitters could hit the ball at least "three sewers," and it was said of Paulie McAleer of the Shamrock Boys that he once hit a ball an incredible five sewers. In memory, the games seem continuous and the days longer, richer, denser, *and* emptier than any others in my life. We did nothing and we did everything. You would wake, the radio playing, the rooms thick with the closed heat (and sometimes the sour smell of drink), grab something to eat — bread and butter covered with sugar, a piece of toast — and then race down the stairs, to burst into the streets. On a perfect Saturday in August, Twelfth Street would be wet from the water wagon, the air fresh, nobody else around, the tenements brooding in Edward Hopper light, and then a door would open and Billy Rossiter would appear with the bat and the spaldeen, and that was all we needed. We'd play off the factory walls until the others came down; we'd play ten hits a piece until there were enough players to choose up sides. And then we'd play until dark.

After stickball, or wedged between the ball games, there were other games too: kick the can, off the point, box ball and punchball, Johnny on the pony (*Buck buck, how many horns are up*), and the greatest of all: ring-o-levio.

One Saturday, we were playing ring-o-levio on Twelfth Street and one of the players on the other side was Frankie Nocera. He was a lean black-haired wild-tempered kid who lived in one of the corner tenements. A few years earlier, hitching a ride on a trolley car, he fell off and his foot went under a steel wheel; he lost the tip of his right foot and became known as No Toes Nocera. Winter and summer, he wore an ankle boot with a steel tip that replaced the missing toes. Because of my father's leg, Frankie and I should have been friends. Frankie, after all, was a cripple. For some reason, he had become my nemesis, the way Dr. Sivana was the nemesis of Captain Marvel or the Joker of Batman. On Thirteenth Street, Brother Foppiano was my nemesis. Now, on Twelfth Street, it was No Toes Nocera. It must have had something to do with the great struggle between the Irish and Italians. Or maybe it was just chemistry.

Unlike Arnold, Frankie didn't make me feel that I had opened a curtain and glimpsed Hell. But he was always *there*, pinching, leaning, nudging, harassing. I'd be playing marbles in the lot and he'd grab a peewee and walk off; if I went after him, he'd drop the marble, or roll it toward a sewer, and laugh. I'd be on a stoop after a game, reading a comic book, and he'd snatch at it, run away, force me into a losing tug-of-war over the comic, as if sensing that I wouldn't risk tearing the cover. He'd squirt water pistols at me; he'd ask for a ride on a scooter and go off for an hour; he was one of those kids who was always grabbing your hat. He wasn't *bad*. But he was a misery.

Naturally, when we played ring-o-levio, Frankie was on the opposing team. The rules of the game were as primitive as warfare. We divided ourselves into two teams, or sides. After a coin toss, one team went out, scattering around the immediate neighborhood, looking for hiding places. The second team would then hunt down the first, capturing each opponent and returning him to a pen whose walls were marked on the tarred street with chalk. The pen was called home. When the last man was captured, the sides switched roles, the hunters becoming the hunted. Imprisonment, however, wasn't permanent. If you were one of the hunted, and could elude capture through guile or deception, you could make a sudden dash, race directly at the wall of defenders around the border of the pen, crash through them, shout the magical phrase *Home free all!* and liberate all members of your side. Most of the time it was impossible to breach the wall of defenders, who stood there with arms locked. But if you succeeded, it was a moment of sheer power and glory.

On this day, I was the last man out. I had evaded all my pursuers and then, gathering strength on the slope above Seventh Avenue, I started my run for home. I dodged left, feinted right, zigzagged, and twirled, never stopping; saw the crowd of defenders guarding home, under the lamppost in front of Mr. Dix's house; saw my side waiting inside the pen, all of them tensing, the defenders crouching, then stepping forward, Frankie Nocero among them; saw them forming a human wall; saw them getting larger as I came closer. And then I leaped, high and strong, feeling that I could fly, saw a blur of bodies and faces, rammed into shoulders and elbows and torsos, and was through! Shouting *Home free all!*

My side scattered into freedom. I whirled to escape. And then saw Frankie Nocero rising from the tangle of defenders. Saw Frankie's eyes wide in rage. Saw him coming at me. Then felt a numbness in my face as a punch hit my nose, then a sharp pain on the side of my head as he threw another.

I backed up, numb, my ears ringing, the world suddenly filmy, and he threw another punch and missed, and someone yelled *Right hand.* I threw the right hand and hit him. Then threw it again, and missed. And again, and hit him, still backing up, Frankie making a snorting sound, his teeth bared, his hair all spiky. Someone else yelled: *Jab, jab, use da jab.* Then I remembered the PAL gym, and Graziano, and the pictures of Sugar Ray, and I raised my hands in the boxer's stance; and when Frankie came at me again I speared him with a jab and threw a right hand behind it. For the first time in my life I heard cheers. A crowd was now gathering. I saw them as a blur, a presence, heads and bodies and no faces; but they were *there*, and they made the fight even more important. I couldn't be humiliated in front of a crowd; I couldn't run; I absolutely could not cry. I remember coiling into an almost ferocious concentration. I jabbed and hit Frankie, and jabbed again, then feinted the jab and threw the right hand and amazingly, Frankie went down. I went down on top of him, battering him with punches, until he started screaming *Stop stop I give up stop okay stop.*

I got off him then, rising slowly, my hands still fists, afraid of a trick, and then heard more cheers, and suddenly my brother Tommy was there and Billy Rossiter and Billy Delaney and they were hugging me and clenching fists in approval and then I saw the crowd of men outside of Unbeatable Joe's and they were clapping and laughing before going back to the bar. I had fought a street fight and won. Not with kids from camp whom I'd never see again. Here at home. On the court. In the Neighborhood. And men cheered. I hoped they would tell my father what I'd done.

Then I saw Frankie Nocera walking into his building. He was holding his face. There was blood all over the front of his shirt. Very red blood. He was absolutely alone, limping on that gimpy foot. I started to go to him, suddenly feeling sorry for him. I wanted to be gracious, the way winning prizefighters were after boxing matches. But Frankie vanished into the dark hallway. We all went to Sanew's then and bought bottles of Frank's Orange or Mission Bell Grape, drinking them greedily, passing them around. Soda had never tasted better. And someone said, *That Frankie, he needed a good fuckin' beating and you sure give it to him.* But even in triumph, something bothered me about the fight.

The next day I saw Frankie again. He was sitting alone on his stoop. Both eyes were hidden behind pads of swollen purple flesh; his nose was thick and crooked. My brother Tommy told me later that Frankie had to go to the hospital because his nose was broken. So I went to him, my mind a confusion of power and pity, a bit nervous that he would lash out at me with the steel toes or come up with a knife.

I didn't want the fight, Frankie, I said. You started it.

Fuck it, he said sadly, with a little wave of his hand.

Let's forget about it, I said.

He looked at me as if knowing that he would never forget about it and neither would I.

Come on, I said. We'll go read comics.

He stared at me for a long moment and then got up, and we walked off to look at stories of heroes and perils in a simpler world.

10

ON SUNDAYS, the family sometimes went visiting. That's what it was called: visiting. You went to someone else's house and brought along some cold cuts or Italian bread or beer and entertained each other. We almost always went to visit my father's relatives; my mother had friends but no relatives in America. After Mass, the whole family would walk down to Fifth Avenue, still dressed in Sunday best, and get on the trolley and rattle out to Bay Ridge to see Uncle Tommy or Uncle Davey, Aunt Louie or Aunt Nellie, and all my cousins. We couldn't play in the street because we were in our good clothes; but visiting wasn't play to us, it was a show. There would be food and drink and singing in the parlor. And here, as in the bars, my father was always the star. The kids were called upon to perform too, singing songs or reciting poems. I was too shy to sing; how could I compete with my father? But every time we went visiting, I was asked that most awful question: What Are You Going to Be When You Grow Up? And during that crowded year, I started answering: a cartoonist.

Usually, they would laugh and someone would get paper and a pencil and ask me to draw something, and I would be forced to draw in a state of anxiety that was worse than fighting Frankie Nocera. I gave them Dick Tracy. Or Flattop. Or Batman. They were the easiest, the faces I could draw without copying. And they would laugh and say, *That's good, Peter,* and then I was free, off the stage, released, and I could ease away from their attentions.

But I was telling the truth. That summer when I was eleven, I first conceived the idea of becoming a cartoonist. There wasn't any special moment that I remember, no Shazam-like bolt of explosive insight that told me this. The ambition was, I suppose, tentative at first, whispered, a wish in the dark while the trolley cars ding-dinged through the night. But going back to Simon and Kirby and *Captain America,* I had learned that comics were written and drawn by men and those men were paid very well for their work. The money wasn't the most important thing; it was something else: they were being paid for doing what they loved to do. My father had a job, and he was paid. But he wasn't working at something he liked. Nobody paid men to drink in saloons.

The focus of my fantasy was Milton Caniff, who was in his last year drawing and writing *Terry and the Pirates.* Suddenly, I got it. The locale was something that my grandfather must have known: the coasts, rivers, plains, and mountains of southern China. I identified with Terry Lee, the blond young pilot. I wished I could talk as fast as the wisecracking Hot Shot Charlie, with his red hair, freckles, Boston accent, corncob pipe, and flight cap worn with a swagger on the back of his head. I wanted to have someone around who was like Pat Ryan or Flip Corkin, a guy who knew the world and could show me how to live in it.

There was something else: Caniff's women put me in a kind of fever. Every one of them exuded a lush sexuality that no other cartoonist has ever matched and did so without ceasing to be a specific individual. They weren't just pinups. Not one of them was a doormat. Every one of them made her way through the world of men without complaint. There was Burma, all blond and shimmering, like women in the thirties movies at the Minerva, a mixture of Sadie Thompson and Jean Harlow, always singing the "St. Louis Blues," sometimes for money and sometimes for love, always smoking, tough with bad guys, soft on Pat Ryan, burning brightly in Terry's life for a while then abruptly vanishing, only to turn up again in some other exotic Asian port. And even larger, grander, more powerful, was the Dragon Lady, Caniff's most famous creation. Sleek black hair framed her oval Dolores Del Rio face with its almond eyes and high Eurasian cheekbones, the eyebrows reduced to fine lines that lay angrily on her face like tiny daggers. Usually the Dragon Lady wore a scarlet cape and under the cape, in fancy gowns or military trousers, she had the full-breasted body of a million wet dreams. The Dragon Lady was not only beautiful; she was often evil — venomous, treacherous, violent — and in a dark and scary way, that made her even more desirable to me.

I began to devour Caniff, driven by a sense of sudden urgency. It had been announced in the *Daily Mirror* that this was Caniff's last year doing *Terry* for the *Daily News;* he would create a new strip that would run in the *Mirror.* I wanted to preserve *Terry* before it was gone forever. I clipped *Terry* from the *Daily News* every day and filed the strips in letter-sized envelopes. I saved the Sunday pages, with their beautiful colors and spectacular action panels. Then I started buying scrapbooks, oversized books made of cheap coarse paper, and began filling them with the *Terry* strips, using the pale yellow glue called mucilage. But there was a problem. In Caniff's wonderful comic strip, time actually passed; Terry got older (although the women didn't). The characters lived in the real world (or so I thought), the world of war and women and airplanes, the world described each day in the front of the newspaper. They didn't inhabit Captain Marvel's world of magic lightning or the garish places where Captain America pursued the Red Skull. *Terry and the Pirates* was like some long picaresque novel, and in 1946 I felt that I had started reading it near the end. The newspaper sequences were self-contained, each story taking about two months before shifting into another combination of heroes and villains. But I wanted to read the novel's early chapters too. Caniff often brought back characters from Terry's youth; the Dragon Lady, Pat Ryan, April Kane, Burma, made more than one appearance. I wanted the whole story, not just its final episodes.

The task of piecing together that story was like the search for the full run of the Bomba books (and resembled the basic task of reporting). I had to work backwards. In tiny type at the bottom of each strip there was a copyright line that supplied the year of its first appearance; a hand-lettered date gave the month and day: 4/1, say, or 6/24. Unfortunately, there were almost no old newspapers in the neighborhood; like my skates, they'd gone to the war, bundled up for scrap paper drives. But many of the newspaper strips had reappeared in the brightly colored pages of *Super Comics*, which also reprinted other strips from the *Daily News*. They had also been converted into Big Little Books. So I followed the same route taken in the Bomba search, exploring the archipelago of secondhand comics shops and bookstores. I was driven by fundamental questions. How did Terry Lee get to China? Who was Pat Ryan? When did they meet the Dragon Lady? Why on earth would Pat Ryan fall in love with prissy Normandie Drake if Burma was around? I wanted to read it all, to keep going back until I found the beginning. In a good story, something happened and as a result, something *else* happened. You went to China or to Fox Lair Camp, and you were changed by what happened to you. I wanted to know what happened to Pat Ryan and Terry Lee.

My obsession with *Terry and the Pirates* was different in one sense from the long pursuit of the Bomba books. I wanted to know Milton Caniff. In a way, *he* was the true hero of the comic strip. I would sit at the kitchen table and try to copy his figures and always failed; drawing Flip Corkin wasn't as simple as making an image of Flattop or Batman, and the Dragon Lady was impossible. I would get the general shapes down on paper but there was always something wrong: the original expression changed into an empty smudge, the ears were in the wrong places, the hands looked thick and clumsy. But I kept trying. After all, Caniff was the best. Like Sugar Ray Robinson. And there was no point in trying to be less than the best, was there?

In 1947, Caniff, as announced, left *Terry* to another artist, George Wunder, and started *Steve Canyon* in the *Daily Mirror*. There was a great burst of publicity. Caniff appeared on the cover of *Time*. The *Mirror* did a series of ads building up to the debut of the new strip. I learned that Caniff was an Irish-American too, from Ohio; had gone to college; wanted to be an actor; came to New York to work for the Associated Press, where he drew a strip called *Dickie Dare*, and went on to do *Terry* in 1934 for the *Daily News*. He was syndicated in more than four hundred newspapers and now lived in a beautiful house in New City, New York. The photographs of the studio showed a room that was larger than our entire flat. I saved all this publicity, staring at Caniff's face, looking at examples of his work going back to his childhood, and then, from the first great Sunday page, clipped every *Canyon* strip until I went into the navy in 1952.

That first Sunday page of *Steve Canyon*, dated January 18, 1947, was as good as any movie. For five panels, we don't see Canyon's face, but his character is established by various people who greet him on his way into an office building. An Irish cop thanks him for stopping off to see his sister in Shannon; the doorman thanks him for sending a souvenir from Egypt to his son; a blind newsdealer, called only "sarge," and obviously a war veteran, thanks Canyon for backing him in setting up the newsstand; a flower girl offers him a carnation for his buttonhole, but when he turns her down he says that she and her mother are due for a movie on him; the elevator girls stammer a hello and say that for him, they won't wait for a full car. So we know immediately that Canyon is a good, generous man, a world traveler, thoughtful, personal, attractive to women. We see his face for the first time in the sixth panel; it's lean, and there's a black streak in his blond hair. Wearing a checkered overcoat, he opens the door with his company's name on the glass: Horizons Unlimited. Beyond the door is his secretary, a Polynesian woman named Feeta Feeta, with lovely breasts under a polka-dotted blouse, flowers in her hair, talking on the phone. On the line is Mr. Dayzee, the formal and officious male secretary to a woman named Copper Calhoun, "the big she-wolf of the stock market." Dayzee virtually orders Canyon to come immediately to Calhoun's apartment; Canyon refuses the order, objecting to the tone of the demand, and tells Dayzee that "the click you hear will mean you're soloing." Feeta Feeta looks resigned; the office rent is due, "but I guess it's bad form to get into regular habits like that. . . ." In the final panel, Copper Calhoun, with sleek black hair, the arched eyebrows of the Dragon Lady, a long cigarette in one hand, says: "I want that man!! . . . Get him!"

I loved this and sat down to labor over a long letter to Caniff, telling him how great it was and how I wanted to be a cartoonist too. A few weeks later a package arrived in the mail from New City. Inside was a note from Caniff himself, a copy of a brochure he'd written for aspiring cartoonists, "A Guide for an Armchair Marco Polo," and a colored picture of Steve Canyon. I was hooked. If *Terry* belonged to my mother first, *Steve Canyon* was mine from the start. On the street, nobody else cared much about my obsession, so this became another part of my secret life.

Later in 1947, I found a book called *The Comics* by Coulton Waugh, who back in the 1930s had succeeded Caniff on *Dickie Dare*. His book told the story of American comic strips from their beginnings in the 1890s with R. F. Outcault's *The Yellow Kid* to the triumph of the comic books. There was, of course, a chapter on Caniff and his imitators, and for the first time my faith in the great man's talents was shaken. Caniff was being imitated by hundreds of other cartoonists, with more appearing every day. Did I want to be just another imitator? *Could* I be an imitator? In Waugh's book I saw the immense variety of possible cartoon styles: Roy Crane's *Buz Sawyer* and *Captain Easy*, George Herriman's *Krazy Kat*, Cliff Sterrett's *Polly and Her Pals*, Hal Foster's *Prince Valiant*, Crockett Johnson's *Barnaby*. There were so many different ways to be a cartoonist. So when I failed once more to capture the sultry pout of the Dragon Lady, I would console myself by thinking, Hey, so what, I don't want to be just another hack imitator of Milton Caniff.

But I didn't just want to draw the characters the way Caniff did. I didn't really want to have his studio in New City. The truth was that I wanted to live the way his creations lived. I didn't want to spend a lifetime doing a comic strip about husbands and wives, or the distant past, or funny animals. I wanted to see the exotic places of the world. I wanted to go where my grandfather had gone. In a notebook, I copied a sentence from Waugh's book that described Roy Crane's creations: *In the old days tubby Tubbs and lanky Easy were loose-footed soldiers of fortune, a big and little stone rolling through the romantic places of the earth, usually broke, sometimes fabulously wealthy, but always ready for fight, frolic, or feed.*

That was it. To be a rolling stone. In the romantic places of the earth. Ready for a fight, a frolic, or a feed. And since I was Irish, since I was Billy Hamill's son, since I was from Brooklyn: a drink too.

11

AROUND THE SAME time, a sign painter named Jim Brady opened a shop on Seventh Avenue off the corner of Thirteenth Street, just past the swirling pole of Fortunato's barbershop, where my father got his hair cut. One summer morning I walked past the shop and stopped short. In the window was an enlarged photostat of the first *Terry* daily, drawn by Caniff in a much more cartoony style than the richly brushed strip that had become my obsession. There were also mounted photostats of characters from *Terry* and some *Terry* comic books arranged in a display. The shop was closed. But I came back that evening and saw a heavy-set man with reddish hair working on a sign for a butcher. He had a red handkerchief tied across his brow to prevent his sweat from splashing on the posters. His eyes were hidden behind thick horn-rimmed glasses. He only had one hand, and held a paintpot in the crook of the injured right arm. He must have felt my eyes on him.

Can I help you, kid? he said.

Uh, I — Well, I saw the Milton Caniff drawings in the window.

He paused.

You a Caniff fan?

Yeah.

Come on in.

He let me watch as he worked on the sign, and asked me questions. Did I draw every day? Was there a drawing class in my school? Where did I live? Oh, so you're Billy Hamill's kid. Hell of a guy, your dad. What do you do after school? Well, maybe you could work for me. Sweep the store. Deliver the signs. . . . But I can't pay much, kid.

So began my apprenticeship. I came back every day. And in that hot, narrow shop, smoky from Brady's Pall Malls, with beautifully lettered signs for pork chops and lamb roasts appearing in black and red paint on rolls of poster paper that unfurled across a tilted plywood worktable, Brady told me tales of the world of comics. Before he became a sign painter, he explained, he was a professional letterer for comic books. That is, he was part of that mysterious and powerful world across the river in Manhattan, where they did the work that I loved so much. He showed me his collection of originals, by Alex Toth (*He's the best around and he's only a kid.*) and a man named Edmund Good (who worked for a time as the artist on *Scorchy Smith*) and some other artists whose names I no longer remember. These were oversized two-ply Strathmore pages in black and white, the blacks very black, with corrections made in china white. Brady explained how in comic books, one man wrote the script, another penciled all the panels (*Usually with a pale blue pencil, 'cause that blue don't photograph when they reduce the page to comic book size*), another inked the pencil drawings, and another, the letterer, did all the balloons. Caniff himself used a fabulous letterer named Frank Engli: *A great cartoonist in his own right, ya know, but a master letterer.* Brady said he loved doing lettering for comic books. *But my eyes started going so I had to stop. . . .* He shook his head sadly, then removed his thick glasses and rubbed his eyes with the elbow of the bad arm. He didn't explain what had happened to his hand, and I didn't ask. But I felt pity for him; like my father, he had lost part of himself on the way to Seventh Avenue in Brooklyn.

Sometimes I brought him the latest old *Terry* comics I had discovered in the bookstores. He would look at them and point out what Caniff was doing.

You see, it's like a movie, like a *frozen* movie, he said. Long shot, medium shot, closeup — see what I mean?

I said I did (and when I went to the movies, I started seeing Caniff in everything). Brady explained about lettering: thick verticals, thin horizontals. *If you have a lettering pen, the nib does it, but ya gotta do it over and over again to make it look natural.* He explained the difference between serif and sans serif. He showed me how Roy Crane and Will Eisner (in *The Spirit* comic books) used lettering to create sounds: Ka-BONG, Padda-POW!

Ya gotta draw and draw, he said, and when you're old enough, ya gotta go to art school.

In a way, that was exactly what I was doing in Jim Brady's shop. His art school even had a small library: old comics, books on drawing and lettering. One day, in a cardboard box, I discovered a book of cartoons by Caniff that I'd never seen before. He had drawn them every week for *Stars and Stripes*, and they weren't meant for civilians. Or for kids. The strip was called *Male Call*, and it featured the most arousing woman of my young life: Miss Lace. She was dark-haired, sloe-eyed, with a lush body that seemed to struggle for release from her clothing. Lace was sexy, funny, generous; it wasn't clear what she was doing in the various theaters of operations but she was certainly making the fighting men happy. Lace reminded me of Rita Hayworth (or, more precisely, the sultry Rita Hayworth provoked in me even more lavish images of Miss Lace), and whenever Brady left me alone in the shop I took out the book and stared at Miss Lace and her hair, mouth, teeth, breasts, and hips in an agony of desire. She didn't exist anywhere in the world, and I didn't care.

Then one afternoon I came into the shop and Brady didn't seem to know me.

What the fuck do *you* want?

I didn't know what to say. And then I realized he was drunk. He was trying to letter an O. But he couldn't hold the curve. He stopped, took the brush in his teeth, and furiously crumpled the paper.

Goddammit, he said, goddammit, goddammit.

I backed up quietly and slipped out into the night. I felt like crying, but couldn't; everybody on the street would see me. I walked in a blur to Prospect Park and back, thinking: They're all drunks. All of them. Every last one.

12

IN THE YEARS after the war, I stopped worrying about my father. He was there, all right, and I talked to him about baseball, or boxing, or the weather. But it was as if I understood that I would never get from him what I wanted most: the kind of casual affection that is a sign of love. I protected myself with indifference, dreams of substitute worlds, a belief in a limitless future that didn't depend upon him. I certainly never talked to him about Jim Brady's sign store, or cartooning, or art school. I knew better.

Instead, I moved back and forth from the street to the Little Room (where Tommy and I now shared bunk beds), from stickball and fistfights to blue pencils, Higgins ink, and the mysteries of the crow quill pen. This wasn't easy. Suddenly, down in the street, it was the time of the gangs.

The street gangs were all over New York then, and the newspapers wrote about them every other day. In Brooklyn, there were immense black gangs in Bedford-Stuyvesant called the Bishops and the Robins; the Navy Street Boys from the waterfront in Fort Greene; tough Jewish gangs from Brownsville and Coney Island. And there were street gangs right in the Neighborhood.

The gang at our end of the Neighborhood was called the Tigers, most of them Irish. Their great rivals were the South Brooklyn Boys, most of them Italian. They all wore variations on the zoot suit, brightly colored trousers with a three-or-four-inch rise above the belt, ballooning knees, tight thirteen-inch pegged ankles. The rear pockets were covered with gun-shaped flaps of a different color, called pistol pockets; sometimes a bright saddle stitch would run down the seam of the trouser leg. If the trousers were a bright green, the pistol pockets, narrow belt, and saddle stitches might all be yellow. Or the combination would be maroon and gray. Or black and tan. Or purple and pale blue. The colors and combinations were drastic, radical, personal, at once an affirmation of their owner's uniqueness and a calculated affront to those locked in the gray dark memory of the Depression, the khaki and navy blue palette of the war, or suit-and-tie respectability. In summer, the gang members wore T-shirts with the sleeves rolled high on the shoulder and a cigarette pack folded into the roll. In chillier seasons, they added garish shirts, wide Windsor-knotted ties, belted jackets with wide padded shoulders called wrap-arounds, and wide-brimmed, narrow-crowned, pearl-gray "gingerella" hats. And like the boys at camp, they were all masters of the Walk. They would come down our avenue in groups of fifteen or twenty, walking with that practiced roll, their faces frozen in impassive masks, all smoking cigarettes, a few holding bats, their trousers billowing like visions from the Arabian Nights. The mixture of power and menace was thrilling.

On the street, we learned their names and their histories and heard the legends of their wars. Tigers and South Brooklyn Boys lived by primitive codes, most of them outlined in what became their catechism: *The Amboy Dukes* by Irving Shulman, published in 1947, probably the best-read novel in the history of Brooklyn. The codes demanded that all loyalty go to the gang, ahead of family, church, city, or country. Everybody had to drink hard and fight to the death; the women had to "put out" for the men. Although they supported themselves with burglaries and other minor crimes, they despised the mugger, they would never hurt old people, they would not ambush drunks in the dark or roll lushes in bars. My father liked some of the Tigers, but he spoke of them sadly.

The Tigers don't stand a chance, my father said one evening. They're fighting the guineas. That means they're fighting the Mafia.

He was right; dozens of South Brooklyn Boys ended up in the Mob. But for five or six years, the Tigers and South Brooklyn fought some epic battles, over women or insults (real and imaginary) or turf. One of the leaders of the Tigers was a handsome young man named Giacomo Fortunato, the dark blond son of the mustached barber next to Jim Brady's sign shop. The son was a great stickball player, an elaborate zoot suiter, and seemed always to have a girl on his arm. One evening in 1950, the Tigers met South Brooklyn at the Swan Lake in Prospect Park, in a full-out prearranged rumble. And at one point, as they battered each other with fists, bats, and pipes, someone from South Brooklyn fired a gun. The cops later said that the shooter's name was Anthony Scarpati, better known as Scappy. Everybody ran, except Giacomo Fortunato. He was dead.

That evening, I was in the street with my brother Tommy and some of the other kids, playing cards under a lamppost. Dozens of people were out on the sidewalks, fanning themselves, cooling off with hot tea, talking about baseball and the weather and each other. Then an invisible wave that seemed made of billions of electrons — a charged mixture of fear, shock, and apprehension — came rolling down the avenue, shaking the thick hot air, penetrating every man, woman, and child. Police cars raced up and down Seventh Avenue. Mothers looked for their children. The poolroom closed. And the words were carried on the electric wave: *Giacomo's dead, they killed Giacomo, Giacomo's dead.* Nobody went to bed. *They killed Giacomo!* And I remember the early editions of the *Daily News* and *Mirror* coming up, people grabbing them, looking disappointed when the story of the killing of Giacomo Fortunato wasn't there, saying, *Maybe it ain't true, maybe they're lying, the bulls . . .*

But it was true, all right; the cops weren't lying. In the morning, the story was in the late editions of the *News* and *Mirror,* and on the front pages of the afternoon papers. *I told you*, my father said. *They can't beat these people.* It seemed impossible that someone I saw every day, someone only five years older than I was, someone so handsome and daring: impossible that someone like Giacomo could be shot to death. And that his death could be recorded in the newspapers. That morning, I walked along Seventh Avenue and saw a wreath in the window of the Fortunato barbershop and a sign saying they were closed until further notice due to a death in the family. Across the street, about a dozen Tigers were reading the papers under the marquee of the Minerva. One of them was Noona Taylor, the toughest and bravest of the Tigers. He was sobbing, great body-wracking sobs. Even long-legged and curly-haired Millie, the sexiest of the Tigerettes, could not console him.

After a few days, the story vanished from the newspapers. On a few mornings that winter I passed the barbershop and saw Giacomo's father sitting alone, smoking cigarettes.

13

IN 1947, I went to work in the grocery store that had once been a Roulston's branch and then was taken over by a fat sweaty man named Ruby. I was there every day after school for three hours and all day on Saturday and was paid six dollars a week. In addition, I earned about three dollars in tips, delivering orders to people all over the Neighborhood. Every Saturday, I gave my mother half this money, an act that made me feel I was growing up, bringing home money to the family. I was determined not to be that species of lowlife who stood just a niche above the wino or informer: the freeloader.

There was another reason for working: I wanted to be free of dependence upon my father. No matter what he did, how drunk he got, how indifferent he was, I wanted him to know that I could get along without him. I still remember telling him that I didn't want an allowance anymore.

What, are you a big shot now? he said

No, I just don't need it now, Dad. I have my own money.

He gave me a long look, as if trying to decide if this was some sort of challenge, and then said: Good for you.

Now I paid with my own money for drawing paper and ink and comics. I saved for books. I would sit down in the crowded kitchen (for we had no space for a table in the Little Room) and get lost in the act of drawing. I also felt I was living a dozen lives at the same time. At any given hour, I was a student, an altar boy, a son, brother, street fighter, Dodger fan, storyteller, cartoonist. I was, by most definitions, a "good" boy; but the gangster style kept calling. Sometimes I trembled with fear when the Tigers marched by on the way to the battlefield or when South Brooklyn launched a sudden invasion. Then I would think that the only way I could ever be safe would be to join them. Not now, not yet, but soon, in a few years, when I was old enough. And that scenario was also scary. Every possibility was imagined. I saw myself facing the South Brooklyn Boys at the Swan Lake, fists clenched, eyes narrow, ready to punch and stomp; saw myself pulling a gun; saw myself being dragged out of the house in handcuffs by two thick-necked bulls; even saw myself walking the last mile to the chair. Every image was as real as breakfast. Along with the stories in the newspapers and my body laid out in Mike Smith's funeral parlor and my mother weeping and my father getting drunk, both of them consumed with shame.

I was saved from the hot seat by a glorious palace of books called the Prospect Branch of the Brooklyn Public Library, known to us simply as the Library. I went there every Saturday morning, during my break from the grocery store, following the familiar route along Seventh Avenue, my blood quickening as I crossed the trolley tracks on Ninth Street and passed the stately brownstones and small synagogue and saw up ahead the wild gloomy garden of the Library. I was always relieved, glancing through the high windows, to see that the lights were on, the leathery cliffs of books still there. The majestic mock Corinthian columns of the main entrance always made me feel puny but inside, behind walls as thick as those of any fortress, I always felt safe. Of one thing I was certain: in the Neighborhood, the bad guys never went to the Library.

I loved that old high-roofed building. It was warm in winter and cool in summer, and although it seemed built to last forever, and the sense of space was unlike anything I knew except the lobbies of movie houses, the attraction of the Library was not merely shelter. I was there on a more exciting mission: the discovery of the world.

To be sure, the *idea* of the Library alarmed me. Those thousands of books seemed to look down upon me with a wintry disdain. They were adult; they knew what I did not know; they were, in a collective way, the epitome of the unknowable, full of mystery and challenge and the most scary thing of all, *doubt*. The harder I worked at cracking their codes, the more certain I was that the task was impossible.

At first, I was condemned to the children's room. I liked the bound volumes of a British magazine called *St. Nicholas*, full of intricate pen drawings and the cheery innocence of the official 19th century. And I also found a book about Milton Caniff, called *The Rembrandt of the Comic Strip*, borrowing it at least once a month, virtually memorizing its pages. In that book Caniff suggested to would-be cartoonists that they study the art of narrative, by reading writers he called "yarn-spinners," such as Rudyard Kipling and Robert Louis Stevenson. I followed the lesson of the master. I memorized verses of Kipling's "Gunga Din" (the movie version played every year at the Minerva along with *Four Feathers*) and read "The Man Who Would Be King" and *The Jungle Book*. As the son of Irish immigrants, I found Kipling a bit too British. But Stevenson was another matter. Of all his books I most cherished *Treasure Island*. How could a son of Billy Hamill resist Long John Silver, with his left leg cut off below the knee? And right there on the first page of the novel was that song of the pirate, the desperado, the outlaw, the song that Noona could sing, or even my father:

> *Fifteen men on the dead man's chest —*
> *Yo-ho-ho, and a bottle of rum!*

I read the novel once. Then again. I was carried away by *Kidnapped*, defeated by the Scotch dialect in *The Weir of Hermiston*. But I kept going back to *Treasure Island*. Tommy and I would sing the tune: *Yo-ho-ho, and a bottle of rum!* And laugh and cheer and call each other matey. Then, tracking down Stevenson, I discovered *Dr. Jekyll and Mr. Hyde*.

I'd seen the movie, with Spencer Tracy and Ingrid Bergman, but the book was even scarier. With his gorgeous images and musical prose, Stevenson carried me into nineteenth-century London, where fog rolled down narrow cobblestoned streets day and night ("A great chocolate-covered pall lowered over heaven. . . ." Or, even better to my inflamed vision: "The fog still slept on the wing above the drowned city, where the lamps glimmered like carbuncles. . . ."). I looked up the word "carbuncles," used it in school compositions ("Musial's eyes glowed like carbuncles"), where I also described fogs that slept and gas lamps that shimmered. But I never used the Stevenson paragraph that chilled my heart:

> *He put the glass to his lips and drank at one gulp. A cry followed; he reeled, staggered, clutched at the table and held on, staring with injected eyes, gasping with open mouth; and as I looked there came, I thought, a change — he seemed to swell — his face became suddenly black and the features seemed to melt and alter — and the next moment, I had sprung to my feet and leaped back against the wall, my arm raised to shield me from that prodigy, my mind submerged in terror.*

I read that passage and thought of my father. In Stevenson's story, Dr. Jekyll says that he had lived "nine-tenths a life of effort, virtue and control"; but the chemical experiment had released Mr. Hyde, "the evil side of my nature." I wanted that to be true of my father. When he first started a drinking session, he was often merry and funny, the joyful Irish singer of funny Irish songs; but as he went on, his face darkened, his eyes grew opaque, his jaw slack. Sometimes, he looked evil. And when he became enraged, I was often afraid of him. I saw the same eerie transformation in the other drunks of the neighborhood. Even Mr. Dix was decent enough until he downed too much of the amber liquid. After reading Stevenson's great story, I could never look at my father the same way; I just hoped he would never come home with a silver-headed cane.

I didn't brood about Jekyll and Hyde or give up reading because the subject cut so close to my bones. I was also collecting Classic Comics (soon to be renamed, for some reason, Classics Illustrated), and they were a kind of road map to the real books. I had all the early Classic Comics in order: 1) *The Three Musketeers;* 2) *Ivanhoe;* 3) *The Count of Monte Cristo;* 4) *The Last of the Mohicans;* 5) *Moby Dick;* 6) *A Tale of Two Cities;* 7) *Robin Hood;* 8) *The Arabian Nights;* 9) *Les Miserables;* 10) *Robinson Crusoe;* and on through *Don Quixote, Uncle Tom's Cabin, Gulliver's Travels, The Corsican Brothers, Huckleberry Finn,* and dozens of others. From the stacks at the Library, I tried reading all of them. Harriet Beecher Stowe, Sir Walter Scott, and James Fenimore Cooper were truly dreadful writers. And I was still too raw to enter *Moby Dick.* But Dumas père thrilled me with *The Count of Monte Cristo* and *The Three Musketeers,* and I found a copy of the tales told by Scheherazade during her Arabian nights; it was beautifully illustrated (probably by Arthur Rackham) and secretly erotic. I loved the writing of Jonathan Swift and Charles Dickens; Don Quixote and Sancho Panza moved into my mind for life, sharing space with

Oliver Twist and David Copperfield. And over and over again, I traveled down the dark river with Huck and the Nigger Jim and dreamed of lighting out for the territory. Tom Sawyer couldn't have lasted long in the Neighborhood. But Huck Finn felt like one of us; after all, wasn't his father the town drunk?

In the comics — even in Milton Caniff — there were no drunks, no scary fathers; it was impossible to imagine Dagwood having a "fair one" with Blondie, the way Mr. Dix once did with his wife. I knew in the Library that in *some* of those books, I was coming closer to the truths of the world. They weren't *The Amboy Dukes*. But then, of course, nothing was.

The illustrators of these classics were often as important to me as the books and obviously served as a transition from comics. The fine-lined Cruikshank drawings in the Dickens books had a spidery texture, creepy and strange, and — in the horrific figure of the drunken Bill Sikes — an ability to make London feel like Twelfth Street in Brooklyn. I also consumed Howard Pyle's *Book of Pirates*, checking it out many times, making pencil copies of the great paintings, reveling in the freebooting lives of pirates, men burnt from the sun, filled with rum, reaching for wenches. And in book after book, I was dazzled by the illustrations of N. C. Wyeth, so rich and thick with golden light; often I checked out books — *Robin Hood* or *Twenty Thousand Leagues Under the Sea* — simply to look at those Wyeth paintings.

But the rest of the books in the children's section meant nothing to me. They all seemed to be about kids living in idyllic country glades, or rabbits who talked, or an elephant named Babar who had adventures in Africa. I was already traveling through Burne Hogarth's fabulous baroque Africa in *Tarzan* (which ran in *Sparkler* comics and the Saturday *Journal-American*) and, of course, I had plunged through the South American jungles with Bomba. After reading *The Count of Monte Cristo*, I began thinking of the children's room as another version of the Château d'If.

That didn't last long. Soon I was a regular in the main reading room. The librarians didn't seem to care about enforcing the rule that confined me to the children's room. And as I moved around those dark aisles, among books sad with dust or placed in some ghetto of the forbidden on high shelves (like that copy of *The Arabian Nights*), I began to find the entrance to the world. At first, I was still trapped in the primary colors of melodrama. But over the last years of the 1940s, the Library took my instincts for the lurid and refined them. The comics, radio serials, B movies, dirty stories, even *The Amboy Dukes*, were part of my experience, the foundations of my own sense of the mythic; I took them with me to the act of reading literature. But slowly the myths started assuming different shapes, a wider context, deeper roots. And reading became a kind of creative act. With each book, I was somehow collaborating with the writer in the creation of an alternative world. I was at once in Brooklyn and in not-Brooklyn. These books were more than simple collections of abstract symbols called words, printed on paper; they described real events that happened to *me*. So I was Jim Hawkins, hiding from Blind Pew. I was D'Artagnan, fighting duels with the henchmen of the evil Milady. I was Edmond Dantès, escaping from my prison cell to extract my terrible revenge. I was Sydney Carton doing a far, far better thing than I had ever done and going to a far, far better place than I had ever known.

I carried those books home, consumed them like food, then brought their stories and characters and lessons down to the streets with me. I couldn't really tell my friends about them. But they were real in my head, they often peopled my dreams, and they helped give me a sense that the streets were not everything. It didn't matter if I never hit a spaldeen five sewers like Paulie McAleer, or if I wasn't the best street fighter in the Neighborhood. Nobody would care if I refused to join up with the Tigers and fight fair ones with the hoods from South Brooklyn. There was a bigger world out there. And by the time I was thirteen, I was sure I was going to see it.

14

I TRIED VERY HARD to believe in God, but I had almost no success. From the first grade on, I studied religion at Holy Name. I memorized endless pages of the Baltimore Catechism and even won religion prizes for reciting in a singsong way the questions and answers of the text. Who made the world? *God made the world.* Who is God? *God is the creator of heaven and earth, and of all things.* What is man? *Man is a creature composed of body and soul, and made to the image and likeness of God.* Why did God make you? *God made me to know Him, to love Him, and to serve Him in this world, and to be happy with Him forever in the next.* Where is God? *God is everywhere.*

The problem was that I didn't believe any of this. On the surface, I was a reasonably good Catholic boy. I took my first communion, was confirmed, finally became an altar boy, memorizing the Latin responses for the whole Mass. *Ad Deum qui laetificat, juventutum meum. . . .* I loved the glazed baroque paintings on the walls of the church. I loved the statues of the flayed Jesus and his grieving mother. I loved the music most of all, with the great booming hymns filling the church on Sunday mornings. I even loved the smell of guttering candles, palm leaves at Easter, pine needles at Christmas. I just couldn't believe in God.

This was one of the heaviest secrets that I carried through those years. I couldn't talk to my mother or father about my terrible failure to imagine God; I certainly couldn't discuss it with the Xaverian Brothers at Holy Name; and down on the street I was afraid that the other kids would think I was weird. So I kept silent. To be sure, the religious education I received taught me some valuable lessons. I didn't care much about the Holy Ghost (though I loved his cartoony name), the Blessed Trinity, or Original Sin. But I did understand the catechism's definition of a mortal sin; it had to be a grievous matter, committed with sufficient reflection and full consent of the will. That is, a mortal sin was a felony. And the Baltimore Catechism taught us that certain mortal sins cried to heaven for vengeance: willful murder, the sin of Sodom, oppression of the poor, defrauding laborers of their wages. For a long time, I didn't know what the sin of Sodom was and couldn't get anyone to explain it to me (not to mention whatever it was they did in Gomorrah). But the rest of the Church's list of abhorrent sins was certainly admirable.

One trouble was that the Church in New York didn't follow its own list of rules, as laid out in the catechism. It certainly didn't seem to care very passionately about the poor. It shamed us into contributing money every Sunday by publishing our names in the church bulletin along with the amounts of the donations. But while altars were heavy with gold chalices and monstrances, and priests drove cars and grew fat, I never saw them down on Seventh Avenue. A Big Shot from the political club helped my father get a job; no priest ever did the same. I never saw priests on picket lines outside the Factory, joining in the fight against the bosses who were defrauding the workers. After sex, most of their negative passion was reserved for communism, which had absolutely nothing to do with life in the tenements of Seventh Avenue. The priests would never try to help a drunken man; all they ever did was judge him.

Still, the Xaverian Brothers at Holy Name tried hard to make me a good Catholic. I was taught the chief sources of sin: Pride, Covetousness, Lust, Anger, Gluttony, Envy, and Sloth. But again, most of the focus seemed to be on Lust. In the sixth grade, Brother Eliot kept me after school one afternoon and tried to explain sex to me. I knew some of the mechanics now from Arnold, the boys at Fox Lair Camp, and the kids from Seventh Avenue. But somehow, in the vague, reverent, whispering way Brother Eliot described it, sex became even more awesome and darkly attractive. It was, Brother Eliot said, a wonderful gift from God. But that didn't prevent the Baltimore Catechism from trying to make it a felony. "Lust," the catechism said, "is the source of immodest looks and actions, which lead to blindness of intellect, hardness of heart, the loss of faith and piety, the ruin of health, and final impenitence." Obviously, this was written by men with a well-developed sense of horror. But they didn't understand that an experience so colossally ruinous could never truly be avoided by the young. Even at the risk of hardness of heart and the ruin of health. In a way, they were offering another dare.

I listened in religion class, and to the fearful whisperings of Brother Eliot, but I just didn't understand it. There were people all over the Neighborhood who were bone poor. Night and day, there was violence on the streets. And I had seen those movies about the concentration camps. Why were the priests and brothers so crazy and fierce about sex? I was a virgin. I had no idea how it felt to fuck a woman. But I just couldn't imagine that someone as all-powerful as God was sitting around heaven on some throne, pissed off about what I might do at night on Seventh Avenue. The good brothers made God sound like some glorified scorekeeper, endlessly filling in box scores and then punishing those who made errors. Since there were billions of people on the earth, it seemed to me that He would have almost nothing else to do. Just writing down the sins of the Tigers would keep him busy; and if he had to do all of Asia, all of Russia, all of Europe, every man and every woman committing sins of Lust, all the movie stars and all the baseball players and all the wise guys in the Mafia, when would He ever get around to noticing what Noona Taylor was doing on the roof with Millie from the Tigerettes?

None of it made any sense. So I carried my disbelief with me, even as an altar boy. I didn't ask to be an altar boy; I was chosen by the brothers in the sixth grade. They probably believed that boys with good grades were also good Catholics; or perhaps they chose us only because we could remember all the Latin responses in the Mass. For whatever reason, I was drafted. But if anything, my time as an altar boy widened my separation from the Church. I learned the Latin; I got up on time every morning, winter and summer, draped my starched surplice over my arms and traveled up the hill to Holy Name. But from the beginning I felt part of a show, giving a rehearsed performance in which the lines never varied. I loved the sound of Latin, the roll of vowels, the way words changed according to their meaning; Latin was another code to be cracked. But even for the priests, it was all an act.

I did like some of the priests, particularly a kind man named Father Ahearn, and another named Father Kavanaugh, who said the fastest Mass in the parish, the Latin falling from his lips as if he were a tobacco auctioneer. But watching them get dressed in priestly garments or smoke cigarettes after Mass, being subjected to their scorn when I made a mistake, I saw them as human beings, not as officers in the army of Christ. I lost whatever sense of awe that I once felt during the Mass. They were men like other men.

At least one of them was like the men of Seventh Avenue, or like my father: a drunk. He had a sweet, smooth, baby's pink face, and eyes without irises. Sometimes he staggered onto the altar. He often forgot some of the Latin, repeated other parts at least twice. His superiors seemed to know he had a problem and gave him the earliest, most sparsely attended Masses. Even at six-thirty in the morning, he was shaky, his breath reeking. The sight of him filled me with pity and anger. It was bad enough that he staggered around; he was forced by his work to do so before an audience. I was angry that nobody from the Church tried to save him from this humiliation.

There was another personal element to the ceremony of the Mass. Wine was central to the ritual. We were taught that during the Mass, bread and wine were transformed into the body and blood of Christ. As an altar boy, I held the wine cruets while the priest blessed them and then poured the sweetish liquid across his fingers during the Offertory. That was the "first act" of the Mass, the section when the priest offered up to God the wine and the small unleavened wafers called hosts. In the second act of the drama, the consecration, he transformed these banal elements, saying his magic words in Latin, holding the host up for all to see; it was the custom in Holy Name to hide one's eyes and bow the head, refusing to look directly at the offered host because that little wafer had become God. Natives often did this in Tarzan movies, when facing their gods, and in *Gunga Din*, the murder cultists did the same with the image of Kali. Then the priest turned his back on the parishioners of Holy Name, ate the host, who was God, and washed Him down with the wine, or His blood. The more I learned, the more I thought that it was all very strange.

15

O N THE RADIO, there was a show called "Truth or Consequences." The announcer would open in egg-shaped tones: *You've gotta
tell the truth or you're gonna pay the consequences.* . . . The price for not telling the truth was usually a public humiliation.

But I couldn't always tell the truth. Just as I couldn't tell anyone that
I didn't believe in God, I couldn't talk to many people about wanting to
be a cartoonist. When I had my first cartoon published, in *Ace Comics* in
1949, on a page filled by young fans, I told nobody at Holy Name; I was
afraid they'd think I was lording it over them. At the same time, I hated
telling lies; even without God I had a sense of sin, and everything taught
me that lying was a sin. So I learned to be silent about most of the deepest
concerns in my life. On the street, I learned to be a tough guy, to curse,
to tell jokes, to play ball. At home, and in my mind, I was someone else:
more naive, more complicated, angrier, more romantic. I wanted to see
the world, to be a man in that world, but a man cleansed of all stupidities.
I didn't want to be like my father. I didn't want to be a drunk.

And yet drinking started to seem as natural to real life as breathing. I
would hear my father and his friends weaving romantic tales of Prohibition, when they were young, and understood that when a country was
made to live under a stupid law then the only way to defy that law was
to do what it forbade; in that case, drinking. I heard Prohibition words
like "rumdum" and "gin mill," "speakeasy" and "needle beer," and loved
their bluntness, their bricklike shapes. The roguish way they came off
the lips of the men made me want to talk that way too. Those words
carried an additional glaze of meaning. The men used them like a code,
one shared by members of an outlaw society. The Prohibition law had
been passed by Protestants to curb the dreadful habits of the Catholic
immigrants (or so they thought), and they had defied that law and won.
In a way, I was a child of Prohibition, even though born two years after
repeal.

Drinking seemed to be part of almost everything else, even politics.
In 1948, Truman was running against Dewey, and in our neighborhood
Dewey was despised. They laughed at him, at his size, his mustache, his
prim image. In the *New York Star,* a cartoonist named Walt Kelly started
drawing him like a bridegroom on a wedding cake. When Dewey's mon-
otonal midwestern voice came over the radio one evening, my father

shouted: *Shut that idjit off!* And when I asked why Dewey made him so angry, he said: *One good shot of whiskey and he'd be on his face on the floor.*

That year, I started moving beyond the comics and the sports pages to the front of the newspaper; there was no war, but there was crime and politics. And my attention was focused by another event. In the used book stores of Pearl Street I made two additional discoveries: a run of a newsletter called *In Fact* by George Seldes, and Bill Mauldin's *Back Home.* On Pearl Street, thirty issues of *In Fact* went home with me for sixty cents. I don't remember anything from them except their format (which resembled the newsletter later published by I. F. Stone) and their suspicion of anything written in newspapers, in particular, newspapers published by Hearst. Mauldin's book, which followed his masterpiece *Up Front*, made me think more sharply about politics. I loved Mauldin's Willie and Joe, and their disdain for officers, regulations, rules; in the *Up Front* cartoons, they were hard-drinking, unshaven, probably bad-talking. But in *Back Home*, Mauldin was looking at the world after the war, the country to which Willie and Joe returned, the nation in which I lived. As he portrayed it, the United States was a country of fearful, ignorant men, bullies with slouch hats and paunches who worked for the House Un-American Activities Committee. Even the name struck me as stupid; would the French have a committee on Un-French Activities? And what was an "American activity" anyway?

Reading Mauldin at thirteen, I felt an odd sense of merger; it was as if I had written these pages, as if I were saying these irreverent things about officers, right-wingers, war profiteers, conservative newspaper publishers, penthouse revolutionaries, professional veterans, and bigots and phonies of all stripes. I didn't really understand some of what Mauldin was writing; but as I read and reread the book, the irreverent attitude felt natural to me. It was as if I'd picked up a glove, tried it on, and found a perfect fit.

None of what I was reading in the newspapers or in Mauldin's book had anything to do with what I was learning in school. From Mauldin I learned that Japanese-Americans had been put in concentration camps during the war, their stores and homes and farms confiscated by white trash, and when the Nisei soldiers came back from fighting courageously in Italy, the whites who stole their property refused to give it up and the government did nothing. I learned how southern white bigots used the poll tax and other legal devices to prevent Negroes from voting. I learned the phrase anti-Semitism, the proper name for the bigotry that had caused Buchenwald. Mauldin confirmed and elaborated many of the lessons I'd absorbed from my mother.

But I heard nothing about such matters in school. Masturbation was a sin; but hatred? Hey, pay attention, young man. Mauldin's world was not far away, in some distant country. Some of it was right there in the Neighborhood, where some people still called Jackie Robinson a nigger and others talked about kikes and yids.

If my mind was full of change, possibility, and notions of justice, other things remained the same. In November, there were great election-night bonfires on Twelfth Street after the voting ended. But the vote for president was very close; the counting went on all night, and some said that the hated Dewey had won. The following day, Truman was declared the winner. My mother wasn't very happy about this. But my father headed for Rattigan's, where the ward heelers were buying. Around midnight, two of their flunkies brought him home. He made it to the second-floor landing. He sat there for a while, crooning about the old country, until I went down and helped him up the last flight.

16

EIGHTH GRADE was a horror. Our teacher was a thick-necked Pole with a jutting jaw and a bent nose. His name was Brother Jan. In the seventh grade, we'd had a soft and saintly man named Brother Rembert as our teacher. We heard scary tales about Brother Jan, but nothing really prepared us for the reality of this snarling, vicious brute. On his desk, Brother Jan kept a thick eighteen-inch ruler called Elmer. He used it on someone every day. He used it if you were late. He used it if you didn't finish your homework. He used it if you smiled or giggled. He used it if you talked back, or copied from another kid during an exam. I would watch him when he bent one of the boys over a front desk, and there was a tremble in his face, a fierce concentration, a sick look of enjoyment as he whacked Elmer on the ass of the chosen boy until the boy dissolved in tears and pain.

He picked on some kids over and over again: a funny guy named Bobby Connors; a slow, sweet boy named Shitty Collins, who lived up the block from me; a tall sly character named Boopie Conroy. Near the end of the first term, Brother Jan started picking on me. Somehow I infuriated him. Maybe it was because I got the highest grades in the class but after school spent my time with the harder kids. I shared my homework with Shitty Collins and some of the slower kids; when Brother Jan discovered this he didn't see it as an act of Christian charity but as a case of subversion; he bent me over the front seat and whipped into me with Elmer. After the first time, he whipped me every week. He broke some other kids, reducing them to tears and humiliation; when he did that, his eyes seemed to recede under his brow and his lips curled into a knowing smile, as if he'd discovered the point at which he could destroy pride and will. I refused to cry. I would wait for the initial shock, then the cutting pain of the second blow, then wait for the next, and tighten my face, clamp my teeth together, feel it again, then again, still *again*, as many as fifteen times, thinking: Fuck you, and fuck you, and fuck you, and fuck you. And Brother Jan would swing again, grunting.

Then he'd be finished and I'd glance at him and sometimes he'd have a film of sweat on his face. And I'd think: You're sick. I'd sit down in pain, and the other kids would look at me, and I would stare up at Brother Jan, thinking: Fuck you, fuck you, fuck you.

Around this time I first sensed that I was my own version of Jekyll and Hyde. In my head, the Good Boy was constantly warring with the Bad Guy. I wanted to be a Bad Guy, tough, physical, a prince of the streets; at the same time, I was driven to be a Good Boy: hardworking, loyal, honorable, a protector of my brothers, an earner of money for the family. The Bad Guy cursed, growled, repeated dirty jokes and resisted Brother Jan; the Good Boy served Mass in the mornings and read novels in bed at night. The Bad Guy practiced walking like one of the Tigers, stole silverware from the Factory, and jerked off; the Good Boy delivered groceries to old ladies who couldn't come down the stairs, memorized poems, and drew cartoons at the kitchen table on cold or rainy evenings. It seems clear to me now that the Bad Guy was demanding respect from my father, the Good Boy acknowledging love from my mother. It wasn't at all clear when I was in my early teens.

There were times when the existence of the Good Boy forced the appearance of the Bad Guy. In the final three years of grammar school at Holy Name, I always finished at the top of the class in grades, averaging 98 or 99, was placed on the honor roll and granted awards for general excellence. But there was an assumption that if you got good grades you must be soft, a sissy, or an AK — an ass kisser. This was part of the most sickening aspect of Irish-American life in those days: the assumption that if you rose above an acceptable level of mediocrity, you were guilty of the sin of pride. You were to accept your place and stay in it for the rest of your life; the true rewards would be given you in heaven, after you were dead. There was ferocious pressure to conform, to avoid breaking out of the pack; self-denial was the supreme virtue. It was the perfect mentality for an infantryman, a civil servant, or a priest. And it added some very honorable lives to the world. But too often, it discouraged kids who aspired to something different. The boy who chose another road was accused of being Full of Himself; he was isolated, assigned a place outside the tribe. Be ordinary, was the message; maintain anonymity; tamp down desires or wild dreams. Some boys withered. And the girls were smothered worse than the boys. They could be nuns or wives, brides of Christ or mothers of us all. There were almost no other possibilities.

But the Bad Guy in me resisted the demand for conformity that was so seductive to the Good Boy. I hated being called an AK. For one thing, it wasn't true. I polished no apples, sought no favors. But worse, to say that I was an AK was to imply that what I had actually done was a fraud. I knew that I got those grades by doing the homework, reading the books, and above all, by paying attention; I didn't get them by kissing ass. So, after a while, whenever I was called an AK, I struck back: punching and hurting my accusers. The Bad Guy shoved the Good Boy out of the way and went to work. By the time I was subjected to Brother Jan's sick furies, nobody again called me an AK. And I'd acquired a vague notion in my head that I could be like Sugar Ray Robinson: a boxer *and* a puncher, smart *and* tough.

By the spring of 1949, seething with anger at Brother Jan, I started hanging out in a different part of the neighborhood, two blocks from Holy Name. In a way, it was a matter of choosing my own place, rather than having it chosen by my parents; they had moved to Seventh Avenue but I didn't have to hang around there. There was another aspect to it too; my brother Tommy was eleven and I was thirteen; eight and ten are somehow much closer than eleven and thirteen; so I was moving away from Tommy too.

The place I chose was called Bartel-Pritchard Square, and it was more a circle than a square. Three different trolley lines converged here, turning around a center island before heading off to Coney Island, Mill Basin, or Smith Street. Off the square on one side were the two tall Corinthian columns that marked the entrance to Prospect Park; we called them the Totem Poles, or the Totes. They rose from cleanly carved granite bases, and in the evenings that spring, after work at the grocery store and after finishing my homework, I would walk up from Seventh Avenue and see the others and we'd gather around the bases, sitting on them, looking at girls, cursing, smoking, making jokes, and drinking beer. First, the Good Boy attended to his chores; then the Bad Guy went out into the evening.

That was when I really started drinking. There were a lot of us hanging around the Totes that spring and summer: Boopie Conroy, Shitty Collins, Mickey Horan, Vito Pinto, Jack McAlevy. Among my friends was a thin, handsome guy named Richie Kelly. He was smart and tough but he always seemed cautious about drinking. Later in the summer, I learned why. His father, Jabbo Kelly, was one of the public rummies, a small group of men who'd been thrown out of their homes and lived on the streets. They slept in the park, or in the subways. They were filthy and panhandled for wine money. There was no way that Richie could avoid seeing Jabbo, because the rummies were always around the park, but I never saw them talk. I admired the way Richie handled a fact of his life that would have shamed others. He was cool and indifferent. For a while, we were close. I thought that with any kind of bad luck, my father could join Jabbo Kelly on his aimless wanderings.

Richie was also our liaison to the older guys, who owned the benches in the center of the traffic island, across the street from the Totes. They played football together as the Raiders and fought occasional gang battles in Coney Island or in the park. Richie's older brother, Tommy, was one of the Raiders. He was built like a safe and was a ferocious puncher but never went out of his way to fight. I never saw him talk to Jabbo either.

I don't know who bought the beer, but it was around, in cardboard containers or quart bottles. At first I didn't join in the drinking. It was as if I knew I would be crossing a line in some permanent way. But I didn't make a big deal out of this; I just shrugged and passed on the offered bottle. Then one evening, all of us laughing and joking, a guy named Johnny Rose handed me a container, casually, easily, and I took a sip.

The first swallow triggered a vague remembrance of the beer I'd sipped when I was a little boy, and was accompanied by a yeasty smell I associated with Gallagher's. I didn't like the taste; unlike the sweet wine I'd drunk in the woods at Fox Lair Camp, the beer had a sourness to it. I passed the container to Boopie Conroy, who took a long swallow. After a while, it came back to me, I took another sip, and this time I picked up a repulsive odor that reminded me of my father's breath when he was sleeping late on weekend mornings.

But as the beer kept coming around to me, I felt oddly proud of myself. The taste and smell didn't matter as much as the act. I was doing something I wasn't supposed to do — drinking under the legal age of eighteen. Just by drinking beer, I was a certified Bad Guy. If the police saw us, and caught us, we'd be in trouble. We stayed on the side of the Totes that faced the park, safe from the scrutiny of passing cars. But several times, I wandered out under the streetlight with my container in my hand. That spring night, and on later evenings in summer, when I had graduated from Holy Name, I *wanted* to be seen. I wanted to be seen by one person: Brother Jan. I wanted him to come over to me. I wanted him to try to stop me from drinking. And then I would crash into him, I'd beat and batter him, I'd stomp him and kick his balls out his ass. He was bigger than I was, heavier, with a fullback's neck; I didn't care. I wanted to hurt him back. On my turf. On the street.

For the first time I began to experience a transformation that would later become familiar: the violent images grew larger in my head and everything else got smaller. It was as if the beer were editing the world, eliminating other elements, such as weather, light, form, beauty. I could hear talk bubbling around me from the others, random words colliding in my head, then a tightening of focus, the faces closest to me having the most solid reality. A few of us talked about Brother Jan and how we'd like to give him a good beating. But all sorts of other talk flew around the beer-tingling air: the Dodgers, the gangs, girls, prizefighters, the songs we heard on the radio.

There were no transistors yet, only clumsy portables, and nobody had one of them. We learned the songs at home, on WNEW's "Make Believe Ballroom," and a nighttime show called "Your Hit Parade." Record sales were smaller then, songs remained in the top ten for months, and the words drilled themselves into memory. Most of the songs were junk. But I can still sing "Slow Boat to China" or "A (You're Adorable)" or "Red Roses for a Blue Lady." On summer evenings, we'd take turns singing the new tunes, even imitating the singers. I could do a pretty fair Nat "King" Cole on "Nature Boy" and what I thought was a smashing Ray Bolger on "Once in Love with Amy" (right down to the arch laugh). I tried to do Billy Eckstine on "I Apologize" and failed; my voice just wasn't deep enough. Above all others, we loved Frankie Laine; each of us could shout every verse of "Mule Train" and we worked hard to sound smoky, sultry, and knowing on "That's My Desire."

Up on the Totes, even while I was learning to like the taste of beer, I never mentioned cartooning. I never tried to discuss the books I was reading. I never let the Good Boy get in the way of the apprentice Bad Guy.

At first, I didn't get drunk. At least I didn't think I was getting drunk. I was always conscious of where I was. I always walked home and didn't stagger (chewing gum or Sen-Sen so that my mother couldn't smell the beer on my breath). I didn't fall down inside the park to sleep, the way some of the others did. But I knew I was being changed. I talked more, postured as badly as all the others, tried on different attitudes as if they were suits. I watched the Raiders — we called them the Big Guys — and the way they dressed (in T-shirts and chino pants, in contrast to the pegged pants of Seventh Avenue) and the way they wore their hair (in crisp crew cuts, instead of the pompadours and sideburns of the Tigers and the South Brooklyn Boys), and I tried to look like that too. I liked the way they held their containers of beer, casually, firmly, passing them around in an open generous style.

I also watched the way they walked up to the Sanders with a girl on a Saturday night, paying for two, the girl waiting to the side, then taking the guy's hand as they walked inside to the dark balcony. I wanted a girl too and had tried to talk to girls in my grade at Holy Name; they didn't share classrooms with us but they were our age and knew the same songs we knew. In their presence, however, I felt clumsy and awkward, and the girls seemed always to be holding back some secret knowledge, exchanging glances with other girls, prepared to dismiss me with a sigh or some form of mockery. It was as if they knew more about me than I did. They certainly knew more about me than I knew about them. I kept hearing about periods and sanitary napkins and didn't understand what any of it meant. I don't think any of the other guys knew either, as they played at being Bad Guys on the Totes on those long summer evenings.

Then one evening that summer, I was home after dinner, drawing at the kitchen table. I had sketched a cartoon in light blue pencil and was drawing with a fine-haired brush, dipping into the Higgins india ink. My father came in. He was drunk and lurching and his eyes were opaque. He bumped into the kitchen table and my hand jerked, ruining a line. And I rose in a fury. I tore up the drawing and threw the ink bottle against the sink and stormed out. I couldn't do this! I wanted to be a cartoonist and this drunk, *my father*, made it impossible! I hated him then, with a white, ear-ringing, boyish hatred, and my rage and hatred carried me to the Totes. Among my friends, I drank to get rid of something.

That gave me a delicious sense of joy. I could drink until I got drunk because it was someone else's fault. If I downed too many beers, it was my father's fault; if I staggered, it was his fault; if I fell down in the grass in the park: it was his fault. The son of a bitch. I didn't say any of this to the other guys. I kept thinking of Bogart in *Casablanca*, sitting at the bar in a pool of bitterness, drinking his whiskey. I would be like that. I would just drink, quietly and angrily, and say nothing. Sitting on the

Totes, with the others laughing and grab-assing around me, I sipped the beer, telling myself that I enjoyed the taste. I didn't want to go home. I didn't want to clean up the mess I'd made with the ink. I didn't want to confront my father or explain to my mother. I wanted to sit there forever, drinking in bitter satisfaction, using someone else as a license. In the years that followed, I did a lot of that.

17

ONE FRIDAY in that spring of 1949, I opened an envelope in the hall of 378 and discovered that I'd won a scholarship to Regis High School. Another boy in my class, Bob McElynn, had won too; four of us had taken the examination together. Regis was a Jesuit school across the river in Manhattan and was said to be the most elite of the city's Catholic high schools. Nobody at Holy Name had ever made it into Regis until McElynn and I did it, and all across that weekend, wondering if I should accept the prize that I'd won, I was happy, pleased, and scared.

The fear was caused in part by the relentless pressure of conformity in the parish. Most of the other boys were going on to Bishop Loughlin or St. Michael's, to Xavier or LaSalle; a few went to Brooklyn Tech; many went to Manual Training, the public high school on Seventh Avenue and Fifth Street. If I went to Regis, I'd be separating myself from all of them. They would walk to school while I took three subway trains to get from my part of Brooklyn to Eighty-fifth Street and Park Avenue in Manhattan. *Park Avenue!* Just the name of the street was a symbol of some other, rarefied existence in the region of the very rich. If the school really *was* an elite school, then I'd be declaring myself part of that elite. I didn't want to join any elite. I wanted to live my life. But the choice of a high school also might have something to do with the way I lived that life. Regis was a prep school; that is, it prepared you for college. But I had never met anyone from the Neighborhood who'd gone to college. Not one. College was for rich kids, not for people from Brooklyn. Or so I thought. Besides, I wanted to be a cartoonist. I wanted to draw, to go to art school. Why should I prep for a school that I would never attend? Why not prep for art school? But in bed one night on that weekend after receiving the acceptance letter, I thought: Milton Caniff went to Ohio

State. Maybe I could go to college *and* be a cartoonist. And besides, wasn't a cartoonist part of an elite? Wouldn't that profession separate me from my friends, from the Neighborhood, from everybody I now knew? Maybe separation was just inevitable.

So I decided to go to Regis, the Good Boy momentarily triumphing over the Bad Guy. The school was rigorous, severe, the teachers dedicated to excellence. I loved Latin, prepared by my years as an altar boy to hear the sounds and rhythms of the language. But there was something else involved: a sense of working on secret codes, discovering the meanings of strange words that linked me to the distant past.

But I couldn't get algebra. It was too abstract, plotless, without narrative or time. I learned enough to pass and nothing more. I was reasonably good in English, bored by grammar, excited by putting stories on paper. It says something about the way difficulty puts its mark on consciousness that I can remember the algebra teacher now, his reddish hair, dry humor, even his name: Purcell. I remember nothing of the English or Latin teachers.

But I do remember another teacher, a heavy-set man in his thirties, who taught the first class after lunch. His face was always glazed with sweat, even when the windows were open to the cold winter air. He was looser and funnier than the others, and one afternoon I understood why. He came in, laughed, started writing on the blackboard, and then seemed to freeze. He turned and hurried out. Someone shouted: *He's drunk!* And so he was. Even here, among the elite of Regis, there were drunks. I laughed with the others, but when the man returned, his face ashen, his eyes wet and rheumy, I felt only pity. I wondered if he had children who wanted to love him.

I wasn't very happy at Regis. I used to think it was the school's fault, that somehow I was a clumsy social fit among a group of upper-class kids. That wasn't it at all. There was actually a leveling democracy of merit at Regis; some of the kids were poor, most were middle class, a few were rich; but no boy could buy his way into the school. You had to pass the test, just as McElynn and I had. There were constricting rules: a dress code, an obsession with punctuality, an assignment of privilege to the boys in the upper grades. But the school wasn't riddled with problems of money and class.

My own problems at Regis were more complicated than the clichéd case of a poor kid thrown in with better-off boys. For the first time, I was in a classroom where everybody else was as smart as I was and many were smarter. That was a new experience to me. I couldn't just sit there and pay attention and come out with decent grades. I had to work. But

there were a number of distractions that made it hard for me to do the
schoolwork at the level that Regis demanded. The distractions all flowed
from the Neighborhood. I was still working after school and on Satur-
days at the grocery store, to pay for the subway and lunch; I couldn't
stay at Regis after school, join the school clubs, play ball in the gym, try
to work for *The Owl*, the school newspaper. When the bell rang to end
the final period, I had to leave for work. At Holy Name, the kids in my
class were the same kids I played with after school or on weekends; at
Regis, I almost never saw the other boys after school, not even McElynn
or two boys from the adjoining parish of St. Saviour's, Jim Shea and
John Duffy. We were friendly, we talked, we joked, we traveled together on the subway and sometimes worked together on homework;
but we weren't friends in that deep mysterious way that marks true
friendships.

So I felt disconnected from the school. More than ever, I wanted to
be with my friends up at the Totes. I was in a growing fever of adolescent
sensuality, trying to find an outlet beyond masturbation, trying to get a
girl who would go with me to a bush or a rooftop or the ink-black balcony
of a movie house. I saw tits in geometry classes and asses in history and
wondered if Julius Caesar was getting laid while he wrote his account of
the Gallic Wars. During the Regis years, I was into a harder contest of
wills with my father. Now he was sneering at my idea of becoming a
cartoonist. *You'd better start thinking about something real. You'd better think
about the cop's test or the firemen or the Navy Yard. . . .* I preferred his indifference to his flat-out opposition. And as the first year at Regis ended, I
was drinking in a more sustained way.

While drinking at the Totes, I asserted myself more often about politics, religion, and sports. In a way, it was simply verbal showing off; I
didn't say as much in the courtyard at Regis, afraid, I suppose, that I'd
be challenged by the kids who were smarter than I was. Safe in Brooklyn,
I said out loud that it was ridiculous that Alger Hiss was on trial or that
Communist party leaders were being sent to jail. How could this be a
free country if you couldn't be free to be a Communist? To which someone would say: Whatta you? A fuckin' commie too? And I'd say No, but
in America you're supposed to be free to be anything, right? In May
1949, the armies of Mao Tse-tung finally won the civil war in China,
driving Chiang Kai-shek and his broken troops into permanent exile
in Formosa. The newspapers were hysterical. On the radio, Gabriel
Heatter told us once more that there was bad news tonight. Up at the
Totes, I mouthed off about how Chiang was a thief, his regime corrupt,
his soldiers cowardly.

The fuck you talkin' about, man, Shitty Collins would say. They were sold out, man, by Truman and the commies in Washington.

No, they just stole the money we sent them, millions of dollars, and when they had to fight, they ran.

How do you know? Was you there?

No, I wasn't there. But I tried to imagine Chiang's troops at the docks, piling into boats, panicky and full of fear, while others were tearing off their uniforms, melting into the shadows, throwing down their guns; in my imagination, it was like some final packed and gorgeous panel of *Terry and the Pirates*. Of course, I didn't really know what I was talking about in those sessions on the Totes; I was retailing opinions I had picked up from the *Star* or the *Compass* or the *Post*, all newspapers of the left. Since everybody in the Neighborhood swore by the *Daily News* or the *Journal-American*, I was going the other way. Against those newspapers. Against the pieties of the Neighborhood. Against the Church. Against my father.

I was lucky in these beery little debates because the others didn't know what *they* were talking about either. It wasn't that I was a fan of Stalin; I didn't like his eyes, which were beady and shifty in the news photographs; and his hands looked too small for his body. More important, I knew that there were no freedoms in the Soviet Union (or Russia, as we all called it), and I was sure that if I lived there I'd have to be against the government, and that meant I'd end up in Siberia. But I thought there was something amazingly stupid about the Cold War; Stalin was now the devil incarnate, only four years after he had served on the side of the angels, namely us. Either we'd made a mistake during the war, or we were making a mistake now. And there was a larger problem, of which Stalin was part: Why were so many Americans so scared, *all the time?* We were the strongest country in the world. We won the war. We had the atom bomb. In May, Truman finally broke the Russian blockade of Berlin with a giant airlift. So why were these people shitting in their pants when they thought about communists? The communists won in China, but that didn't mean they were about to land in Los Angeles. And why did so many people think that the communists might be behind anything that made sense: unions, health care, free education? Even in 1949, there were people saying that we shouldn't have stopped in Berlin in 1945, we should've kept going all the way to Moscow.

George Patton, he knew how to deal wit' dese bastids.

Oney thing they respect is force.

That fuckin' Rose-a-velt, he made a deal wit' Stalin, let the Russians take Berlin, now look at the fuckin' mess we're in. . . .

The talk sputtered on into the night. Drinking beer on the Totes, arguing with my friends (or arguing *at* them), I sometimes even felt as if I understood how the world worked. I was that young. Even that September, when Truman announced that the Russians had tested an atom bomb, I thought that everything would be all right. If we each had the atom bomb, I reasoned, then nobody would ever start a war because nobody could win it. In the newspapers, there was great excitement: if the Russians had the atom bomb they must have stolen it from us. There must be spies everywhere, slipping our secrets to them. Some columnists pointed out that the Russians also had former Nazi scientists working for them, the way we did, and maybe they didn't have to steal anything. Most of the guys couldn't have cared less about politics or communism; they were more angry with the Dodgers, who lost to the Yankees in five games in the 1949 World Series, than they were with anyone on the other side of the planet. They didn't care that Dean Acheson had replaced George Marshall as secretary of state; they were wondering whether Dotty Long's tits were real. Almost all of this talk was just riffs in the night. The wars were over. None of this distant bullshit would ever directly affect us. Even the air raid drills, the warnings about the Bomb, the bombardment of Moscow with Hail Marys, *even the Fall of China,* couldn't convince us that these matters had anything to do with our lives. *Pass the cardboard, Jake, I'm thirsty. . . .* When we got bored with politics (which was quickly), we went on to baseball or what we all called pussy.

I hear Naomi puts out.

Who?

Naomi, from down Seventeenth Street. I hear she does it.

Who you hear that from?

Harry from the Parkview, you know him? Lives down Seeley Street? Tells me she does it for quarters. . . .

Then, on my fifteenth birthday, June 24, 1950, everything shifted again. That Saturday, seven divisions of North Korean troops and 150 North Korean tanks crossed the 38th parallel in an invasion of South Korea.

III

BREAKING OUT

How many bibles make a Sabbath?
How many girls have disappeared
Down musky avenues of leaves?
It's an autocracy, the past. . . .

> — Tom Paulin,
>   "In the Egyptian Gardens"

1

THE SUNDAY NEWSPAPERS told the story of the invasion in a sketchy way. They made clear that there was a crisis. President Truman was flying back to Washington from a vacation in Independence, Missouri, while General MacArthur was huddling with his staff at his headquarters in Tokyo. The secretary of state, Dean Acheson, had called for an emergency meeting of the United Nations Security Council. But that Sunday morning, up at the Totes, nobody talked about war. This wasn't another Pearl Harbor; it was some distant battle between Koreans, a kind of civil war, nothing to do with us. Our war ended in August 1945. Around noon, we got on the Coney Island trolley car, picking up transfers to the Neptune Avenue line, and we went to the beach.

In the summer of 1950, all of us from the Neighborhood hung out in a place on Coney Island called Oceantide. Built on the boardwalk at Bay 22, it was a block-long complex with a swimming pool, lockers, a long packed bar, and a small fenced-off area where the young men danced with the young women to a bubbling Wurlitzer jukebox. Down the block was a shop called Mary's, which sold the most fabulous hero sandwiches in New York, great thick concoctions of ham and cheese and tomatoes laced with mustard or mayonnaise, along with cases of ice cold sodas. Out on the beach we gathered on blankets placed like islands in the sand. One of the Big Guys always had a portable radio, and the music drifted across the hot afternoon as we drank beer and watched the girls lather themselves with suntan oil. Off to the right as we faced the sea was a walled development called Sea Gate, mostly Jewish, the place where Isaac Bashevis Singer came to live in 1935 when he arrived from Poland. And down on Surf Avenue, a block from the beach, there were two Irish bars where everyone did their serious drinking.

On that first Sunday of the Korean War, the older guys were laughing and drinking with their girlfriends on the blankets when there was a sudden roar. From out of the pack, a young man named Buddy Kiernan came running and laughing. He was naked. The others had pulled off his bathing suit and now he was grabbing at blankets and dancing around and the girls were giggling and blushing and the guys yawping and then Buddy Kiernan began to run to the sea. People stood up on all the blankets, watching Buddy run, his black hair wild, his legs pumping, his balls and penis bobbing, until he dived into the surf.

To great cheers.

I thought: *I'll remember this all my life.*

We all got drunk that day, the younger guys sharing the wild exuberance of the Coney Island summer and the glorious performance of Buddy Kiernan. I fell asleep on the cold dark sand under the boardwalk, and when I woke up, everybody was gone. My mouth felt coarse. There was a sour smell to my body that I couldn't erase with the salt of the sea. I went home alone on the trolley car, wondering about the war.

By Monday, everybody was talking about Korea. We were in another war. It didn't matter that there had been no direct attack on Americans. We were part of the United Nations. We might have to go. By Friday, the first American ground troops were on their way to the fighting.

It just goes on and on, my mother said one evening. Brian was now four. My newest brother, John, was less than a year old, crawling on the linoleum. *They just keep on killing each other.* There were no tears in her for this war. She didn't weep at the news on the radio. She just crooned, in a sad way, *It goes on and on.*

By the Fourth of July, the mood of the Neighborhood had radically changed. It was clear now: the older guys were going off to the war in Korea. Truman was calling it a "police action," but everybody else called it a war. If you were eighteen, nineteen, twenty, you could be drafted. In August, the reserves were called up, including many men who had fought in World War II. The war would be tough; everybody said so; Seoul had fallen, the South Korean army was destroyed, and the American troops had poor equipment. If you went away, if you drew a number from the draft board that sent you to Korea, you might die.

That summer, Buddy Kelly died in Korea. He was the oldest son of the Kellys at 471 Fourteenth Street and had been on garrison duty in Japan when he was called up. One evening, I saw his brothers, Billy and Danny, sitting with his mother and father on the stoop where we'd all once lived. They sat in absolute silence, and I didn't know what to say; I didn't even remember Buddy clearly. I kept walking. What could I say? That Buddy Kelly had died for his country? He died for someone else's country. Could I say he was a good man and a great American? I barely knew him. He was one of us, part of the tribe, a man of the Neighborhood; but we never got to know him.

Now there was a lot more drinking, everywhere: in the park, in the bars, at the beach. But the tone had changed. The feeling of mindless exuberance gave way to urgency, even desperation. Every weekend there was another going-away party, and you saw weeping girls walking in pairs as another boy went off to basic training or boot camp. Over the next two years at Holy Name, there were a lot of weddings and too many funerals: the bridegrooms were in uniform and the coffins were draped with flags.

When I went back to Regis in the fall, my mind was scrambled. In the yard, we talked a lot about the war. Many boys had brothers who had been drafted or called up. Almost everybody thought that communism had to be stopped. At the same time, they were attacking Truman and Acheson, blaming them for the war. I tried to make sense of this. If it was important to fight the communists, and Truman and Acheson were fighting them, why were they wrong?

The Red Scare didn't dominate Regis the way it did the Neighborhood. But I do remember seeing a Catholic comic book that showed communist mobs attacking St. Patrick's Cathedral. And there was an extended discussion of a papal encyclical called *Atheistic Communism*. The Church expressed itself in other ways. In the *Journal-American*, and other friendly forums, Cardinal Spellman, chubby and pink-skinned, kept warning about how America was in danger of destruction at the hands of the communists, those in Russia, those at home. In the *Daily News*, there were frantic warnings about pinkos, fellow travelers, New Dealers, and liberals. And even in Regis, where Jesuitical irony and skepticism generally prevailed, I started to hear a lot of favorable talk about the junior senator from Wisconsin, Joseph McCarthy.

Because we still couldn't afford television, I didn't see the way McCarthy moved and talked until much later. But I saw Herblock's cartoons in the *Post*, in which an unshaven McCarthy, his brows kissing in a thuggish way, often worked in tandem with another unshaven character who kept climbing out of sewers: a senator from California named Richard Nixon. Cardinal Spellman loved them both.

In that second year at Regis, my allegiance to the Catholic Church ended. It was bad enough that I didn't believe in God; I thought for a while that I might come around, like Ignatius Loyola himself did, the man who had committed all the sins of the world back in the sixteenth century, before undergoing a conversion and founding the Jesuits. Maybe I would get religion the way I finally got *Terry and the Pirates*. But McCarthy and Spellman finished me off. They merged with Brother Jan to create a collective image of a bullying, intolerant Catholicism that repelled me. If they were the heroes of the Catholic Church, I wanted nothing to do with it. And that deepened my feeling of unease and disconnection at Regis.

The school, of course, couldn't be separated from the other parts of my life. With three brothers and a sister now at home, I had endless trouble working at my cartooning; it was difficult even to get homework done, sharing the kitchen table with Tommy and Kathleen. Worse, because there were now seven mouths to feed, we were even poorer. The boys at Regis were not rich, but they wore creased trousers and neat jackets and ties; I had to shuffle together the clothes I wore. I was now taller and heavier than my father, so I couldn't wear any of his clothes; my brothers were younger than I was, so I couldn't borrow theirs. My mother did her best. She took me to Orchard Street on the Lower East Side and bought cheap clothes; she set up time payments to get me slacks at Belmont's on Brooklyn's Fifth Avenue. But the cheap clothes wore out quickly, holes in the pockets first, then the elbows, followed by chronic, mysterious tears under the arms. She patched and repaired them (hunched over a Singer sewing machine), but she had the other kids to tend to, along with my father. When I went to school I couldn't imagine that the mothers of the other boys were up late at night patching their jackets after an evening of cooking, dishes, and helping with homework.

Shoes were an even worse problem. I never had two pairs of shoes at the same time. I wore one pair until they wore out; when the heels wore down or great holes appeared in the soles, I sat in a little booth at the shoemaker's until he finished attaching new soles or heels. After a while, they could not be saved, the edges unable to take another nail, the cheap leather cracking across the top like overcooked bacon. Then my mother bought me a new pair.

In the beginning, I didn't care much about any of this. But some of the boys — the upperclassmen — started making remarks. *Where'd you get that air conditioned jacket, fella?* Or, *You buy those pants down the Bowery?* They probably did this to other kids; they probably did it with each other; but I sometimes felt as if I were the only kid at Regis being inspected for the mortal sin of dressing badly. I began slipping into the yard as late as possible each morning, hugging the wall, avoiding the more wicked tongues. One rainy day I came to school with cardboard stuffed into my shoes because of the holes. In a corner of the locker room, I removed the shoes, wrung out the socks, and threw away the cardboard. A junior, fat-bodied and thick-necked, saw me, and started laughing, pointing at me and nudging his friends. My face flushed; I thought: *Fuck you, you fat bastard, fuck you.* His polished shoes had thick soles and seemed untouched by the morning rain. Quickly, I tied my laces and slipped away without looking at him. But all day long I kept seeing the Fat Boy's grinning face, and my shame grew into rage. He had hurt me; I wanted to hurt him back. During Latin and German and English, I rehearsed what I would do, over and over again, remembering Frankie Nocera, and other fights on Seventh Avenue, wondering what Noona Taylor would do if the Fat Boy laughed at his shoes. And when school ended, I hurried down to Park Avenue to wait for him.

The rain was falling harder. I saw my friends hurrying across the avenue, then staying close to the wall as they ran to Eighty-sixth Street and the Lexington Avenue subway. Some had umbrellas. After a while, there were almost no kids leaving Regis and I thought that maybe the Fat Boy had taken another route home: along Madison Avenue, or over to Fifth Avenue and the downtown bus. My anger ebbed and I was about to go home. Then I saw him walking quickly, holding an umbrella almost daintily in one hand and his books in the other. He didn't see me until he reached the corner.

Hey, you fat bastard.

He peered at me from under the umbrella and smiled. The same smile, I thought. A fucking smirk.

Without another word, I hit him hard in the face and his eyes got wide and the umbrella flew up and the books fell, and then I hit him again and again, blind with rage. He fell and I kicked him with those shameful ugly shoes and grabbed his hair and punched him in the neck, and then he started to scream. That stopped me. I looked around. The streets were empty, lashed by the hard rain. No cops, no pedestrians, not even a doorman. The Fat Boy sat up, his pants ruined, his jacket soaked, his eyes startled and afraid.

Don't laugh at me any more, you fat fuck, I said.

Then I walked away.

That night, I was sure I was finished at Regis. In the morning, he would go to the principal's office and report me. How could he not? His books were ruined, his notes spattered with rain and dirt. I had hurt him badly. He would report me, all right, and they would call me down to the office and tell me that I'd been expelled.

All right, I thought. *Fuck it. I'll go to another school, to Loughlin or St. Agnes or even to Manual. But I won't whimper. I won't beg them to let me stay. If they kick me out, I'll just walk out of there like a man.*

I tossed and turned, alternately consumed with shame, failure and regret, satisfaction and defiance. I was most worried about what my mother would say. I thought that if they kicked me out, I'd have failed *her*. She had been so proud when I made it into Regis. It was proof to her that you could do anything in this country if you worked hard enough. I just hoped that she wouldn't cry. I didn't care what my father thought.

In the morning, I trembled all the way from Brooklyn to Park Avenue, I couldn't read. I couldn't focus on the Miss Subways sign or the girls who got on at Jay Street. I considered playing hooky, just riding the trains all day. It was Friday, I thought, and maybe by Monday they would have forgotten everything. But in those days, subway cops stopped kids who weren't in school and if the kids didn't have notes or good excuses, they picked them up. I didn't want the police to take me back to Regis. I didn't want faces turning to me as I was escorted down a corridor to the principal's office. So I took my trains and came up into Eighty-sixth Street and walked to school. I waited outside the main gate for a while, where the seniors smoked cigarettes, and then went into the yard. The Fat Boy was there with his friends. His face was swollen but he didn't look at me. I went off to my first class and sat through it, hearing nothing, waiting for someone to come to the door and escort me to the principal's office. Nobody ever came. Not in the first period. Not through the day.

When I left school, the Fat Boy was waiting on the corner. I tensed, ready to fight again. And then he started walking toward me. He put out his hand. I hesitated, then shook it.

I'm sorry, he said. You were right. I made fun of you and your shoes and that was a lousy thing to do.

I didn't know what to say. Maybe it was a trick. Maybe now he would sly rap me. But he didn't.

Okay, I said. I'm sorry too.

I walked off alone. We didn't become friends. But I admired him. He'd done what I couldn't do: admitted he was wrong. Without knowing it, the Fat Boy had accomplished something else; because he'd laughed at me, because I'd then given him a beating that could lead to expulsion, the idea of leaving Regis had blossomed in my head. Drinking that night on the Totes, the notion flowered. I began to imagine myself free of the rigor of the Jesuits. I imagined myself in another school, in classes with my friends from the Neighborhood. Then saw myself in other places, rolling around the world, working on the freighters the way my grandfather did, going to Panama and Honduras to pick up the bananas, traveling to Nagasaki. I imagined myself in the navy, sailing for Korea and the war. I imagined myself drawing cartoons the way Bill Mauldin did in World War II. I drank a lot of beer. The visions, as always, grew grander.

2

THAT WINTER, Steve Canyon enlisted in the air force and Caniff's great comic strip began what most fans thought was a long decline. The *Compass* sent Bill Mauldin to Korea, and Willie and Joe found themselves at another front. The *Post* assigned its star sportswriter, Jimmy Cannon, to Korea, and his stories of GIs in trouble made me feel I was there. In contrast, my own problems seemed puny and childish.

And the comics grew darker. A pair of comic books, *Two Fisted Tales* and *Frontline Combat*, were first published that winter by a company called E.C., and they astonished me. The major artist was Harvey Kurtzman, and he revolutionized the form. Unlike war as reflected by Caniff, these combat stories were hard, bleak, free of rah-rah patriotism. They were about men, not costumed superheroes. In Kurtzman's Korean War, there was no Red Skull. The content wasn't the only change. Kurtzman's drawing style was fresh and powerful: full of stark figures, ferocious action, fat juicy brushstrokes applied with spectacular confidence. Somehow he'd created a new style while I was still imitating Caniff. So I'd be sitting in a classroom at Regis, looking at a teacher and instead of listening to what he was saying, I'd be trying to imagine new ways of drawing. Not like Caniff. Not like Kurtzman. I'd draw like myself, as free as handwriting, using crayons, or big brushes, or a million tiny pen lines. This became still another distraction. My grades started to slide.

Around this time, on other shelves in the comic book stores, I was also discovering pulp magazines, drawn to them at first by the work of their illustrators. In the science fiction books *Amazing* and *Astounding* there was an artist named Virgil Finlay. His drawings were full of voluptuous women, almost naked, their breasts often bare except for seashells or veils or carefully placed foliage. Finlay used a pen, creating form by scalloping the shading with individual lines that were built up, thickened, then thinned according to their density; the drawings were full of wonder, the skies bursting with strange forms, the landscapes of his imaginary planets scary and strange. As hard as I tried, I couldn't imitate him.

The science fiction stories meant almost nothing to me but I couldn't resist the detective pulps: *Black Mask, Dime Detective, Flynn's Detective Fiction*, and *Popular Detective*. The drawings were dark, as full of shadows as the movie melodramas of the period, and the men, women, and guns were interchangeable. The stories carried titles like "Hellcats of Homicide Highway" or "Sinner Take All," but often the writing was a lot better than the titles or the illustrations. The stories took place in a landscape I understood: not sagebrush or the plains of Venus, but bad parts of mean towns, where the streetlights were always dim, the cops always crooked, and nobody had a home. The heroes were tough guys, able to absorb ferocious beatings before shooting their enemies without remorse; they'd have felt little sympathy for Frankie Nocera or the Fat Boy. Almost all the women were bad: devious Delilahs, greedy, selfish, and dangerous. They worked in bars, hotels, the streets, and they usually went to bed with a man only to cut his throat. In a way, this vision of women was a perfect fit with the sinful temptresses portrayed by the Church. Naturally, I wished I could meet one of them.

In all the pulp stories, the dark glamour of the scene revolved around drinking. The men met the women in bars. The whiskey was always warm when it went down. Lights were always dim, the jukebox muted, the bartenders sympathetic. Alone, or with women, the heroes always ended up buying a bottle to bring back with them to the hotel. I began to imagine myself in those pulp magazine bars, far from my father's mundane neighborhood saloons. I put the money down and ordered my whiskey and then the girl came in, out of the rain or out of the fog or out of the past. Sometimes she wanted money. Sometimes she wanted help. Sometimes she wanted sex. I was ready to give her all three. In my reveries, I always bought her a drink, just the way the tough guys did, and after a while I paid for a bottle of rotgut (as they always called it) and took her and the bottle back to the brass bed with the hard mattress. That was life. That was how I would live too.

In the pulps on sale at Sanew's, or among the used copies sold in the stores where I once bought comic books, I began to notice the names of the pulp writers: John D. MacDonald, Frank Gruber, Cornell Woolrich. And I started copying paragraphs from their stories into notebooks, particularly from MacDonald, who described places and people in a style that always felt right. At first I thought I would use these paragraphs as text blocks for my sample comic strips. I'd heard from Jim Brady that to get any kind of work you needed to bring samples to the comic book publishers or newspaper syndicates. The pulp texts would make my pages look more professional.

But copying took too much time and I started writing my own texts. I liked inventing names and characters and plots (most of them out of the memory of the stories I'd read). The people did what I wanted them to do and said what I made them say. It was like a magic trick. In some ways, writing stories was easier than trying to do comics; I didn't need to draw the details of a gun; I just had to say the word "gun." I began to think about pulp stories in bed, on the subway, in class.

Soon I had a major problem at Regis. For an English composition assignment, I invented a pulp story about a man who murders his neighbor and buries him in the backyard, only to be discovered when the grass won't grow above the buried body. There was no detective, no hero. Only a passing cop who gets suspicious. I slaved over the story, lettering each page in a composition book and adding illustrations that were drawn on separate sheets of bond paper and pasted into place. I used 435 Thirteenth Street as the house. I improved the backyard, giving it grass and flowers instead of clay. I picked names I knew: Nocero and Taylor. And that's how I got into trouble. Nocero was the name of the man who was killed and buried. I named the murderer Chuck Taylor. Not Noona Taylor, but Chuck. The principal of Regis was the Rev. Charles Taylor, S.J.

I handed in the story, proud of what I'd done, sure that the English teacher would get the joke. He would smile in a sly way (I thought) and praise me for the work I'd done; this wasn't another of those idiotic compositions about "My Trip To Albany." If he got the joke, he didn't appreciate it. A few days later, he handed back the graded compositions. Inside the hand-drawn cover, on the title page ("Seeds of Death"), he had marked a large F and scribbled beneath it, *Sophomoric contempt for authority.* At the end of class, while the others filed out, he told me to remain in my seat. I still held my book in my hand, but now it felt like something dirty.

You must think you're a wise guy, he said.

No, sir.

Only a wise guy would do this.

I said nothing.

And in this world, there is no room for wise guys. They cause trouble. For everybody. For themselves.

He stared at me. I looked at the cover of my book and the lettering of the title. I hoped that he would now forgive me. He didn't.

Come with me, Mister Hamill.

I followed him down the corridors to the principal's office. The English teacher opened the door, nodded, and then went away. The Rev.

Charles Taylor was waiting for me, seated behind his desk. He did not get up. He made a little steeple with his fingers.

Is that the famous book? he said in a chilly voice.

Yes, Father.

He reached across the desk and took it from me. He stared at the cover, the words "Seeds of Death," then at the text. He began reading it. I waited, afraid to breathe. He read to the end. He closed the book and stared at the cover for a long moment. Then his chilly eyes fell upon me.

You're not happy at Regis, are you, Mister Hamill.

I shrugged. Yes, sir. I mean, no sir. I mean — It's all right, it's hard work sometimes, but . . .

My words dribbled away. I looked at crosses on the wall, pictures of saints, some leather-bound missals.

There is nothing keeping you here, young man, he said. If you feel you aren't up to the work, to our standards, to our *disciplines*, then you are, of course, free to go elsewhere.

He bit off the words.

Your other grades are low. You're failing plane geometry.

It's hard, Father. I have a job after school. I have —

You have time to . . . to do *this*, though, don't you? It must have taken many hours, making these drawings, doing this lettering.

Yes, sir.

He was quiet for a beat. Then:

I'm placing you on probation. If your grades improve, you'll have no problems. If not . . .

He let the alternative hang in the air, unspoken. Then he looked back at my book. On one page, I had drawn a portrait of Chuck Taylor, his name carefully lettered at the side. He stopped and then looked up.

Is that what I look like? he said.

No, sir.

He handed me the book.

Actually, it's not a bad likeness. You've got the nose. You've got the nose.

I left in a daze. He'd told me I was on the brink of flunking out of Regis. But I did get his nose right.

3

THE GIRL'S NAME was Jenny. She had a long face framed by long brown hair. Her nose was long too, and she was self-conscious about it. I hate this nose, she said to me one night. I wish I could cut it off. Her brown eyes were among the saddest I've ever seen. In that dark snowy winter of 1950–51, I fell in love with her.

I'm too old for you, she said. I'm seventeen.

I'll be sixteen in June, I said. A year doesn't matter that much, does it?

To some people it does, she said.

Does it matter to you?

No.

I met her in the back booth of a soda fountain named Steven's, which was just off the corner of Ninth Street on Seventh Avenue. There was a big modern jukebox against a wall, packed with 45 rpm records instead of the old 78s that you still saw in the bars of the Neighborhood. Here, Nat Cole was singing "Mona Lisa," Teresa Brewer was belting out "Music, Music, Music," Don Cornell was telling us that it wasn't fair for him to love her, and Frankie Laine was proclaiming loudly that he was gonna live 'til he died. There were some old songs too, from all the way back in 1949: Frankie Laine's "Mule Train" and "Lucky Old Sun" and Vaughan Monroe's evocation of those ghost riders in the sky. That night, I came into Steven's with someone else, who knew the girl sitting with Jenny. We sat down and stayed for two hours. I walked Jenny home to a house on Tenth Street. She smiled goodnight in a tentative way and hurried into the vestibule. I went back to Steven's the next night and she was there again and I walked her home again and asked her to go to a movie.

That Friday night we went to Loew's Metropolitan and saw *In a Lonely Place*, with Humphrey Bogart and Gloria Grahame. I loved that movie. Bogart plays a Hollywood screenwriter who has been assigned to make a script from a terrible best-selling book. This depresses him and he goes to a bar to get rid of his depression by getting drunk. He starts talking to a hatcheck girl, who tells Bogart that she has read the book. He invites her back to his apartment so that she can tell him the story. That way, he won't have to read it himself. It wasn't clear what else he had in mind, but I could make it up. Drinks, a small apartment, sex. The next day, the hatcheck girl is found murdered and the cops come looking for Bogart . . .

I remember talking all the way home about this amazing movie. Did Jenny think the story had anything to do with all this anticommunist stuff? You know, the way people were being ruined by rumors? Wasn't that what it meant? Jenny looked at me as if I were nuts.

Come on, she said, it's just a movie about this guy who drinks too much and beats people up.

No, no, I insisted. It's about more than that.

She smiled at me and her eyes grew sadder.

You're weird, she said.

In the weeks that followed, during that cold winter, I became a regular at Steven's, seeing almost nothing of my friends on the Totes. I was going with Jenny.

On those first dates, the Good Boy dominated the Bad Guy. I was polite. That is, I didn't grab her tits as soon as we sat down. With the older guys now gone to the war, we younger boys were taking their place; the seventeen-year-old girls had no nineteen-year-old boys to take them into the nights. Suddenly, there was an aura of seriousness about most of us: guys disappearing for days with their girls, saying nothing about what they did or bragging too loudly when next they showed up on the Totes. I sat alone with Jenny in the booths, talking, listening to the jukebox: Tony Martin's "There's No Tomorrow" and "La Vie en Rose" and the Weavers singing "Goodnight, Irene." On that jukebox, there were also two glorious celebrations of drinking: a Wynonie Harris shouting blues, "Don't Roll Those Bloodshot Eyes at Me," and a tune called "Cigarees and Whuskey and Wild, Wild Women." I played them as if they were anthems.

Within weeks, Jenny and I were going steady. This was a formal condition, like being engaged, or even being married. I asked her to go steady right after Christmas, coming home from a party. All the way home, I held her close to me; she was wearing a long brown coat with a curlicued design sewn on the back at her waist. I was sure I loved her, even though I knew virtually nothing about her, except that she lived with her mother in a small apartment on Tenth Street near Sixth Avenue. In the time we were together, I never once saw her mother.

You don't have any brothers or sisters? I asked her one freezing night as we sat on a bench beside the park.

No. It's just me and my mother. She's a nurse down at Cumberland.

And your father?

She shook her head and looked away.

I'm sorry, I said. Is he, uh, dead?

No, she said. He just went away.

That's too bad, I said, thinking: Maybe she's better off.

Yeah, she said. It's too bad.

She started to cry and I hugged her and kissed her neck and her hair. She was the first girl who made me feel protective, the first who provoked in me the treacherous entanglement of pity with love. All that winter, in doorways, rooftops, park benches, we kissed and talked and talked and kissed, holding each other to keep warm. She said she loved me, but her eyes remained very sad; it was as if she could see some awful future. I started buying beer at the grocery store, telling Jack it was for my father, and Jenny and I would drink together on the parkside. She would get teary and cry and then bury her face against my neck. Finally, in the deep shadows of the parkside, she let me touch her breasts through her clothes. Then she let me open her blouse and touch her flesh. But whenever I moved my hand between her legs, she always stopped me.

I can't let you do that, she said. You'll lose all respect for me.

No, I won't, I swear. I love you, Jenny. How could I lose respect for *you?*

She should have laughed out loud — *asshole!* — but she said nothing, just snuggled against me. I suppose she was exercising a kind of wisdom that had nothing to do with respect. I was still a kid. In a neighborhood of cops, firemen, ironworkers, and dock wallopers, I kept conjuring crazy visions of the future: writing comics, going to art school, seeing the world. Everything I talked about to Jenny was the opposite of security; my basic goal, unclear even to me, was to run away from home.

Jenny was probably also sensing my own confused mixture of desire and fear. On some nights, I wanted so badly to put my cock in her that my body hurt (the condition even had a name — "blue balls"). But actual consummation was also scary. I'd never even seen a girl's pubic hair or a vagina, not even in photographs (this was before *Playboy*, and long before *Penthouse*). For all the technical discussions on the street, I wasn't even sure *where* I should put my cock. And even though I didn't believe in God, all those years in Catholic schools surely had helped shape my psyche.

These confusions accompanied me and Jenny to the benches along the parkside, to the darkened hallways and freezing rooftops. But we didn't stay in the cold forever. One weekend, her mother moved them to Bay Ridge and soon after started working a 6 P.M. to 2 A.M. shift at the hospital. That first Saturday night, Jenny invited me to dinner. I took the trolley out to Sixty-ninth Street and picked up three quarts of Ballantine's beer in a deli; the old man at the counter didn't ask for proof of age. I felt like a man as I walked out, the bottles clunking in the paper bag.

Jenny met me at the door of the basement apartment. She was wearing a light brown dress that was tight across her breasts and wide at the bottom. She had crinolines underneath and high-heeled black shoes that made her look older. She put a stack of records on a thick-spindled 45 rpm player: Nat Cole and Don Cornell, Sinatra singing "I'm a Fool to Want You," and Tommy Edwards doing "Blue Velvet." My hands were damp, but when I took her hands, they were wet. There was a candle burning on the table, and she served spaghetti and meatballs and fresh Italian bread. I finished a glass of beer, then another, a full quart while eating greedily. She gazed at me with her sad eyes, as if afraid I'd hate the food. I told her dinner was wonderful (it was) and opened another beer. We danced. She cleared the table. She turned off the lights in the kitchen and the overhead lights in the living room, leaving one lamp burning. She made sure the curtains and drapes were closed. We danced again and then went to the couch. I kissed her, felt her up (as we said then), unzippered the back of her dress, unsnapped her bra, while her protests became whimpers and her breathing got heavier. I moved a hand between her legs, up to the flesh at the top of her stockings and then under her panties while the crinolines made a sighing sound. This time she didn't stop me. She was wet. She fumbled with my belt. She unzipped my fly. She gripped my cock.

And so we did it. It was awful and amazing, clumsy and frantic and inept and vaguely comical. I exploded at the end. Jenny wept. I fell back, my shoes still on, my trousers and undershorts around my ankles. I looked down and laughed. That made her feel worse. She hurried into the bathroom, sobbing. I took off my shoes and pulled up my trousers. I couldn't believe it: I had done it. I had put my cock in a cunt. I had come in a girl. Oh, man. The records had finished playing, so I turned them over and started playing the flip sides. I took another Ballantine's from the refrigerator, and when I turned around, she was walking naked out of the bathroom.

I bet I'm pregnant, she said.

Nah, I said.

I know I am.

I'd never seen a naked woman before and I just stood there, gazing at her, at her breasts and belly and great black vee of pubic hair. I thought of Virgil Finlay's women and Miss Lace and the hot women in the pulp magazines. She came over and kissed me, holding my face in both hands. I held her heavy hard-nippled breasts in my hands.

If I'm pregnant, will you marry me? she whispered.
Of course, I said, struggling with my panic.
Then, come on.
We went to her bedroom. I took the beer with me.

4

THE YEAR 1951 was terrible. I was at least six people: the schoolboy at Regis, the hardworking delivery boy after school, the opinionated angry young man raging at the world, the aspiring cartoonist, the lover of Jenny, the apprentice drinker and Bad Guy. In Latin class, I was struggling with the subjunctive; at night, I was fucking my brains out. Drinking became an integral part of sex. I'd drink three or four beers to feel confident; Jenny would drink three or four beers to have an excuse for letting me do it once again. It was as much a ritual as the Mass. Sometimes I bought condoms; sometimes I had to choose between a pack of Trojans or a quart of Ballantine's. I always settled for beer and risk.

At home, I was miserable. My mother was trying to feed, clothe, and civilize the whole brood, while holding down her new part-time job as a cashier at the RKO Prospect movie house. She got little help from my father. He was drinking as hard as ever, particularly on the weekends. He began to go on binges, sometimes missing work on a Monday or Friday, thus granting me the self-righteous joy of despising him. I was too young and self-absorbed to ask him why he was drinking so much, what he feared, what made him weep, who he *was*. We worked out a ritual too. We made remarks about the weather. We talked about baseball. He predicted that Ray Robinson would beat Jake LaMotta for the middleweight championship, and he was right. But there was nothing else I could say to him.

I certainly couldn't tell him, or my mother, about Jenny. I couldn't tell anyone else either. If I told my friends, they'd immediately tell everybody in the Neighborhood that Jenny "put out." If they thought she put out, they wouldn't respect her. And how could I love a girl my friends didn't respect? Besides, I didn't think of it as putting out. To me, it was a love story.

The key word, of course, was "story." After the fiasco of Chuck Taylor, I stopped writing my versions of pulp stories. But I wasn't writing comics anymore either. One reason was the physical impossibility of doing it in the apartment. The kids were the infantry of disorder; they moved from room to room in a sustained campaign of disruption. At eleven, my sister, as the only girl, took title to the Little Room. I couldn't lay out paper or board, ink, pens and brushes, on the kitchen table. Gradually, I just gave up. That long slow surrender ate at my guts, but I convinced myself that I had no choice. As long as I live here, I thought, I'll be unable to work.

Instead of creating stories, I created Jenny. I invented her in my head, supplying her with qualities no girl could possess, granting her a perfection that had more to do with literature than with the scared, lonely girl who gave me her body. In some primitive, inarticulate way, our love story was driven by my need for narrative, for drama, for a sense of beginning, middle, and end. It was a better story than the ones I had invented out of comics and pulps; I just didn't know how it would end.

In the spring, many things began to unravel while others took shape. I was doing worse at Regis. In March the Rosenbergs were convicted of espionage, and I read in one of the newspapers that there'd be a rally in their defense in Union Square. I tried to get some of the guys from school to meet me at the rally, and one of them said: What are you, some kind of communist? I said no, I wasn't a communist; but this was a kind of history and I wanted to see it. Are you crazy? the guy said. You get arrested, you end up on some list, your life is ruined. I went anyway, alone. The crowd was small. But the sense of defiant energy was thrilling. I saw young women who didn't look like anyone from the Neighborhood; they were older than I was, but I wanted to come back, see them again, know them. They cheered at the speeches. They smiled at people and asked them to sign petitions. They didn't ask me.

When the rally ended, I wandered downtown to find the subway station at West Fourth Street. Along the way, I discovered two places that were to pull me back again and again: Book Row on Fourth Avenue and the neighborhood called Greenwich Village. The first was like a series of treasure houses, one used book store after another, the cheapest books stacked outside in stalls, selling for a nickel, the interiors dark, musty, packed from floor to ceiling with more expensive books. I was afraid to enter, afraid I'd see some glittering bauble that would exhaust the few dollars I had in my pocket — money for the beer that would grant me admission to Jenny's bed. I ran my hands over the books as if they were holy objects and moved on.

Walking into the Village was like entering a movie set. The elegant houses, blooming trees, intimate bars, and scattered bookshops were lovely to look at, but I was even more enchanted by the way the people looked. They were completely different from the people in the Neighborhood or those I saw uptown near Regis. That first day, I saw bearded men with paint-spattered clothes lugging wildly painted abstract canvases into buildings with skylights on the rooftops. Women wore hair down to their hips, bright ceramic earrings, long black stockings, and they smoked cigarettes as they walked. Men carried books and talked to friends with excitement and passion. On Eighth Street, there were theaters showing movies from Italy and France. I passed coffee shops, cafeterias, and bars filled with people deep in argument, engulfed by cigarette smoke, and all of them looked different from the men in the bars of Brooklyn. I wanted to come back. And stay.

That day the unravelment at Regis and at home receded as I glimpsed the possibility of another life, only a subway ride from Brooklyn, in a place where I could fill my life with politics, art, books, and women. I didn't want to wait. This was where I could live. Far from Brooklyn and my father and Rattigan's and the insistence on being a plumber or a cop. I could be a bohemian! I'd read the word somewhere and looked it up in a dictionary, and it sounded romantically perfect. A *bohemian*, free of all the stupid dumb-ass constraints of the world! With a huge studio, my own drawing table, a bookcase full of books, a skylight. I'd work all day and go to the cafés at night, to drink brandy and listen to poetry. A free man. The vision excited me all the way home on the subway. Jenny was nowhere in it.

That vision didn't help me at Regis; it might have accelerated my decline. I simply couldn't concentrate. I'd sit in geometry class and think of Jenny's nipples and get an erection. I'd be in a civics class and want to know why the Rosenbergs had been sentenced to death. I'd be in the English class, with a teacher discussing the assigned text, and see myself in a café reading books of my own choosing. Each morning, I would linger in bed, filled with resistance and dread. I didn't want to get up, didn't want to go to school. If I'd seen Jenny the night before, and drunk too much beer, I'd be physically logy and sometimes emotionally hung over too. I'd try to remember if I wore a condom or not; sometimes I hadn't, and that filled me with dread as I thought of Jenny pregnant. I don't know if my mother suspected anything about the drinking; I tried to hide it, brushing my teeth or chewing gum. If she did, she said nothing. In a way, that made it worse for me, because I had to carry the burden of the drinking by myself. The effort of hiding it made me feel even more separated from my classmates at Regis.

That spring, failure entered me like an infection. My grades were falling and I had already been placed on probation by Father Taylor. I was certain I would suffer the humiliation of flunking out at the end of the term. That meant I might have to repeat my sophomore year at some other school. And *that* would delay my life.

Finally, I went to see the school counselor, a kind man named Father Burke, and explained most of it to him. I left out Jenny. I didn't mention the drinking. But I told him that I just wasn't able to do the work at Regis and wanted out.

Have you discussed this with your parents? he said.

No.

What will they say?

I don't know.

Then you'd better tell them.

I don't want to ask their permission, I said. I just want to do it.

But you'll have to transfer to another school, he said. You're not even sixteen yet, so you can't just drop out.

What school would take me?

I'll see, Father Burke said. If your mind is made up, I'll try to find you another school.

That night, I told my mother that I wanted to drop out of Regis. She was concerned, sweet, apologetic.

I feel I didn't help, she said. I feel that I should've given you more help.

No, Mom. It wasn't you. It was me.

She made tea, and said that she didn't want me to be unhappy, and if I wasn't happy at Regis, then maybe I should go to another school. I was relieved. I just didn't want to see her crying. That night, she seemed too tired to weep. Her hair had turned gray, her face was pale. She was only forty and starting to look old.

The next day was my last at Regis. I didn't say good-bye to any of my classmates. I didn't stop in to see Father Burke. I just packed my books and went home. But I didn't feel free. All the way back to Brooklyn, I felt that I'd done something unbelievably stupid. Because of my laziness, distraction, fear, and drinking, I had walked away from the best Catholic high school in New York. As the F train came up out of the tunnel after Bergen Street, I looked down from the train and saw the Gowanus Canal beneath me and knew that the building where my father had worked as a clerk for Roulston's was nearby. I remembered going there with my mother when everything was still in the future, even the war. Then I looked in the other direction and saw the skyline of Manhattan, rising from the harbor, stone-gray and indifferent, beautiful and unattainable, and I began to weep.

That night I went to Jenny's and told her what had happened and then tried to get rid of my failure in her body. I drank too much beer and fell asleep. She woke me later, shaking me in desperation, frantic that her mother would find us, shouting that she had to make the bed and air out the room. *You're drunk*, she said. *Don't you understand me? Are you too drunk to know what I'm saying?* Carrying the empties, I left in a rage, at her and at myself. She was giving me *orders*, her panic transformed into wide-eyed fury that seemed like the opposite of love. But I was at fault too; I'd had too many beers and was sluggish and confused, like my father on the second-floor landing at 378. Down by the subway, I hurled the empty beer bottles at a parked garbage truck, enjoying the way they smashed and splintered.

On Monday, I started at my new school, St. Agnes on Forty-fourth Street, in midtown Manhattan. It was dark and gloomy after Regis, the classrooms smaller, the desks more battered. But on the first day, I knew that I would do well. Even with my terrible record at Regis, I was far ahead of most of the students at St. Agnes. By the end of the week, some of my broken ego was restored. And I loved the physical act of going to that school. I came up out of Grand Central and then walked east, passing under the massive rumbling structure of the Third Avenue El. There were Irish saloons on every corner of Third Avenue, with men standing at the bars all day long.

Some of the drinkers were newspapermen. The *Daily News* was on Forty-second Street between Second and Third, and I liked going into the lobby to look at the immense globe and the polished floors; it was like visiting the *Daily Planet* (and years later the *Daily News* building served as the setting for that imaginary newspaper in the first *Superman* movie). Sometimes I saw men I was sure were reporters (they all wore hats) hurry out the door, straight to the bars. A few blocks away, on Forty-fifth Street, was the *Daily Mirror*. I once saw their sports columnist, Dan Parker, a huge man with a pencil-thin mustache, walk out of the newspaper and stroll down to Third Avenue, whistling all the way. I felt connected to the *Mirror* by *Steve Canyon*. But I never saw Caniff come out of the building. Still, the sight of Dan Parker was enough. I loved the idea of a newspaperman who whistled.

I also came to love the gloomy light under the El and wished I could walk into the bars and order a drink. At one point, with some other kids from St. Agnes, I started watching the Kefauver hearings through the windows, seeing various gangsters and politicians talk in black and white, and watched Frank Costello's hands. I wanted a television set now. And a telephone. And a room with a door. Far more than we could afford at 378. Most of all I wanted to walk into a Third Avenue bar and drink like a man.

5

THEN ONE NIGHT, Jenny and I went to the Avon, a third-run movie house on Ninth Street. One of the two movies was *Portrait of Jennie*, with Joseph Cotten. I thought he was great in *The Third Man* and we laughed about how those people out in Hollywood couldn't even spell Jenny. In the movie, Joseph Cotten was a painter. He lived in the Village and had an amazing studio, with easels, a fireplace and, of course, a skylight. One day, he's in Central Park and meets Jennifer Jones, who is young and shy and beautiful. She sings a strange little song:

> *Where I come from nobody knows,*
> *And where I'm going, everything goes . . .*

Joseph Cotten keeps meeting the girl over the next month or two, and each time she's older. He paints her portrait and tries to learn more about her. But in fact, she's dead, killed years before in a storm. At the end of the movie he meets her on the anniversary of her death. He gets to kiss her and hug her; the music builds to an amazing swell; she is swept out to sea to die again.

Jenny was crying at the end. I kept thinking about Joseph Cotten's studio. We didn't stay for the second feature. All the way to her house on the Fifth Avenue trolley, Jenny was silent.

That's the way life is, isn't it? she said.

Like what? That movie?

Yeah.

Oh, sure. We always fall in love with ghosts we meet in Central Park.

No, she said. I mean that things always turn out lousy.

Hey, Jenny, it's a movie.

We reached her house. She asked me not to come in. It was too late. Her mother would be home soon.

You keep saying you're an artist, she said. Why don't you draw me?

I will.

When?

Tomorrow night?

My mother's home tomorrow night.

Next Friday.

You swear? she said, smiling.

I swear.

That Friday night, she served me another dinner, this time of baked ziti. I sipped my beer slowly, cleaned my plate, and had seconds. After dinner, she stacked the dishes in the sink, ran water over them, left them to soak, then washed her hands and primped her hair. She seemed very nervous.

Maybe you shouldn't try this, she said. You don't have to draw me if you don't want to.

No, no, I said. Let's try it.

She sat on the edge of the couch in the muted yellow light of the table lamp and I sat across from her and started to draw. In my head I saw Joseph Cotten making his portrait of Jennifer Jones, and I wished we were in some great high-ceilinged garret in the Village instead of this basement in Bay Ridge. But I worked hard, using a number 2 pencil on a pad of white paper, outlining her head with very light marks, blocking in the eyes and the nose and the mouth, loosely indicating the hair, the neck, and the collar of her white blouse. I was soon lost in the act, erasing, shading, smudging with a finger, but the picture was not going well. Jenny's hair looked fine, and I'd captured those sad eyes; but there was something wrong with the mouth, and the nose looked enormous. I erased again, trying to make the nose smaller, but that wasn't right either; I couldn't put someone else's nose on Jenny's face. I paused, sipped my beer, stared at her, trying to figure out what I was doing wrong, then tried to outline her nose with absolute exactitude. This time I thought I had it right. With the nose recorded properly, the mouth was easier to fix. I hurried to the end, blocking in the hair with what I thought were bold strokes, then finishing the neck and blouse. I exhaled, then took a deep breath and finished my beer.

Can I move? she said.

Yeah, I said. I'm finished.

Can I see it?

Sure.

I handed her the drawing pad. She looked at the picture, her eyes wide. And then burst into tears. She stood up, bawling, and threw the pad at me.

I'm ugly, she sobbed. You think I'm ugly!

No, Jenny, I don't think you're ugly. I was —

Look at my nose!

She turned away and buried her face in the pillows of the couch. I tried to console her, petting her hair, hugging her. She stopped crying and then sat up slowly, saw the picture on the floor before the chair and started crying again.

That's the way you see me, she said. I'm ugly, ugly, ugly!

No, Jenny, I love you.

You love my — you love what I give you! You love what I let you do to me!

I stood up and closed the pad, so she wouldn't see the hated picture. She wiped at her eyes with the sleeve of her dress and then saw the pencil and it started again. I didn't know what to do. I'd tried so hard to make the drawing real, and she obviously was wounded by it. A gift had become an instrument of torture. Joseph Cotten didn't have this problem. I stayed a little longer and then took my pad and my pencil and fled.

That was the end of it. Suddenly, shockingly. We saw each other two days later outside Steven's. She didn't want coffee or a soda. Standing on the sidewalk, she announced that she was "breaking off" with me. She talked about needing "freedom" and how she was too young to get married or settle down and how she was afraid of getting caught by her mother or ending up pregnant.

You're only fifteen, she said. It's not right.

Her eyes looked sadder than ever. She turned her back on me and hurried down Ninth Street to catch the Fifth Avenue bus. I felt absolutely alone, engulfed by a delicious melancholy. Now, I thought, this story has an ending.

So back I went to my friends and the Totem Poles and drinking beer from cardboard containers. I listened to my friends talk about the glories of pussy, knowing they were almost all virgins. I started truly listening to Sinatra. I did almost no homework, drew no cartoons, attempted no portraits. The war ground on in Korea, back and forth with little gain. I saw more young women in grave little knots, going out together on Saturday nights. I didn't call Jenny; she couldn't call me. Suddenly, Tony Bennett was on all the radios and crooning from the jukeboxes: "I Won't Cry Anymore" and "Cold, Cold Heart." I would sing with him:

I've shed a million tears since we're apart,
But tears will never mend a broken heart.

One night, I saw Jenny waiting to the side at the Sanders while the men lined up to buy tickets. She glanced over at the Totem Poles, but then turned and smiled at her date: a big dumb guy from Seventh Avenue who could hit a spaldeen about four blocks. She took his arm and they went in to see the movie. I never talked to her again.

6

I WAS BORED in St. Agnes and started playing hooky, the empty spring days spent wandering the city. Sometimes I sat in movie houses. Other times I worked my way through the dark caves of Book Row. In May, Willie Mays came up from the minors to play for the Giants.

They say he's the greatest thing on two feet, my father said.

What do you think?

We'll see, he said. We'll see if he can hit the curveball.

Suppose he can?

Then the Dodgers are in trouble.

We talked about the Dodgers and about Kid Gavilan beating Johnny Bratton. But we talked about nothing else. He went to work and then to Rattigan's. I went to school and then to the Totem Poles. In June, I finished at St. Agnes. I never went back.

Instead, I took an examination to get into the apprenticeship program at the Brooklyn Navy Yard. My uncle David worked as a sheetmetal worker in the Yard (as it was called) and he told my father about the program. One night over dinner, the kids all there, my father mentioned it to me.

It's a goddamn good thing, he said, if you can get into it.

My mother shook her head.

Ach, Billy, she said, let the boy finish high school.

But he went on explaining it to me. The program was simple: you worked for four weeks, then went to school for a week, right there in the Yard; when you finished, you got a high school diploma, and you got paid for the weeks you went to school; eventually you moved up to become a journeyman at your trade. I listened carefully; it was the first thing I'd ever heard my father approve for me. I could escape from the drudgery of high school. I'd start earning a living, no matter how small. Hell, he explained, you could have a job at the Yard for thirty years, and retire with a good pension. And remember, he said, it's a *federal* civil service job. There's nothing better than civil service, except federal civil service.

If there's another Depression, he said, you'll always work.

My mother said nothing. I was beginning to understand what the Depression had done to both of them. I took the test for the Navy Yard and passed.

That summer, I was in another kind of depression. Day and night, I felt that I'd lost my way. It was as if some long steady tide were flowing out of me, the waters rising in my skull and then tumbling me along with that tide I couldn't control. It seemed absurd to think anymore about being a cartoonist. Or a bohemian. Maybe everybody was right, from my father to Brother Jan: it was arrogant, a sin of pride, to conceive of a life beyond the certainties, rhythms, and traditions of the Neighborhood. Sometimes the attitude was expressed directly, by my friends or the Big Guys or some of the men from Rattigan's. More often, it was implied. But the Neighborhood view of the world had fierce power. Who did I think I was? Who the *fuck* did I think I was? Forget these kid's dreams, I told myself, give 'em up. Do what everybody else does: drop out of high school, go to work, join the army or navy, get married, settle down, have children. Don't make waves. Don't rock the boat. Every year I'd do my Easter duty, whether I believed in God or not. I'd drink on the way home from work and spend most weekends with my friends in the saloons. I'd get old. I'd die and my friends would see me off in Mike Smith's funeral parlor across the street from Holy Name. That was the end of every story in the Neighborhood. Come on: let's have a fucking drink.

7

I DIDN'T KNOW it at the time, but I had entered the drinking life. Drinking was part of being a man. Drinking was an integral part of sexuality, easing entrance to its dark and mysterious treasure chambers. Drinking was the sacramental binder of friendships. Drinking was the reward for work, the fuel of celebration, the consolation for death or defeat. Drinking gave me strength, confidence, ease, laughter; it made me believe that dreams really could come true.

Drinking also made me change my feelings about my father. In the Navy Yard, I worked with men who knew him. And after a day of labor, buried inside an aircraft carrier that was being converted for jets, or lugging angle irons on my shoulders across Shop 17, I would go to the bars on Sands Street with them and hear tales of young Billy Hamill.

He was a great soccer player, one of them said, a man named Hugh Delargy. He was fast and he was tough. Jesus, was he tough. Smart too.

I was there the day he got hurt, said Eddie McManus, a short, powerful balding welder. It was out at the oval in Bay Ridge, on a Sunday. We were playing a German team. Our team was called Belfast Celtic, after the team back home. And there were teams from the different countries, a Spanish team, a Jewish team called House of David. We were playing the German team that day and your father was at center forward. He was having a great day, bloody great.

And then, Delargy said, that German fucker came at him . . .

Kicked him so bloody hard, McManus said, it sounded like a board breakin'.

Delargy sipped his whiskey and said, He went down and we all knew he was hurt and everybody ran out on the field. They wanted to kill the fuckin' Kraut.

They took Billy over on the side, McManus said, and it was pitiful, fuckin' pitiful to see. The leg was broke beneath the knee and the bone was sticking out through the blood. And Billy was cryin' like a baby, My leg, he kept saying, my leg, my leg, my leg . . .

DeLargy and McManus told me this in grave voices, sipping whiskey while I drank my beer. I remember trying very hard not to cry, then excusing myself and hurrying into the men's room. I sat on a bowl in a locked stall and bawled for my father. And despised myself for the way I'd often sneered at him. When I went back to the bar, I gulped the beer and ordered another, engulfed in a sweet bitterness, knowing that all my life I would see my father on that hard winter playing field, crying like a baby.

After that talk, and other tales told in the bars near the Navy Yard, I began to love my father again. Pity allowed me to see him as a man, instead of a father who could not play the role that my childish imagination and need had assigned him. I could see him in Belfast as a boy, running streets and fields with his twin brother, trying to eat in a kitchen with a dozen other kids, listening to commands from his own father. There was a photograph of his long-dead father in our house now, recently sent from Ireland, where it had been found by Uncle Frank in an old steamer trunk. It was cracked with age and very formal, showing a somber long-faced man whose white beard made him look like George Bernard Shaw. He looked as capable of silence as my own father.

What was he like, your father? I asked him one evening.

He was a mason. A stonemason.

No, I mean what kind of *man* was he?

Billy Hamill shrugged and lit a Camel.

He was stern, he said. He was very stern.

Then I saw my father in flight from the stern white-bearded man, smoking Woodbines in the Belfast night, watching British soldiers patrol streets, hearing endless talk about Catholics and Protestants, playing soccer in frozen fields, and learning to drink. Was it whiskey or was it beer? Or did they drink the dark liquid called stout? And was he drinking when he joined Sinn Fein? Did he and his friends drink the night the bomb was planted and the British soldiers were killed and they all took the night boat to Liverpool and then America? After the bomb, did he shiver in fear? Was he afraid of being caught and turned into an informer? Or did they all go somewhere and get drunk and sing the songs he now sang in Rattigan's?

In a new way, Billy Hamill came alive to me, a person cobbled together from sparse facts and my imagination, and in that summer of my own defeat, I pitied him, with the glibness of a child, and felt the permanent grieving hurt in all his black silences.

We still could not talk in any easy way. But in the bars near the Navy Yard and on long evenings at the Totem Poles I would speak to him in imagination and he would speak to me. I have fucked up my life, Dad; I've quit high school and gone to work in the Navy Yard and I don't want to be there. Well, he would say, do something about it. What can I do? Do what you want to do, Son. Make yourself happy, Son. Live every day of your life, Son. And I'd say, Love me, Dad. And he'd answer, Let's have a drink.

But we never had that conversation. And I knew I had to save my life on my own. I was taking home forty dollars a week from the Navy Yard and giving my mother ten. But I couldn't do at home what I still wanted to do. I couldn't draw. I couldn't read. And I began thinking about a place of my own. A place where I could leave unfinished drawings on the table until I got home, with no fear they would be ruined. A place where I could drink beer and slide girls between sheets. Maybe I could even go to school at night. Maybe, in spite of my dreadful failure, I could still try to be an artist.

On the subway one morning I met a guy I knew in Holy Name. His name was Ronnie Zeilenhofer. He was smart and decent. His father owned a delicatessen on Prospect Park Southwest. We talked and joked for a few minutes, but when I told him I'd dropped out of high school, his face went oddly slack.

Jeez, I figured you'd be one of the guys that went to college, he said. I can't believe it, you dropping out.

I felt suddenly small and diminished. In two years I'd gone from being the smartest kid in the class to another guy from the Neighborhood, trudging off to work with his hands and his back. Another loser from Brooklyn. I started talking wildly about how I was just starting, I was gonna go to art school and was looking for a place of my own. Panic and shame produced something resembling the truth. Zeilenhofer and I weren't close, so in an odd way I could tell him what I really felt. Then he said that if I was serious there was a small place for rent upstairs from his father's deli. Eight dollars a week, with a bed and a refrigerator.

That sounds great, I said.

Call me, and I'll show it to you.

A week later, I moved in. Three months after starting in the Navy Yard, I was off on my own.

8

THE ROOM was small and bare, with flowered wallpaper stained by old glue. There was one picture on the walls: a framed magazine photo of the Rockies. The bed was narrow, the mattress lumpy. But there was a bureau for my clothes and I set out my inks and pens and brushes on a small table and stacked some books on the windowsill and I was happy.

The room was in the back, overlooking a chilly treeless yard. On weekends and on cold evenings I would sit at the table, deep in the luxury of solitude, and draw pictures of aviators and pirates, of detectives, and villains with scarred faces. I loved the feeling of standing up and going to the sink and washing the india ink from the brushes, pushing them into a bar of soap, rinsing them, then forming a perfect needlelike tip with my mouth. I bought a small lamp. I Scotch-taped my drawings to the walls. I learned to carry dirty clothes to the launderette and feed myself in greasy spoons.

Downstairs, to the left, was a bar called the Parkview, and when I came home in the evenings from the Navy Yard I could see faces staring from the windows. The faces were almost the same as those in Rattigan's: pouchy-eyed and tight-lipped. One evening I ran into Mickey Horan, one of the crowd from the Totes. He invited me in for a drink. The bartender served us without asking for draft cards. Soon I was walking in on my own, and the faces from the windows acquired names. Like the men at the Navy Yard, they seemed to accept me. I was sixteen. But I could put my dollar on the bar with the others. That was enough. They talked over and over again about Bobby Thomson's home run in the play-off game at the Polo Grounds and how it had destroyed more than the Dodgers, it had wrecked *them*. They talked about Ray Robinson's revenge against Randy Turpin, and how he battered the Englishman into a stupor at the Polo Grounds. They talked about Rocky Marciano's destruction of Joe Louis. They didn't talk about Korea. As the year moved toward Christmas, I would come up to the room, gassy with beer, and the ceiling would move and the table bob and I would hold a pillow to my chest as if it were an anchor. Sometimes, for no reason that I understood, I would weep.

On Saturday mornings, I would go to Seventh Avenue and climb the stairs to the apartment and give my mother eight dollars. The Good Boy, of course. She would talk to me as best she could about going on with my schooling, maybe at night. But it was hard to sustain such talk; the kids were running around; the shopping must be done; she had to be on the job at the movie house by five. I knew she was right. But I didn't know what to do about it. I walked back up the slope to the Totes. I talked with my friends. I went to the Parkview and drank beer and listened to the jukebox. The Four Aces were singing "Tell Me Why." Tony Bennett was singing "Cold, Cold Heart." Rosemary Clooney was singing "Come On-A-My House." I didn't sing with them. After a while, I went upstairs to the room and napped and woke up and drew pictures. Sometimes the music would drift up from the bar. Sinatra. *I'm a fool to want you . . .*

The newspapers fed me in a different way. And everything I learned from the newspapers seemed to lead to something else. In one of them, I saw a story about the death of a painter named John Sloan. He was 80 years old and a member of a group called the Ashcan School, the paper said, and it showed one of his drawings of people under the Third Avenue El. I went to the library and found books that showed his paintings and etchings and copied them into my own sketchbooks. Those pictures had nothing to do with comics. Instead, they were about a world that I recognized, even if most of them were made in the 1920s. The El. The streets of Manhattan. The dark city looming at twilight. I loved Sloan's lumpy Irish face too; he could have stood right at the bar in the Parkview, talking or singing. He even painted bars, for the books showed several works about a place in Manhattan called McSorley's. He caught the dark snug safety of a bar, the golden warmth it could give you on a cold night. His bars had no jukeboxes or shuffleboard machines in them. But I had seen places like them all over Brooklyn. One Saturday afternoon, I went over to see McSorley's, down the street from the Third Avenue El. The oldest bar in New York, a sign said. I was thrilled; it was exactly the way Sloan had painted it, dark and romantic, with old pictures on the wall and a potbelly stove and lumpy men at the bar and tables. I took a breath and went in. But the bartender asked me for a draft card and I left in a mixture of humiliation and panic. Still, John Sloan had his effect on me: I started sitting in booths at the Parkview and drawing the men at the bar.

Who the hell is that? a guy would say.

You.

I don't look like that, come on, kid.

You look worse than that, Jerry, another guy would say.

If I did, I'd fuckin' kill myself.

The older men seemed amused by me, the kid from upstairs who worked in the Navy Yard and drew pictures in the bar.

You oughtta do that for a living, kid, said a bartender named Brick.

Brick, don't encourage him. He'll end up in the fuckin' Village wit' the faggots.

Impossible. He's a fuckin' Catlick!

They all laughed. I drew their pictures and they asked for copies and I handed them out as if they were my tickets to the show. In the Navy Yard, I could drink with men because I worked with men; in the Parkview, I could drink with men because I drew their pictures. The world was a grand confusion. Finally, when I was bleary, when my hand wouldn't do what I wanted it to do, I went home. I would lie alone in the dark, feeling that I was a character in a story that had lost its plot.

Then one Sunday before Christmas I saw a story in the *Journal-American* about Burne Hogarth, the artist who used to draw *Tarzan*. He and some other people had started the Cartoonists and Illustrators School on Twenty-third Street in Manhattan. There was a picture of Hogarth in a classroom full of easels, just like the photographs of John Sloan at the Art Students League. He was teaching in a real school. Now. Not in the distant past. Not in some remote place. Here. In New York.

Suddenly, after months without a narrative line for my own life, I felt the story again. The next day after work, I went to Twenty-third Street and after twenty minutes of hesitation, walked into the Cartoonists and Illustrators School. It was located then on the corner of Second Avenue and Twenty-third Street (later it became the School of Visual Arts and moved up the street to grander quarters). I was dressed in my rough work clothes from the Navy Yard, but that didn't seem to matter; almost everybody else was dressed the same way. There was a wonderful pungent odor in the air (a mixture, I learned later, of turpentine and linseed oil) and a busy sense of purpose and direction, people carrying large manila portfolio envelopes or stretched canvases or pieces of unfinished plaster sculptures. There were dark-haired girls with vivacious eyes. There were young men with paint-stained dungarees. They talked and laughed and smoked until a bell rang somewhere and they all hurried away to unseen classrooms. In the office, I was given a catalog, which I accepted clumsily. Then I turned around and walked out.

All the way home on the subway, I read the catalog over and over again. The newspaper story was true: the great Burne Hogarth was teaching three nights a week. Drawing and anatomy. The term started in the first week of January. The tuition was thirty dollars a month. Almost a full week's pay. But I could do it. Somehow. If I ate less. If I didn't spend money drinking. I could do it. Yes. *Do* it.

9

AND SO I DID.

The classroom was a large studio on the top floor. Easels were scattered everywhere, facing a wooden model's platform, while one easel faced us. There was an empty stool on the platform. The floors were scabbed with dried paint, a thousand drips and spatters of color. Most of the students were young men, all of them older than I was; there were three young women. They seemed to know each other and laughed and joked in an easy way. I found an empty easel and watched them set up their newsprint pads and take out their black chalks. I did the same. I was very nervous.

A few minutes before seven a gray-haired woman walked in, dressed in a blue-gray smock. She sat on the edge of the platform, smoking a cigarette and reading a book. She was wearing slippers. Her hair was pulled back tightly and tied into a pigtail. She was about forty. Nobody seemed to notice her. Three guys near me were looking at some yellowing pages of Hal Foster's *Prince Valiant*. I looked at the woman's face, her long nose and dark eyebrows, and wondered how Foster would draw her.

Then, at seven o'clock sharp, a compact mustached man arrived. His hair was a shiny black, combed straight back. He wore a button-down shirt, dark tie, sharply creased slacks, and polished loafers. The room hushed as the man placed his own large newsprint pad on the easel beside the stand. He looked more confident than anyone I'd ever seen. This was Burne Hogarth.

All right, folks, he said, let's get started.

I realized that my hands were already black from a mixture of sweat and compressed charcoal. I saw the guy next to me tear the cover sheet off his pad and I did the same. The woman put out her cigarette in a small ashtray, then took off her robe, stepped out of her slippers, and went to the center of the platform. I gazed at her body, her small hard breasts, the thick ridges of pale flesh around her stomach and thighs. Jenny's flesh was smoother and darker. The woman looked cold under the blue fluorescent lights. I could see veins in her legs. Her pubic hair was gray.

We'll do some one-minute poses to loosen up, Hogarth said. All yours, model.

Suddenly everybody was drawing furiously, as the woman assumed one pose after another, bending, twisting, stretching, firing invisible arrows from invisible bows. My drawing was cramped and tight, as I started at the top of her head and worked my way down. I was used to small drawings, penciled first, then laboriously inked. Every time I moved down from the head, she changed the pose again. I heard the others tearing pages off their pads. I saw that one student was as stiff as I was; another was bold and swift. I felt clumsy. Suddenly Hogarth was beside me.

Forget the eyebrows, he said. Just get the gesture, the big shape. Scribble it, but make the big shape fit on the page. No details.

He moved away. I tore off the page, then scribbled in a big bold shape.

Use the side of the chalk, not the point, Hogarth was telling another student. Big and blocky, nice and bold.

Now I could hear chalk on paper all over the room. I didn't look at anything except the model, locking in, me and her and the chalk on paper. Now I saw that she had a long beautiful neck, and I wondered how she had come to this room.

Hogarth said, Okay, now look at her and remember what you see, then close your eyes and draw what you remember.

I tried what he asked and drew the memory of the woman bending one knee and extending the other. When I opened my eyes, I was amazed. There was a big brutal form on my page, bold and strong. Then Hogarth said, All right, the quick poses are over, let's do a twenty-minute pose.

The model sat on the stool and posed with one foot on the second rung, the other stretched out behind her on the floor. There was no expression on her face.

I started drawing but I cramped up again, starting at the top in a linear contoured way. When I stopped to look at it, everything was out of proportion. Her neck was too short, her shoulders too broad, her stomach too thick. Worse, she didn't seem to be sitting on the stool; she looked pasted to it. Then Hogarth was beside me again.

You didn't think this out, he said. The big forms have to come first. Look.

He took my chalk and made a few bold strokes over my labored drawing, showing me that the way I was going, the model's feet would be off the page. He made them fit. And he showed me where the big forms were.

You lay it out in big quick forms, he said. Even if the forms are light, make them the basis. Later you can get into the details. Just don't start with the details or you'll get lost in them. It's the old business about not seeing the forest for the trees. Or the trees for the leaves.

He was talking to me *and* talking to the full class. But he didn't seem to be trying to make me feel small; there was no Brother Jan in him. He said his few words, in a sharp precise voice, and then moved on to another student. Everybody listened; we all learned.

When the twenty-minute pose ended, Hogarth called a break. The model slipped on her robe and slippers and took out a pack of Chesterfields. She glanced at some of the drawings but not mine. I watched her go. She must have felt my eyes on her, because at the door she smiled in a polite way and walked into the hall. I wandered out to the hall too. I didn't smoke then, but everybody else did. They were all talking and laughing and smoking. I wandered around the hall, looking at notices for art shows and foreign movies, glancing into classrooms where other students worked on oil paintings. I didn't see the model anywhere.

The break ended, and now Hogarth was in front of his own newsprint pad, giving us an anatomy lesson. He explained the basic shape of the torso, how it was essentially several wedges, one large, one small; or, in a shorthand, more fluid way, a kind of peanut shape. He showed us how, if we established the peanut, there was a logic to the way you added shoulders, arms, and legs.

The head is the basic measure, Hogarth said. The ideal figure is seven heads high, although fashion illustrators — or our friend El Greco — make it nine heads high. Forget about them for now. Forget about short people or infants too. For our classes, seven heads should be the measure. And remember, your task isn't to copy what's in front of you. Any camera can do that. It's to understand what the figure is *doing* and *why* it can do it. You learn anatomy to understand what's beneath the skin. And you don't express the figure by what it is, but by what it *does*. It *is* what it *does*.

I was awed by the man because it wasn't just talk; he also put on a show, starting with the peanut, the shoulders roughed in as a kind of barbell, the hands beginning as mittens, then acquiring startling power. *It is what it does*, he said, making his own drawings look both easy and impossible, the chalk obeying his commands, providing shape, volume, and power to the figures. He luxuriated in foreshortening, in making the figure seem to leap off his pages. Sometimes he made forms simpler; at other times, he made them more complex, showing unseen muscles, bones, structures, beneath the sheath of skin. Those figures didn't look like our models; a Hogarth drawing resembled nothing on the earth. But he seemed to be saying that it didn't matter. The model was where you began, nothing more; the drawing was the result. The model was a collection of facts; the drawing was the truth.

When that first evening was over, my mind was a roar of words, bodies, drawings. I remember Hogarth saying to the model, Goodnight, Laura, and thank you. She pulled on the smock and fumbled for her cigarettes and left. I went home in a blur of exhaustion and excitement, thinking: My life has changed. Here. Tonight. This morning I was just another fuckup, a high school dropout from Brooklyn. Tonight I became an art student.

And hey, maybe I was going to be good at it. On the breaks I walked among the other easels. Some drawings were beautiful. Some were pretty good. Some were dreadful. Mine were at least okay. I was the youngest student in the class, but I was better than a lot of them. I thought: I can do this.

Back in the room beside the Parkview, I looked at the drawings I'd made, tearing up the truly dreadful ones, seeing a progression, an improvement. Lying in bed later in the dark, hearing the trolley move down Prospect Park Southwest for Coney Island, I thought about the model. What did Hogarth call her? Laura. Like the Stan Kenton record. *Laura, on the train that is passing through* . . . I wondered if she had a husband or boyfriend or children and what they would think of her sitting naked every night in a roomful of strangers. I wondered what she thought as she held herself still for this group inspection and the only sound was chalk on paper. I wished she would come here to this place in Brooklyn and let me draw her. Slowly and lovingly. Until I got it right. I was tracing the outlines of her body in my mind, her small hard breasts and thickening hips, when I fell asleep.

So I worked in the Navy Yard days and went to C&I nights. On the weekends, there was drinking, openly in the Parkview or clandestinely in my own room, joined by some of my friends from the Totes. There was one difference. In the fall, I had drunk out of a sour sense of waste and failure. Now I was drinking exuberantly, certain I had earned that right. I felt that I was on my way.

Hogarth was a great teacher. He had a critical intelligence that could be sardonic but not devastating; I never saw him destroy anybody's ego or try to establish his own worth by humiliating a kid. At the same time, he set up high standards of excellence and let us know when we weren't pushing ourselves hard enough. Most of us failed, most of the time. But he encouraged us to try again, and although most of the students wanted to be cartoonists, he always reminded us that there were other options.

You might become a painter, he said. You might become a sculptor. You might make murals. Just work at the top of your talent and keep pushing past it. And remember: The figure is the key to everything.

I bought a small composition book and started writing down some of what he said, his phrases, the names of the artists he mentioned. During the week, there was no time to go to museums or galleries; on weekends, the rhythm of the Neighborhood seemed to eat my time — taking my clothes to the laundry, cleaning the apartment, visiting 378, drinking on the Totes or in the Parkview. But I did find time to go to the main library at Grand Army Plaza. In the reference room, where they kept the art books, I looked at pictures by Michelangelo and Rubens, Rembrandt and Caravaggio, Leonardo and Velázquez, Picasso and Matisse. I realized I'd seen many of the paintings and drawings before, in magazines, or in religion books in grammar school, even in advertising; but now they were works made by men, calculated, planned, made by hand, in the same way that Steve Canyon was made by Milton Caniff.

They call them masters, Hogarth said. But they all started with the figure, with drawing. Among other things, they all understood the principle of contraposition. They understood that all forms become dynamic by moving in opposition to each other. The shoulder moves up, the biceps and triceps move to the front and the back . . .

I didn't get everything that Hogarth was saying, but it thrilled me. Drawing wasn't just God-given, like a voice; it was something that could be learned, it had rules, axioms, formulas. As crude and unfinished as I was, I would get better. All it took was work.

At night, when I came out of the subway beside the Totes, or stopped for food in the back booths at Lewnes', my drawings became a hit. *Naked broads!* Duke Baluta shouted, taking the drawings from my portfolio envelope. The other guys grinned lewdly.

You mean to tell me, Baluta said, that you sit there looking at this broad, naked, tits out and all — and you don't get a *hard-on?*

Duke, I said, it's like, I don't know, you're so involved in getting the drawing right that —

That you don't want to *fuck* her?

Uh, I, well —

See, Duke said, he *does* want to fuck her!

No, it's like it could be apples or pears or something, I told him, my head filling with half-baked Hogarthisms. You're trying to get the contrapos — the basic form. You want to get to the core of the shape.

You mean you want to get to the core of her *pussy*.

Usually, they all guffawed and I laughed with them. Sometimes, they called over a few of the girls and showed them the drawings and the girls giggled or blushed or got huffy. Some of the girls thought I was weird. Living alone at sixteen. Drawing naked women. In that neighborhood, it was too strange, too dangerous.

10

AT SCHOOL, the models changed every week, sometimes from night to night. Laura was gone after a few nights and I didn't see her around. Then one chilly night, I went out on the break and saw her down the hall, wearing her smock and sandals, smoking her cigarette. I walked toward her, glancing into a painting classroom, and nodded at her. She smiled back.

You must be cold out here, I said.

It's colder in there, she said. Here, I get to wear this.

Your name is Laura, right?

Right, she said. She seemed surprised. Cigarette?

Thanks, I don't smoke. Would you like a coffee or something?

She smiled, in an amused way; it was the first time I'd seen her smile and it made her seem younger.

Sure. After the last bell?

Okay.

That wasn't what I'd meant; I meant that I could go downstairs and get coffee from the machine. Now, somehow, I had a date. Tonight. Dressed in my Navy Yard clothes. Back in class, my heart was thumping. We were drawing from a black male model, but I kept thinking about that last bell. And Laura. Who was she? How old was she? If she asks, how old am *I*? An artist and a model! Jesus. But what if she's just playing a game on me? Calm down. She probably won't show up. She'll think it over and just come and shake my hand and tell me something came up, she had an appointment she forgot, maybe next week or next term.

But there she was at the end of the last class, waiting for me in the lobby. She was wearing a navy pea jacket, dungarees, a wool cap pulled over her hair, and sneakers. She looked much younger.

There's a coffee shop over on Lexington, she said.

It had begun to snow. Big white flakes fell into Twenty-third Street, turning briefly black against the streetlamps, before melting on the roofs of cars.

Oh, *great!* she shouted, in an almost girlish voice. I *love* snow!

We sat in a window booth, facing each other and watching the snow falling steadily. She ordered an English muffin and black coffee; so did I (as in so many other things, I followed the lead of those who seemed to know what they were doing). Laura told me that she'd come to New York to be a dancer (and I wondered, When? Before the war?). But dancing hadn't worked out. She married a photographer who took pictures of radios and refrigerators for catalogs; that didn't work out either. But before it ended, the photographer introduced her to some painters, and after a while she started painting too.

The trouble is, there's maybe twenty thousand painters in New York now, she said. Maybe more. That GI Bill, that made everybody think they could be painters. So it's hard to make a living. That's why I model. To make ends meet.

She smiled in a matter-of-fact way and sipped her coffee and lit another cigarette. I could see her nipples in my mind and her pubic hair and the thickness of her hips.

How do you feel, I said, with everyone looking at you up there?

Most of the time, I don't feel anything. I think about the painting I'm working on. Or the book I'm reading. Or the landlord. Or the laundry.

She took a deep drag and then smiled, glancing at the snow.

But to tell the truth, Laura said, sometimes I get hot. I can feel all those eyes on me and I know some of the men must want to fuck me. Maybe some of the women too. And what happens is, I start thinking like them, some kind of transference, I *am* them, I'm them fucking me, kissing me, pressing against me, licking me; and I get hot. And then I'm afraid I'll turn a certain way and you'll see that I'm wet. Do you have a hard-on now?

Yeah.

Let's go to my place.

Laura had a two-room apartment on Tenth Street, three buildings away from the Third Avenue El. The shades were drawn but I could hear the train rumble through the snowy night. One room was a kitchen with a table and two chairs beside a window that opened into an air shaft. The other room was studio and bedroom, cramped and messy. There were books packed on shelves, lying on the paint-spattered linoleum floor, used to hold open a door. There was a record player, a radio, stacks of records; a toolbox full of brushes and tubes of paint; a huge wooden easel; a long table covered with tomato cans full of paint, linseed oil, turpentine, and other cans holding big fat brushes; and dozens of canvases covered with shimmering abstract paintings, most of them in great splashy variations of a single color: blue.

My Billie Holiday paintings, she said. Want a drink?

Sure.

She poured an inch of Canadian Club into each of two water glasses. I felt unreal, as if I'd walked into a novel.

Okay, Laura said, now it's my turn.

For what?

She sipped her drink and said, Take off your clothes.

I laughed.

You've been drawing me, she said. Now I draw you.

I'm sure I must have blushed. I took a sip of the whiskey, which burned into my stomach, and then put the glass on a table. I took off my shirt and undershirt, then my boots and socks and trousers. The paint-spattered floor felt pebbly. So did my skin in the chilly room.

Everything, she said.

So I slipped off my shorts and tossed them onto a chair, trying to look casual. In the chill, I was sure my cock had shrunk to its tiniest size. I was afraid to look. She was placing a newsprint pad on the easel, an amused look on her face.

Now what? I said.

Just like Hogarth's class, she said. Quick poses.

I tried to remember what she did, bending, twisting, holding the pose. All I could hear was the chalk moving on paper, sheets being torn off the pad, ice clunking in her glass. Then she asked me to hold a longer pose, seated on a chair, right leg extended, left leg curled along the side of the chair. She brought me my drink; I sipped it and she took it away and put Billie Holiday on the record player. The recording was a worn version of "Strange Fruit." I worked at holding the pose, knowing she was looking straight at me, sensing her presence but not seeing her. Then I remembered what she'd said in the coffee shop, how she'd imagine us thinking about fucking her. I tried to see myself on this chair, tried to *be* her, looking at my body, at my shoulders and belly and legs and cock, and then I could feel my cock getting hard. I tried to stop it then, shifting my imaginings, trying to will it away; but I only got harder.

And then Laura was there, on her knees, gripping my cock in a chalk-blackened hand. Then she took it in her mouth, gripping it more tightly, her hand moving slowly, as I held to the edge of the chair, looking at the slow movement of her head. She looked up at me, her eyes wide, her mouth stuffed with my cock, and I started to come. Violently. My whole body erupting as my pelvis thrust up off the chair. Laura held on as an involuntary roar rose from my throat and I went back again and over the chair to the floor.

Silence.

And then Laura began to laugh in a crazy way.

Jesus Christ, she squealed. Jesus H. Christ, that was *amazing!*

I got up slowly, my back aching. Laura sat there, sitting on her ankles, still fully clothed.

How old are you anyway? she said.

Almost seventeen, I said.

Jesus H. Christ.

I stood up, trying to look casual, and she went to the bathroom. I looked at her drawings. They were scribbled and loose, made up of hundreds of small lines that built up form and volume; later, I'd see a similar style in the drawings of Giacometti. I was shivering and sipped my drink and was warm again. Then Laura was back, wearing a thin robe, carrying a hot washcloth that gave off steam.

First things first, young man, she said, and began to wash the charcoal off my cock. She dropped the cloth on a table, switched off a lamp, then another, and then she came to me from behind and rubbed her hand on my stomach and began kissing and sucking on my neck.

Okay, she whispered. Now we can fuck.

11

THAT SPRING, I felt as if some enormous ice jam had broken. I was alive again after a long dead time. The feelings of failure, impotence, loneliness, ruin: all were washed away. Art school made me feel that I could do something that was valuable, special, part of me. Laura made my body tremble with sensuality, and that went into my drawings. Through the long days at the Navy Yard, I could handle any drudgery, full of the luxuries of the evening.

Then at a Saturday-night birthday party in the Neighborhood, I met a girl named Maureen Crowley. She was tall, thin, dark-haired, with a slouching walk and bright dark eyes. For a long time, I was in love with her in that diffuse, ambiguous, and obsessive way that can never be explained to strangers. Laura was from the world outside the Neighborhood; Maureen was part of it. I knew that Laura wasn't part of some limitless future; I wanted to believe that Maureen was. She was the middle daughter in a respectable family that lived in a private home near where I had my room. Her father owned a grocery store and later ran a bar. It was clear from the beginning that he didn't want his daughter to be going out with the likes of me: a high school dropout from Seventh Avenue, and perhaps worse, a son of Billy Hamill.

Much of this disapproval was surely about class. The Irish from Seventh Avenue were "shanty": low, common, often violent and alcoholic. The Crowleys were "lace curtain"; the father worked for himself, wore a necktie to his job, had moved at least one step past the immigrant generation. When I first came calling at the house, I wore my best clothes. Or the clothes then considered the style on Seventh Avenue. The clothes of the hoodlum: pegged pants, shirts with wide Mr. B collars, wraparound jackets. I couldn't afford a suit, or a tweed jacket; most of my spare money was going to tuition and art supplies. Gradually I adopted the chinos and plaid shirts favored by the Big Guys, but it was too late. With Maureen's parents, first impressions were everything. To them, even art school was a negative; what sort of foolish dreamer went to art school?

But the very obstacles charged this new love story with an aching romanticism. I wanted to prove my worthiness; that meant I had to live a lie. I never told Maureen about Laura. I saw Maureen on Wednesday nights, when there were no classes at C&I, and on weekends. On the other weekday nights, I almost ran to Laura's place.

Laura was amused by me, I suppose; I was a kind of earnest, untrained pet. I never found out whether she had other lovers; I knew almost nothing about the way she lived outside school and the studio on Tenth Street. At school, she seldom talked to me in the hallway; she would see me in the hallway and nod Yes or shake her head No and that would tell me all I needed to know for the night. If it was No, I'd be stabbed by jealousy; I'd try to see if she left alone or if she was sitting in the coffee shop with another student. Once, I waited in the shadows near her house, to see if she came home with someone else. That night, she never came home at all.

But if she nodded Yes, Laura always had something new for me. She'd tie me to the bed with cord or pieces of clothesline and lick my body until, as I did one memorable midnight, I ejaculated without being touched by anything but her tongue. She'd paint my cock with watercolors or have me apply lipstick to the lips of her vagina. She had me fuck her on tables and the floor and against the kitchen sink, sometimes while I wore only my work boots. Once she asked me to tie her to the easel and fuck her from behind. On several nights, she took me into a hot soapy bath, the walls perspiring, and sat on my cock until she came. Meanwhile, I couldn't get much beyond Maureen's breasts. And then one night, while I was frantically fucking Laura, she whispered to me:

What's her name?

What's *whose* name?

The girl you're thinking about while you're fucking me.

She had me. My erection started dying. I must have smiled in some dumb way, because she looked at me, her eyes squinting. I rolled over on my side, feeling as if I'd been unfaithful to Laura.

Hey, young man, she said. Hey, don't feel bad. *Everybody* does it.

She began playing with my cock, and when it was hard again she whispered: Call me by her name.

I turned to her, seeing the outline of her face in the light from the street. I ran my fingers on her nipples and drew close to her.

Maureen, I whispered.

Yes, Laura murmured.

Maureen, Maureen.

Say my name. Come in me, baby.

Maureen, Maureen, Maureen.

She started twisting and heaving in a ferocious orgasm, pulling my hair, biting my neck and shoulders, jamming her heels into my thighs, digging her fingers into my ass.

My name!

Laura, Maureen, Laura, Maureen, Laura, Laura, Laura . . .

Then I exploded into her.

We lay there, very still, for a long while. The El rumbled by. She lit a cigarette and sipped from a drink.

You'd better go home now, she said.

I want to stay here tonight.

That would be a mistake, she said.

Please, I said. I want to sleep with you. I want to wake up with you.

You do that once, she whispered, and you'll never come back.

Why?

She got up and switched on a small lamp. She pulled on a robe and started fixing me a whiskey and soda.

Why? You'll see me in the cold light of day, that's why. You'll see I'm old enough to be your mother. You'll want your nice little virgin from Brooklyn. That's why.

I see you in Hogarth's class, I said. With all those goddamned fluorescent lights!

That's different, she said. I could be three lemons in a bowl.

Come on, Laura. I love you.

She turned on me, snarling.

For Chrissakes, don't say that! Don't ever say that to me again!

It's true.

You don't even know what the word means! You'll find out, one of these days, and you won't say it so easy. Love gets everything all screwed up. It's one of those lies that ruin the world.

I thought, in a thrilled way: *Jesus, that's like a line from a movie.*

I said: Then what do you feel about me?

I'm fucking you, kid, she said bitterly. But I don't have to love you to fuck you.

That was not a movie line. She drained her glass, then poured another, staring at the floor. Her face was clenched. I started getting dressed. I noticed a new canvas against the far wall, leaning against the windowsill. She had sketched in a naked young man. His heart was outside the skin of his chest. Everything was blue, even the heart.

For a few weeks, she signaled me No. Twice, she modeled in Hogarth's class, and I pulsed with jealousy. I stayed at an easel to the side, but was jealous of those who could see between her legs. I had been *in* there. I didn't want her to be imagining them imagining entering her. On the second night, at the end of the second week, I tried to loathe her. Her gray pubic hair. The small breasts. The ridged white flesh around her hips.

But I couldn't make the loathing work. I kept drawing her the way I knew her, remembered her, wanted her to be: in writhing Hogarthian movements. Hogarth himself took notice.

Pretty sexy, fella, he said. Now try it the other way. Not a pinup. Make her ugly. Make her a hundred years old.

I don't know if I can, I said.

Invent it, he said, walking away. Use your imagination.

I didn't know if Laura heard him, but I tried. I made her a wrinkled crone. I made her toothless. I made her immensely fat. Nothing worked. I still wanted her. My last drawing was made up of hundreds of small scribbles, like one of her own drawings. When the bell rang, she walked past my easel and glanced at the drawing. I started to say something but she kept moving.

I waited for her outside the school. An icy wind was blowing off the East River. The streets looked dark and shiny, as if they'd been glazed. Then she came out.

Laura, I —

Come on, she said, and took my arm.

We went to Tenth Street and drank and fucked and fucked and drank. I stayed until morning.

She woke me with scrambled eggs on a plate and buttered rye toast. I suddenly panicked. It was Friday and the kitchen clock said it was eight thirty-five. I was due at the Navy Yard at eight.

The hell with it, she said. So you miss a day, so what?

Yeah. So what.

I looked at her more closely now as she made coffee. She was dressed in a loose flowered dress and sandals. Her hair was wild, but her face was clean and shining. The winter light threw cold shadows on the walls. I pulled a blanket over my shoulders and began eating greedily. She brought me a steaming cup of coffee and then sat at the end of the bed and looked at me in a forlorn way.

You'll be going away, she said.

No, I said. I'll stay here. Maybe we can go to a museum or a movie or something.

I have to work today. Besides, I wasn't talking about today.

She got up and poured herself the first whiskey of the morning.

You're the type who is always going away, she said.

Come on, I said. You know better. You gave me the brush for two weeks and here I am.

Temporary insanity, she said, and smiled. She stared into the glass.

I think you want me to go.

No, she said. Not yet.

12

THE ROOM in Brooklyn became my center, and from that center I tried to sort out all the different strands of my story: art school, the Navy Yard, the Neighborhood, my father, my brothers and sister, my friends, drinking, Maureen and Laura. I couldn't do it, and there was little time left for anything else. McCarthyism was gathering its dark force but I wasn't thinking much about it; I had no time anymore for reading seven newspapers a day, for clipping the comics and filing them into envelopes. The comics themselves seemed small and cramped now, and I kept wanting to draw the way Hogarth did, with great sweeping movements, my body involved in the act. I had no money for paint and canvases. And the room was too small for truly gigantic canvases. All of that was up ahead somewhere.

But while I wanted a future, I also wanted my identity in the Neighborhood. The drawings gave me part of it. So did the room. And that winter of 1951–52 I found a place where the guys from the Totes could meet on frigid nights.

Boop's was on the corner of Seventeenth Street and Tenth Avenue. Tommy Conroy and Mickey Horan took me there for my first visit, entering through a side door on the Tenth Avenue side. There were booths and an unused kitchen. We moved through a dark passageway, past the restrooms, and into the saloon itself. It was dark and golden, like a John Sloan painting, with a long bar, a TV set near the windows, a shuffleboard machine, a lone table, and a jukebox. Behind the bar, the bottles glistened. On the same shelf, the cash register was in the center, with a toaster for making hot dogs at one end and signs for the Miss Rheingold contest at the other. That first night, the bar was packed and warm and smoky from cigarettes. The windows were opaque with steam.

Boop himself was a heavy-set mild-mannered Italian guy who years later was head of security at Madison Square Garden. That first night, Conroy ordered three beers and Boop pulled them without asking for draft cards. He was too busy. I still remember the feeling, standing at a bar with my friends, paying my own way. In the Parkview I was the kid from upstairs. This was to be my own bar, a place to drink or sing, my first club. That night I got very drunk. In the morning, I woke up happy.

Soon, my routine got more elaborate. If I wasn't with Laura, I usually stopped off in Boop's on my way home from C&I. Part of this must have been a need for approval. I wanted them to marvel at my drawing skills, to recognize that I was different, that I wasn't just another high school dropout. But I also wanted to be part of the widening fraternity of drinkers. On weekday nights, I didn't get drunk; I didn't have enough money and I had to be up early to go to the Navy Yard. Laura drank more than I did. But on weekend nights, I usually went out with Maureen, early in the evening, to see a movie at Loew's Met or the Sanders or Prospect. I would take her for a soda, or coffee, at Lewnes' and then walk her home. She was in before midnight. Then I'd walk up Prospect Avenue to Boop's and all the other young men would be gathering. They'd almost all had Saturday nights like mine. They hadn't gotten laid either. So with the jukebox blasting and the beers flowing, we'd all get roaring drunk.

There are permanent holes in my memory about most of those nights. I remember lurching home. I remember the streets rising and falling and

lampposts swaying. Or lying in bed while the ceiling moved like the sea. Most of all, I remember the great heady closed feeling in the bar, pushing quarters around in the wetness, the *confirmed* feeling when the bartender bought me a free round after I'd paid for three. Beers were a dime and a tune on the jukebox cost a nickle (or six for a quarter). You could get drunk for a dollar and a half. Through the night I was filled with talk about fighters and ballplayers and the war, guys we knew who'd been hurt, and others who'd been arrested, and a few who'd just gone off somewhere. And the music of the jukebox drove into me. I sang along with Sinatra on "I'm a Fool to Want You" and joined everybody in the bar on Johnnie Ray's "Cry."

Nobody talked politics, except to make occasional remarks about politicians in general. And none of the others talked much about the future. The war in Korea got in the way. They would mention taking the tests for the cops or the firemen; someday, later. But first they had to decide what to do about the war. The draft waited for all of us. For some of the older guys, it was only months away. So they discussed the relative merits of the army or the navy, the Marine Corps or the air force. They didn't question the reasons for Korea. It never occurred to them to protest it. There was a war on. When it was your turn, you went too.

Most of the time, I listened. These were my friends and I didn't want to argue with them. But in certain ways I was already separated from them. I couldn't tell them about Laura, because they wouldn't believe me, and if they heard I was having sex with an old woman (she was forty-one!), they'd probably laugh. On the nights when I wasn't at Boop's, or on Saturday or Sunday mornings, I started making drawings for myself again, filling newsprint pads instead of making cartoons. I made great violent drawings of prizefighters, starting with photographs from newspapers or *Ring Magazine*, then abstracting them, then drawing them from memory, repeating alone the exercises from school. I took stiff classroom drawings of Laura and thinned her out and added Maureen's face, smudging the features with my fingers to protect her from the judgments of my visiting friends. I began imagining Maureen's body in detail, seeing her on the model stand instead of Laura, her pale skin blushing, her pubic hair dark and shiny. In those drawings she seemed more real than she did when she sat beside me in the Sanders.

Somehow, making those drawings, I knew that I could lose the Navy Yard, lose Laura, even lose Maureen, but I couldn't afford to lose art school. That would be losing my life.

13

BY APRIL, even Laura thought I was getting better.

You've got talent, she said one night, but you don't know anything yet.

What do you mean?

I mean you're intelligent, you learn fast, but you're amazingly ignorant. You're too much in love with being a mug from Brooklyn.

The words wounded me. She was right, and I knew it.

What should I learn? I asked her.

Laura smiled and said, Every fucking thing you can.

She would never go out anywhere with me, obviously (I thought) because she didn't want her friends to laugh at her with a young man. But she began to show me drawings in art books and from folders of reproductions she'd torn from magazines. None of them looked like Burne Hogarth's work or Milton Caniff's or Jack Kirby's. But I began to sense what Picasso was doing, and Matisse; I saw George Grosz for the first time and Otto Dix and a wonderful draftsman, now unjustly forgotten, named Rico Lebrun. Seeing my boxing pictures, she showed me *Stag at Sharkey's* by George Bellows. She showed me pictures by Ben Shahn and Yasuo Kuniyoshi. And then she pulled out some drawings by a man who was doing what I wished I could be doing: José Clemente Orozco. He was a Mexican and drew figures with thick black lines and great bold power.

You're a draftsman, she said. So study the great draftsmen. You can get to color later. Most artists use color to hide things they don't understand. Photographers do it all the time.

She smoked her cigarettes and sipped her Canadian Club and rummaged through these files, which she kept in folders in a Campbell's soup box, and there was always a running commentary.

Jesus H. Christ, I have saved an amazing amount of crap. I oughtta just throw it all out.

Where'd you get it all?

She held up a copy of *Art News*.

Magazines like this, she said. But do yourself a favor, don't read these rags. Just tear out the pictures. The writing is usually the most amazing bullshit.

Then she gave me a copy of a book called *The Art Spirit* by Robert Henri, and I devoured it. I felt connected to Henri because he was a friend of John Sloan. His book was a collection of notes about the study of art, written down by students in his classes at the Art Students League, and first published in 1923. As I read, I heard Henri speaking in Hogarth's voice, and he seemed to be speaking directly to me.

The work of the art student is no light matter. Few have the courage and stamina to see it through. You have to make up your mind to be alone in many ways. We like sympathy and we like to be in company. It is easier than going it alone. But alone one gets acquainted with himself, grows up and on, not stopping with the crowd. It costs to do this. If you succeed you may have to pay for it as well as enjoy it all your life. . . .

This struck me as absolutely true; I knew, for example, that when I was alone I made drawings that went beyond the work I did in class. And I hoped I had the courage and stamina to see it through. I would sometimes remember these words while drinking in Boop's — receiving what I thought Henri meant by sympathy, a kind of generalized human warmth; being, as he said, in company — and know that I should be home at work. Henri's words became a kind of sweet curse. In my mind, the desire to be an artist had been a desire for freedom: from the routines of life, from the Navy Yards of the world. Until I read Henri, it had never occurred to me that there could be a cost, that an artist must pay a price in loneliness. That idea gave me a romantic thrill.

An art student must be a master from the beginning; that is, he must be master of such as he has. By being now master of such as he has there is promise that he will be master in the future. . . .

Was I a master of what I had? That is, had I pushed as hard as I could against my crudities, my clumsiness, my lack of skill? I knew I hadn't. But nobody else at Boop's had either. Most of them seemed content to go along, get a job, join the army. Who did I think I was anyway? Who was I to think I could go beyond myself?

You can do anything you want to do. What is rare is this actual wanting to do a specific thing: wanting it so much that you are practically blind to all other things, that nothing else will satisfy you. . . . I mean it. There is reason for you to give this statement some of your best thought. You may find that this is just what is the matter with most of the people in the world; that few are really wanting what they think they want, and that most people go through their lives without ever doing one whole thing they really want to do. . . .

In the Navy Yard, I met men who were doing hard work because they had to do it; to support wives, children, pay rent. In Boop's, the guys who were working weren't doing what they wanted to do. Most of them didn't even *know* what they wanted to do. And what about my father? What did he want to do when he was my age, and how had it turned out? What could he have become if he hadn't left Ireland or if he hadn't lost his leg? What about my mother? I knew almost nothing about her, except that she was there, she worked, she was smart, she encouraged me to do anything I wanted to do. As Henri did.

An artist has got to get acquainted with himself just as much as he can. It is no easy job, for it is not a present-day habit of humanity. That is what I call self-development, self-education. No matter how fine a school you are in, you have to educate yourself.

Yes.

14

IN THE LATE spring of 1952, as the Dodgers tried in the new season to recover from the Home Run, and the war in Korea was grinding on, and the papers said that Eisenhower was planning to run for president, everything shifted again. Laura disappeared.

For two nights, I didn't see her at school, didn't receive her Yes or No. On the third night, I asked about her at the office. The secretary was annoyed because Laura hadn't even called. They had to cancel one painting class because they couldn't find a substitute.

I was suddenly panicky. In class that night, I imagined her burning with some fever, alone in the studio without a telephone. I imagined her careening around the studio, drunk and falling, the blood running from a gash in her head. Or she flipped a cigarette in a careless way and it landed in the files or the turpentine and exploded and she was burned alive. Or a man climbed in through the air shaft window, to hold her prisoner, and was even now hurting her. The lurid scenarios filled my head while I tried to draw a lithe young brown-nippled Puerto Rican model in class. The model was exquisite, with sad brown eyes, and a thin trail of hair from her navel down her stomach to a thick black vee between her legs. But I couldn't even focus my lust. When the bell rang for the first break, I packed my things and hurried down to Tenth Street.

The door to Laura's studio was unlocked. I opened it slowly, remembering all those film noir scenes of the horror within. The rooms were black, but I knew where the kitchen light cord was and pulled it on.

Everything was gone except the bed.

The easel was gone. The paintings. The brushes and paints and tomato cans. The sumptuous art books. The folders full of reproductions. Laura.

The linoleum floor now looked like an immense abstract painting. Under the sink, there was a bag of garbage. Inside it were two empty pint bottles of Canadian Club. I stood there for a long moment. How could she just go like this, without a word? *I'm fucking you, kid. But I don't have to love you to fuck you.* Why didn't I see this coming? I looked everywhere for a note to me, even on the bathroom mirror where they left notes in the movies. Nothing. She was gone. I imagined a man coming to the door and the two of them laughing. She was already packed, the clothes folded into suitcases, the canvases wrapped and tied together, the easel broken down for shipment, and he helped her to the street with her things and shoved them into his car. A convertible. I was sure of that. The easel sticking up from the back like a cross. And off they drove, smoking cigarettes and drinking whiskey and laughing, laughing.

She would never tell him about me, some kid from Brooklyn, some boy out of art school. She might never tell anyone about me, might already have forgotten my existence. I slammed the icebox door with the flat of my hand, then did it again and again. Then turned around and saw the bed, stripped of sheets and covers, the striped mattress as naked as a corpse. I walked over and ran my fingers along its edge. Then I fell upon its vast emptiness and heard the distant rumble of the El and wept.

A chill came into me. For weeks, I couldn't read Henri, or look at the artists Laura had introduced me to. It was as if the whole world that she knew had walked out into the night. My need focused more than ever before on Maureen. We were now going steady. That was supposed to give me a sense of structure, and a shared intimacy on the inevitable path to engagement and marriage. Instead I was full of uncertainty and one huge silent lie: I couldn't tell Maureen how numbed I was by the disappearance of Laura.

The notion of marriage was scary; it made me see an apartment in the Neighborhood, kids, noise, a job I might hate. For a while I tried to merge the notion with my vision of life as an artist. We'd live in the Village and have children later. Maureen would be my model and we'd spend our evenings together in the company of painters and poets. I must have been a hugely egocentric boyfriend. I remember almost nothing about what she wanted from life, but I'm certain I spent many hours talking about what I wanted. I do remember that she didn't take seriously my grand plans. Or so I thought at the time. She might have simply been what most girls then were: a supreme realist.

When the school term ended in June, my life started to unravel again. Without Laura, I had no outlet for my sexuality. Maureen was a Good Girl and with her I usually played the Good Boy. It was only late at night, after I'd dropped her off, that the Bad Guy came to life. Neither Boop's nor the Parkview was any help; there were almost no available women in the Neighborhood, and those who were free knew I was going steady with Maureen. One evening, I called the school office to see if Laura had returned for summer sessions. No, she wasn't part of the modeling pool anymore. What about Gloria, the Puerto Rican girl? The secretary laughed.

What do you think this is, a dating service?

No, no, I lied. During the summer, some of the guys from class, we're planning some life sessions, just to stay in shape for the fall.

She gave me a number for Gloria Vasquez. I called. A man answered in Spanish and I hung up.

In the lunchtime bars along Sands Street, some of the guys from the Navy Yard talked joyfully about the whores who showed up in the evenings. But I had seen them, painted, lacquered, with huge piles of hair and alarming mouths, and they made me afraid. Afraid of disease. Afraid of their experience: thousands of blow jobs, thousands of fucks. And besides, I couldn't pay them.

So I got drunk a lot and into fights, drowning my cock in rivers of beer. Drunk, I called Gloria Vasquez again one night, my head full of her brown nipples and thick lustrous hair, and this time she answered. She was sweet. She was polite. But she knew I was drunk and soon hung up. I was too embarrassed ever to call again.

The summer came and we all went back to Bay 22 and Oceantide. I remember strutting too much under a Saturday sun, getting bleary with beer, and falling asleep on a blanket beside Maureen. I woke with a furry tongue but I wasn't very ashamed of myself: everybody else from the Neighborhood was doing the same thing. For all of us, boys and girls, drinking was natural. It was also woven together with sex; you drank in order to get sex or you drank if you didn't have sex. In those years before the Pill, sex was also woven together with fear. The girls surely wanted it as much as we did, but they would pay a tougher price. Instead of fucking, we got drunk.

On the beach, among all those oiled bodies, with Maureen beside me but untouchable, I sometimes tried to distract myself with books and allow a novel to lift me into some other world. But then someone would come over and say, Whatta you, studying for a test? And I'd put the book away and play the role to which the Neighborhood had assigned me. I went to the bar at Oceantide (where they *did* check draft cards) and sat on the side at a crowded table and sipped beer that older guys had bought. I talked much bullshit. Sometimes I even danced with Maureen.

On my seventeenth birthday, I stopped at 378. I brought my father some drawings I had made of Duke Snider and Sugar Ray Robinson and he seemed happy with them but didn't know what to do with them. He rolled them up and put them in a closet. My mother had a cake for me and the kids all cheered. Then my mother saw something in my face.

You're unhappy, aren't you? she said.

I'm all right, I said.

What's the matter?

I shrugged and didn't answer.

Maybe you should come home, she said.

Maybe, I said.

But I didn't want to go home. When I said goodnight, there were tears in her eyes, but she didn't cry.

From the pay phone in Sanew's, I called Maureen. Her father answered.

Who's this? he said.

Pete.

She's already asleep.

Could you tell her I called, Mr. Crowley?

He sighed and hung up.

I was a mess of emotions and I wanted to get drunk. But I knew that wouldn't help. I went back to the room, and for the first time since Laura left, I read *The Art Spirit*.

Find out what you really like if you can. Find out what is really important to you. Then sing your song. You will have something to sing about and your whole heart will be in the singing. . . .

I was soon asleep.

15

MICKEY HORAN joined the navy in July. A few weeks later, he was followed by Jack McAlevy. And Joe Griffin. Suddenly, among the guys in Boop's, it was our turn.

The radio and the newspapers were still full of the war. In my room, I was reading Harvey Kurtzman's *Two Fisted Tales* and *Frontline Combat*. Even Ted Williams, the greatest hitter in baseball, was back in the air force, joining Steve Canyon. I imagined myself in Korea. Or on ships plowing through icy northern waters.

You're the type who is always going away, said Laura, before she went away herself.

And I thought: Maybe she was right. She was right about a lot of other things. Maybe I have to go away. It wasn't just destiny; there were practical reasons too. The money I earned at the Navy Yard just wasn't enough for me. I had to pay for rent, food, and carfare; I needed money for drinking, to see friends, to have a little enjoyment; and I was going steady with Maureen. In the fall, when school started again, I'd need tuition along with money for paint and canvases, because I was supposed to move on from the basic drawing course. But I didn't even have a bank account. I couldn't afford a telephone or a television set. Two days before payday, I always had to borrow a few dollars, just for carfare and hot dogs. I knew what I wanted: enough money to pay for art school, to buy paint and brushes and books. Without those things, I couldn't imagine a life, even with Maureen. I just couldn't afford the wanting.

In August, I decided to join the navy.

But *why?* Maureen said.

I can finish high school in the navy, I said. And when I get out, I'll get the GI Bill. You know, they pay you to go to school. They give you loans to buy a house. I can save a lot of money while I'm in, and we'll be in great shape when I get out. It's for *us*, Maureen. For *us*.

She knew otherwise. She began to weep. I talked to her, caressed her, kissed her almost desperately. I hedged, layering doubt into my words, making it sound as if my mind wasn't made up. She cried inconsolably for a while and then stopped. I walked her home. She ran inside without another word.

But the idea of the navy had possessed me, and the possession wasn't based on the benefits of the GI Bill. That summer, I couldn't see myself clearly; it was as if the mirror was warped. The navy would provide me with a clear identity, no matter how temporary. Once I could say I was an *Eagle* boy and everyone knew what I meant; now I could say I was a sailor. In the navy, I would earn my space in the world and in this country; the act would certify that I was American, not Irish, not simply my father's son. Joining a group larger than myself would cause my hobbling ten-cent miseries to recede and vanish. Above all, the navy offered escape. I would escape the stunted geography of Brooklyn, going where nobody knew about my father, my drinking, my failure at Regis, my limitless uncertainties. I would escape the grinding pressure to pay my way in the world. Above all, I would escape the strained demands of choice. I wouldn't have to choose between life as a cop or a bohemian, a plumber or an artist. I wouldn't have to choose between art school or an early marriage and the baby carriage in the hallway.

In addition, there was the truant spirit of romance. I would be going from the known to the unknown, the safe to the dangerous. Alone at night, I saw myself on a cruiser, rocking in deep blue water as the heavy guns fired salvos at the dark Korean coast. I saw myself moving through radiant tropical ports with palm trees blowing in the wind and bars full of dark abundant women like Gloria Vasquez, with brown nipples and black hair. I thought about visiting all the ports where my grandfather had gone, drinking in his bars, and then, dressed in navy whites, tougher and older, walking into the sunlight and seeing Laura. She would stop and squint and say, Is that you? And I'd look at her in a bitter Bogart way and say, Not anymore, and turn to take Gloria Vasquez by the hand.

And Maureen? I made a different set of pictures, conjured another shadow-self. Maybe we'd get married. Not right away. Eventually. When Korea was over or something. She'd come and live with me in my home port, in Hawaii or San Diego, some bright gleaming place far from Brooklyn. Or we'd wait until I was discharged. Sure.

Because I was only seventeen, I needed to be signed into the navy by one of my parents. But when I told them one evening in 378, my mother was horrified.

They'll send you to the *war*, she said.

Everybody's going to the war, Mom.

Buddy Kelly is dead in this war, she said. Buddy Kiernan is dead. Every week, more of them are dead.

They were in the army, Mom. I'll be in the navy.

Can't you wait a year? Until you're eighteen? Maybe the war'll be over by then.

I don't want to wait, Mom.

She shook her head in sorrow and frustration. But my father was looking at me in a different way.

Don't listen to her, he said. It'll be the best thing you ever did. You can learn a trade. It'll make you a man.

I don't understand it, my mother said.

You're not a man, Annie.

And so he signed the papers.

I was told to report three weeks later, on Monday, September 8, at eight in the morning. The recruiter said I could "strike" for a yeoman rate, which meant I might be able to work as an artist or cartoonist on a ship's newspaper. There were no guarantees, he said, but since I'd gone to art school, it was possible. This inflamed me even more; with any luck, I could become the Bill Mauldin of the navy!

A week after signing up, I left the Navy Yard, saying good-bye to the men, who all wished me well. I wrote to C&I, explaining that I wouldn't be back until I was out of the navy. Then I packed all my things, gave up the room next to the Parkview, and went home to 378. I didn't show off the nude drawings; I sealed them with Scotch tape into the big portfolio envelopes. I got cardboard boxes from the grocery store and packed my art supplies, comics, and other books, including *The Art Spirit*. I stacked them all in the woodbin in the cellar, explaining to my brother Tommy that eventually he might send them to me when I was out at sea. He was now at Brooklyn Tech, a brilliant student, with plans to be an engineer. He took the assignment as if it were a sacred duty.

Then I went on a summer binge, ten days of tearful scenes with Maureen, wild nights at Boop's, sunburns at Coney. The art school interlude was behind me; I had been reclaimed by the rituals of the Neighborhood. Everything culminated in a going-away party for me and three other young men in a VFW post down by the Venus theater. I arrived with Maureen and we clung to each other through the long evening. Now there was no going back; the papers were signed; my friends were here to say good-bye. The hall was packed, the tables stacked with whiskey and set-ups and pitchers of beer. The jukebox blasted. Maureen and I danced, her small breasts pushing hard against me, her hands tense and sweaty. She said very little, but at some point I made a joke and smiled and she turned away in tears. Her girlfriends came over and hurried her into the ladies room. I downed a cold beer and poured another. Goddammit, Maureen, I'm a *man*, I thought (incapable of irony or self-mockery); I have to do this because men do these things. When Maureen came back, her eyes were red. I took her hand and we went to dance. Jo Stafford was singing "You Belong to Me."

She began to weep again, and I put my arm around her and waved good-bye to my friends and went into the cool autumn air. She lived a few blocks away, and we walked together with my arm around her waist. Suddenly, I didn't want to go. I wanted to repeal everything: the decision to join, the signing of the papers, the surrender of room and job, the departure from the only school I'd ever loved. And I wanted to take back everything I'd said to Maureen.

But when we reached her house, huddling on the bottom step out of view of anyone inside, I couldn't find the right words. There was no going back. Staying would be scarier than going. I kissed her. She cried. So did I.

Maybe I've made some terrible mistake, I said.

She didn't answer. I said I'd write every day. She said she would too. I said I'd be home at Christmas. She said she'd see me then. I asked her to wait for me. A light went on inside her house, and she kissed me one final time on the cheek and moved quickly up the steps, opened the front door with a key, and vanished. I stood there for a long moment, wondering if I should go back to the VFW and get roaring drunk.

Then I started walking home through the Neighborhood, along the parkside and the dark brooding forest beyond the granite walls, past the Totem Poles and the Sanders, down past the shuttered synagogue and the gated armory to Seventh Avenue. The lights were out in most of the apartments. Even at 378. I wondered if any of them were doing what they wanted to do. I wondered if Maureen was asleep. I wondered where Laura was.

In the morning, I went off to the navy.

IV

TO THE GATES
OF EDEN

The Consul had not uttered a single word. It was all an illusion, a whirling cerebral chaos, out of which, at last, at long last, at this very instant, emerged, rounded and complete, order.

— Malcolm Lowry, *Under the Volcano*

       the whole pasture looked like our meal
       we didn't need speedometers
       we could manage cocktails out of ice and water

— Frank O'Hara, "Animals"

There are periods and occasions when drinking is in the air, even seems to be a moral necessity.

— Alfred Kazin, "The Giant Killer"

1

DURING my time in the navy, drinking became more deeply ingrained in my nature. If I'd served my apprenticeship in Brooklyn, in the navy I became a journeyman. I learned much about race, sex, the South, literature, music, and all of it was absorbed in a delicious heady delirium of drink.

During a one-day liberty from boot camp in Bainbridge, Maryland, I careened around the flesh joints of East Baltimore Street, lusted for a stripper named Tempest Storm, threw up in an alley and laughed about it with my friends in the morning. I received a Dear John letter from Maureen, wrote her anguished letters, came home at Christmas, made a fool of myself over her, joined my father in a winning us-against-them fistfight in Rattigan's, and was moved to beer-soaked tears when he said afterward, *This is my son, Peter, in whom I am well proud.*

Then I was off to Norman, Oklahoma, to airmen's school (there turned out to be no great demand for yeomen who were high school dropouts). I arrived on the morning of New Year's Eve and ended up that night in a tough Indian bar where I took a whore's tits out of her bra under her sweater in a side booth and later followed her upstairs. She was very fat and we drank hootch from an unlabeled bottle. She blew me and I fell asleep and woke up at dawn with the door locked from the outside and my money gone. I had to move a bureau and climb out through the transom and then wandered the frozen streets until I found a bus to take me to the base. Then I was in Jacksonville, Florida, training for a storekeeper's rate, learning to type, seeing palm trees for the first time, and the southern sun. Eisenhower had been elected, the North Koreans were negotiating, and I would see no war. In Daytona one weekend, I stood on the beach with another sailor, named Stamps, and watched the cars roll by on the hard-packed sand. Two college girls came along in a convertible and Stamps and I leaped into the back seat and then we were in their motel room, drinking beer and fucking them for hours. I was almost eighteen. At night in the enlisted men's barracks, I longed for Maureen — O wounded vanity! — and in my fantasies was once again in the Tenth Street apartment with Laura tied to an easel.

From Jacksonville I was sent to Pensacola, to a helicopter training base at Ellyson Field. In the small base library I discovered Hemingway, Fitzgerald, and the myth of the Lost Generation. The discovery was set off by a single sentence by Malcolm Cowley in his 1944 introduction to a small compact Viking Portable that contained *The Sun Also Rises*, excerpts from other novels, and a selection of Hemingway's short stories.

> *Going back to Hemingway's work after several years is like going back to a brook where you had often fished and finding the woods as deep and cool as they used to be. . . .*

I was a city boy; I hadn't seen a brook since Fox Lair Camp, had never fished in any serious way, associated woods with the place where Arnold hid his bottle of wine. But something about that sentence pulled me in: a vision of clarity that was liquid and moving and cool.

Part of the appeal came from reading it in the heat of Florida. But I had never thought of a writer that way, making words as clear as flowing water. Cowley allowed Hemingway himself to talk:

> *All good books are alike in that they are truer than if they had really happened and after you are finished reading one you will feel that all that happened to you and afterwards it all belongs to you: the good and the bad, the ecstasy, the remorse and sorrow, the people and the places and how the weather was.*

I knew that was true; the stuff of many books already lived in my mind as if it had happened to me. I didn't remember the bad books.

And if the Hemingway world of Paris and Pamplona, the slopes of Kilimanjaro and the eddies of the Big Two-Hearted River had nothing concrete to do with my life, Cowley described a part of that world that surely did. The Hemingway heroes had one thing in common.

> *They drink early and late; they consume enough beer, wine, anis, grappa and Fundador to put them all into alcoholic wards, if they were ordinary mortals; but drinking seems to have the effect on them of a magic potion.*

Yes! I had sampled that magic potion myself. And Cowley then quoted from Hemingway's *For Whom the Bell Tolls*, whose hero, Robert Jordan, finds that a cup of absinthe

> *took the place of the evening papers, of all the old evenings in cafés, of all the chestnut trees that would be in bloom now in this month . . . of all the things he had enjoyed and forgotten and that came back to him when he*

tasted that opaque, bitter, tongue-numbing, brain-warming, stomach-warming, idea-changing liquid alchemy.

For weeks I tried to find absinthe in the dirt-floored bars of O Street, and failed. There were other forms of liquid alchemy, and so the lack of absinthe did not matter. I was soon in the Hemingway world, carrying his stoic ethic with me off the base, to sailor bars where drinking was sport, entertainment, clarification, and pleasure. I went on to Cowley's *Exile's Return*, about the Lost Generation that Gertrude Stein had named and Hemingway had made famous, and learned that drinking could be something more than mere fuel for a wild night out. It could be a huge fuck you to Authority.

The writers, artists, and poets of the 1920s, Cowley explained, were faced with one mammoth idiocy of Authority: the mistake called Prohibition. Then, as in my own 1953, right-wingers, bigots, bluenoses, and puritans ruled America. They used goons to break labor unions. Like our current political gangster Joe McCarthy, they sniffed around for people they called subversives, silenced them, jailed them, deported them. If people like that passed a law making it a crime to drink, you had only one choice: to get roaring drunk.

Cowley led me to Fitzgerald and *The Great Gatsby*, to the world of bootleggers and speakeasies, and I remembered my father's friends sitting in the kitchen that time talking about rumrunners. Nothing could have been more romantic. James Cagney lived in that world, in the old movies that kept playing in the Minerva and the Sixteenth Street; so did Bogart and Robinson and Raft. And now Wolfsheim the gambler was there and Nick Carraway and Jay Gatsby, along with Fitzgerald himself, and Billy Hamill.

And Billy Hamill's oldest son too.

All of them staring across the water at the green light on Daisy's dock.

2

FROM HEMINGWAY, I stole the guise of the stoic drinker, mixing it up with Bogart and some old salts who had come through the war and knew that a helicopter base in the Florida panhandle was Mickey Mouse duty. These men carried deep wounded feelings beneath the tough exteriors (or so I thought), but they taught us that the only unforgivable sin was self-pity. A girl broke your heart? Fuck her. Get another one. Break *her* heart. You lost a fight? Fuck it. Get up. Wipe off the blood. Have another whiskey and go get him again.

Most of them knew a lot about life in a concrete way. And they laughed out loud at the oratory of the politicians. That, too, fit in with the codes of Hemingway.

> *I was always embarrassed by the words sacred, glorious, and sacrifice, and the expression in vain. We had heard them, sometimes standing in the rain almost out of earshot, so that only the shouted words came through, and had read them, on proclamations that were slapped up by billposters over other proclamations, now for a long time, and I had seen nothing sacred, and the things that were glorious had no glory and the sacrifices were like the stockyards at Chicago if nothing was done with the meat except to bury it. . . . Abstract words such as glory, honor, courage, or hallow were obscene beside the concrete names of villages, the numbers of roads, the names of rivers, the numbers of regiments and the dates. . . .*

That was from *A Farewell to Arms,* and in that romantic novel, I first came across the notion of a separate peace. In the climax of the drama, Frederic Henry deserts to join his woman, Catherine Barkley, leaving behind the abstractions of patriotism, loyalty, and solemn oaths. Living was more important than dying; loving a woman was more important than loving a country. And from Cowley's *Exile's Return,* I realized that there was another way to make a separate peace: departure. Faced with an America dedicated to sobriety, thrift, puritanism, and commercialism, many Twenties writers and artists became expatriates. I loved that word. The expatriate Fitzgerald went to the Riviera, T. S. Eliot to London, Katherine Anne Porter to Mexico, Hemingway to Paris. They lived the expatriate life among civilized people (or so I thought), in countries where food and shelter and drink were cheap and the women were beautiful.

In my imagination, searching for absinthe among the Hank Williams–Webb Pierce jukeboxes, Paris became the golden city of my imagination. It was so in the 1920s, I thought; it must be so now. I envisioned café tables on summer afternoons, smoky dives in the winter, painters on the slopes of Montparnasse, and there, coming in the door of the *bal musette,* striding right out of *The Sun Also Rises,* was Lady Brett Ashley.

> *She wore a slipover jersey sweater and a tweed skirt, and her hair was brushed back like a boy's. She started all that. She was built with curves*

*like the hull of a racing yacht, and you missed none of it with that wool
jersey. . . .*

Around this time, I first saw Vincente Minnelli's *An American in Paris,*
and here was Gene Kelly, living on the GI Bill after World War II —
that is to say, *now* — telling me that if you can't paint in Paris, you might
as well marry the boss's daughter. He had a studio in the Quarter that
was smaller than Laura's, with a bed on pulleys that he raised in the
morning to the ceiling, and windows open to the spring air, the Paris
rooftops, the cobblestoned streets, the bookstalls, and the fresh bread
and, of course, the cafés. Oscar Levant was his best friend, a piano
player, and they met each day in the Café Bel Ami. The girl he loved
was Leslie Caron. His music was by George Gershwin, full of charm and
confidence and bittersweet regret. This wasn't the Paris of Jake Barnes
and Robert Cohn from *The Sun Also Rises*. But it was bright and gay and
full of painters and music and beautiful women and I wanted it.

And began to think I might even get it. When I finished with the navy,
I too was entitled to the GI Bill, just like Gene Kelly. I could go to Paris
and see all the great paintings in the Louvre and read all the writers whose
names were scattered through Cowley's book: Joyce and Pound, Proust
and Valéry, Verlaine and Rimbaud and Baudelaire. Why not? I'd find the
Café Bel Ami and sit at a table and order Fundador and read little magazines too. And study at the Académie Julien or the Sorbonne. And paint
in the street. All night long, I'd discuss with my fellow theologians the
canon law of the religion of art. And sample other pleasures.

The only things that matter, said Gene Kelly, *are women and wine.*

And absinthe. Of course.

3

BUT I DIDN'T GO to Paris. The Korean War ended in a grim
stalemate, and a year later the navy ended for me too, and I went back
to New York. I found a job as a messenger and then proofreader in the
production department of an advertising agency that specialized in industrial accounts. Everybody in the Neighborhood thought I was crazy.

You got a good job in the Navy Yard, Duke Baluta said. They gotta
count your navy time toward your pension too.

I want to try something else, I said.

You could be there for life.

That's what I'm afraid of.

Back home, I didn't go very far. I found a new room, this one next to a synagogue on Ninth Street in Brooklyn, a half block from the library. I was soon going steady with another girl from the Neighborhood, this one named Catherine. I didn't go back to C&I; there was some problem about the GI Bill. I enrolled instead in evening classes at Pratt Institute, where an English teacher named Tom McMahon looked at my compositions and encouraged me to write. McMahon was a fine teacher with a probing theatrical style. He was an expert on Hemingway, an admirer of Nathanael West and Horace McCoy, a cigarette smoker and wearer of trench coats, and at one point he urged me to try to get into Columbia University, where I could study literature *or* art. I went up to Morningside Heights and saw the registrar, a bald polished man. He looked at my academic record, such as it was, and suggested in a condescending voice that I consider going to a vocational school.

I hear there is a big need for dental technicians, he said.

Fuck you, I said, gathered my papers and walked out the door.

All the way back to Brooklyn from Morningside Heights I kept saying, Fuck you, I'll do it some other way. Fuck you, I'll do it anyway.

I was reading newspapers again, the comics behind me, but enthralled by Jimmy Cannon in the *Post*'s sports section and by Murray Kempton's column on the editorial page. After Pensacola, the seven New York newspapers were a gorgeous feast. I no longer wanted to be a cartoonist. But the dream of painting in Paris also began to fade under the gray pressure of earning a living and a feeling of rejection. I wrote to the Sorbonne in Paris. I wrote to the Académie Julien. I never received answers. Fuck you, I said to Paris. Fuck you too.

Now everyone in the Neighborhood had a television set — even my father — and on summer nights the streets were emptier, as each apartment lit up with a pale blue glow. I still listened to Symphony Sid and got drunk when Charlie Parker died and sneered at the arrival of rock and roll.

In Brooklyn I felt stalled again. Most of my friends were still in the service; they'd gone in after me and stayed later. My best friend was Tim Lee, a brilliant guy who had boxed in the amateurs at Thomas Aquinas and came home on weekends from his army base in Maryland. In Boop's or Rattigan's or the Caton Inn, we talked a lot about going to college, *doing* something with our lives. Everything seemed possible over a beer. But in 1955, such talk was always interrupted by other matters. In Boop's, we cheered in September when Archie Moore knocked down Rocky Marciano before getting knocked out himself. We were thrilled when Sugar Ray Robinson ended his amazing comeback in December by knocking out Bobo Olson in two rounds. At the bar there was a lot of talk now about heroin, which was claiming its first victims in the Neighborhood.

Who brought this shit around anyway? I asked one night in Boop's.

The guineas, who else? said Vito Pinto.

Hey, Vito, Duke Baluta said, *you're* a guinea!

You know who I mean, Vito said.

Everybody knew, all right. The racket guys from South Brooklyn had started slowly peddling heroin, and now it was coming in a flood. The streets that once had the most drunks — Twelfth Street, Seventh Avenue, Seventeenth Street — now housed the most junkies. The South Brooklyn wise guys did to the Tigers with heroin what they couldn't do with fists, bats, or guns: wasted them and robbed them of their pride. Seeing that, I was never tempted by hard drugs. But now drinking acquired another quality: it was the normal, healthy, even *moral* alternative to smack.

That year, I also started hanging around with a tough funny ironworker named Jack Daugherty. He loved sentimental Irish songs, practical jokes, and fighting. He was the hardest-punching street fighter I ever knew. And soon, in bars and coffee shops all over Brooklyn, we were in fights every night. We fought strangers over change (*I had t'ree quarters here when I went to take my piss*) or looks (*The fuck you lookin' at, prickface?*) or women (*Whatta you, own this broad?*). Sometimes Tim Lee was there; usually it was Jack and me. I broke my right hand twice and had a stabilizing pin inserted through my knuckles, forcing me for a few weeks to draw with my left. There were wild fights in Bickford's cafeteria on Ninth Street and wilder ones on the sidewalks outside Nathan's on Coney Island. I was drinking every day but seldom got drunk and never had hangovers; it was a matter of deep pride in the Neighborhood to be able to hold your drink.

One night in the Caton Inn, a dark joint on Coney Island Avenue with a huge horseshoe bar, a booming jukebox, and a dance floor, I was drinking with my girl, Catherine. My broken right hand was in a cast. Then a guy grabbed Catherine's ass on his way to the men's room and I spun him around and hit him between the eyes with the cast. His head bounced off another guy's foot, breaking his toe. It became known as The Night Pete Hamill Broke Frank Christie's Toe with One Punch.

Catherine was sweet, funny, a drinker, with dark hair cut in a bob, long legs, and smooth skin. All around us, people were getting married, as the men came back from Korea. It was assumed that we would be married too. My father knew her father; she lived two blocks from 378; I was told in a dozen different ways by several dozen grown-ups that there was nothing better than a good neighborhood girl. That year, Catherine went to a lot of baby showers. We went together to some weddings. She didn't mind my drinking or fighting; that was what men did. She gushed about the drawings I took home from Pratt, giggled at the naked women, but looked blank when I tried to talk about a life as a painter. She didn't dismiss the subject the way Maureen had; it just didn't register with her. I could have been discussing the rings of Saturn. We ordered beers. We danced. She laughed at my jokes. We groped each other in the kitchen of her parents' flat. I went home. Or stopped for a nightcap in a bar.

One day in the *Daily News* there was a story about the ongoing demolition of the Third Avenue El. The work crews were moving uptown from the Bowery and were about to reach Fourteenth Street. I felt a pang; a piece of the world I knew was going to disappear. But there was more to it than that. After work, I went down to Tenth Street and Third Avenue, secretly hoping that Laura had seen the same news item and would feel the same pang. A half block from the El, we had pleasured each other on winter nights. I told myself that I wasn't in love with her; I didn't even want to take her to bed; I just wanted to see her again and hear from her what had happened. From the Astor Place subway station, I walked slowly east along Tenth Street. At her building, I went into the vestibule and looked at the mailboxes, but someone else was living in the old studio. Then I walked to the corner. Third Avenue felt empty and hollow without the great dark iron structures of the El and the steel growl of the trains. I went into a bar and sat there for a long time, sipping beers, watching the street. But I never saw Laura again. I never saw her name in the art magazines. She wasn't listed in the directories of American artists. She was gone forever.

4

BY EARLY 1956, I began to feel that I was vanishing too. The production manager at the agency had quickly decided I wasn't what he needed; he about to fire me. The art director, Ernie Waivada, saved me, out of an excess of Christian pity, and from him I started to acquire some minor skills. I could draw a straight line with a steel T square, for example. I could do simple pasteups and mechanicals. I could "spec" type and do some primitive lettering (taming my cartoony instincts). I knew about repro proofs and photostats and Photo Lettering. I was trusted to black out cut lines on negative photostats, to cut mats, to "gang" various small pieces of art for photostats. I managed to keep the job and was even given a small raise.

But at night in the dark, alone with myself, graphic design seemed a chilly discipline. It was basically a function of the intellect, and I was still in the sweaty grip of romance, full of Hemingway, reading the poems of García Lorca, soaking up James M. Cain, discovering the drawings of Heinrich Kley, copying George Grosz and Orozco. I still loved drawing human bodies, hair and teeth and flesh. I had much less interest in squares, circles, triangles, or the delicacies of Caslon Bold.

In the small studio, upstairs from a rug importer on Fifth Avenue and Forty-seventh Street, there was another man who came to work three or four days a week. His name was Dave Hills. He was in his sixties, with age freckles on his hands, his back hunched from years bent over drawing boards. He had been the first art director of the agency but now worked as a part-time freelancer on some of the minor work, such as employee newsletters. He had a few peculiar specialities, one of which was lettering that looked like rope. But he never talked about the glories of design. His fundamental medium was the Job. He had started out long ago and come through the Depression and the war; he was happy to be there at all. Then one day he announced that he was going to retire. He was packing up and moving to Mexico.

Why Mexico, Dave? I asked.

Oh, I don't know, he said. I like the people. I like the country. I like the booze. And besides, it's cheap.

At almost the same time, I received a letter from a navy friend who also wanted to be a painter. He enclosed a catalog for a school called Mexico City College, approved for study on the GI Bill, with an art department offering a bachelor of fine arts degree. The language of instruction was English, but there were extensive courses in the Spanish language. *Maybe this is our Paris*, my friend wrote. *And besides, it's cheap*, said Dave Hills.

Suddenly Mexico cast a voluptuous spell. If a sixty-five-year-old man could pack up and go to Mexico, why couldn't I? I sent the catalog to my friend Tim Lee, who was still in the army. Maybe, I wrote him, we could go there together. So what if nobody in the Neighborhood ever went to college; why shouldn't we be the first? And in *Mexico!* The notion would not go away. In the agency, I was trying to letter a line of copy in Clarendon Bold and suddenly Orozco tore across my mind. I sat at the bar in the Caton Inn with Catherine and imagined hard brown mountains, cactus, distant volcanoes; bandidos out of *The Treasure of the Sierra Madre*; pyramids and lost cities; cantinas full of music and tequila and brown-skinned women.

Are you okay? Catherine said.

Yeah, yeah.

You're not drunk?

No, I'm not drunk.

I hope you're not thinking about some other girl.

No.

Or one of those naked women from school.

No. No women. I swear. . . .

In February, Tim got out of the army. And we ended up one night at the bar in Boop's.

What do you think? I said.

About what?

About going to Mexico.

He laughed out loud.

You're nuts, he said.

I know, I said. But I'm serious.

He downed a beer, his brow furrowing, and said: Hey, why not? Why fucking not?

In May, we sent the application forms to Mexico, just to see what would happen. Weeks passed. The Mexico fever ebbed as I assumed that I faced still another rejection. Then, on a Friday, a plump letter trimmed with orange and green arrived in my mailbox. The stamps were from Mexico. I tore it open and discovered that I was accepted. So was Tim. After the cold rejection by Columbia, and the silence of Paris, I was giddy with jubilation and went off to Boop's to celebrate. They did not have tequila at the bar so I got wrecked on vodka. On Monday, I gave my notice at the agency, telling Ernie Waivada that I would leave in late August. I gave no notice to Catherine. I just couldn't tell her anything that was not a lie, so I said nothing. To save money for the trip, I took a second job, as a page at NBC, starting at six in the evening and working until one in the morning. That summer, every hour seemed packed with excitement and discovery, as I learned about the world of television while dreaming of Mexico. There was an added benefit: the long hours kept me from facing Catherine.

Meanwhile, Tim and I applied for U.S. passports and Mexican student visas. The summer raced by. Until the week before we left, none of it seemed real. We didn't learn any Spanish, except the words for bread (*pan*), water (*agua*), and beer (*cerveza*). Three days before we left, I finally told Catherine. There were tears and scenes. I behaved badly.

On the last weekend of August, Tim and I went to the Greyhound station and waited for the bus that would take us to Mexico City. I had eighty dollars in my pocket and a bag of sandwiches.

Pan, I said to myself. *Agua. Cerveza.*

5

THE BUS from Transportes del Norte was climbing slowly, breaching one final ridge as it drove into a gigantic scarlet dawn. Suddenly we could go no higher. And there in the distance, spread out before us in the great valley of Anáhuac, was Mexico City.

I remember the tumult of the bus station, the air drowned with vowels, and the taxi driver staring at the written address and then driving wildly to the house where we would stay, with a family arranged by the school. The address was Melchor Ocampo 288, an apartment house on the corner of Río Tiber. At the door on the fourth floor, an old woman smiled and nodded, speaking no English; her two homely daughters examined us discreetly and led us to the clean, bright rooms. We unpacked, had soup and rolls, trying to be polite. *Pan*, I said, *agua*, adding *por favor*, and ending with *gracias*. We bowed. We nodded. We smiled too much. Then we went out in search of *cerveza*.

We found a bar three blocks away, where the Mexicans stood on the rail and so did we. Later we learned that they first thought we were making fun of them; they used the rail because the bar was high and they were short. There was a great pot of shrimp soup in the place, and our fellow drinkers laughed as they explained mezcal and the worm at the bottom of the bottle and tried to describe what pulque does to the human brain. That first night, a soldier came in with his girlfriend and placed himself in the doorway leading to the john, which was an open trench with a steel bar upon which you hoisted yourself if you had more to do than urinate. His girlfriend went in to hoist herself on the steel bar and the soldier held his rifle at the ready, glaring at all of us. Nobody said a word. A rifle is a useful guarantor of good manners. Then the woman was through and the soldier nodded gravely and said *Buenas noches* and they went into the night.

The bottles of Carta Blanca beer were cold, *bien fría, señor*, very cold, sir. And from the great jukebox I first heard José Alfredo Jiménez growling his cantina poems and Cuco Sánchez with the harp and the bass guitar singing "La Cama de Piedra":

> *De piedra ha de ser la cama,*
> *De piedra la cabecera . . .*

And everyone joining in the mournful line *Ay, ay: corazón porque no amas*. My heart is broken. Because you don't love me.

Dos más, por favor.

I had grown up in New York and visited Baltimore and Miami and New Orleans. But Mexico City was the most beautiful city I'd ever seen, as we walked in the cool nights along the hard-packed earth of the great wide Paseo de la Reforma. Ash trees climbed high above us. One-peso cabs hugged the curbs. Thick-bodied pigtailed maids met their boyfriends in the shadows and sat on stone benches to listen to the music drifting from the fancy supper clubs. There were elegant office buildings and great Victorian mansions from the days of Porfirio Díaz; cafés on the sidewalks of the Zona Rosa and tiny restaurants where they served octopus in its own ink and shrimp flown in from the Pacific ports. Freshly arrived from the countryside, campesinos in straw hats and white pajamas stared at the great light-bathed statue of the Angel of Independence in the center of the circular *glorieta* where Río Tiber intersected with the Reforma.

In the crisp mornings, the air thin and clear at 7500 feet above sea level, we walked seven blocks to the school bus, passing shopkeepers washing their sidewalks, and schoolgirls in uniforms hurrying to class. We bought the sports papers, *Esto* and *Ovaciones*, and read about how

Floyd Patterson, from Tim's high school in Brooklyn, had knocked out Archie Moore in five rounds to become at twenty-one the youngest heavyweight champion in history. We were the same age as Floyd; wasn't everything now possible for us too? We also read about the great Mexican fighters, the bantamweight Ratón Macias, who could box and punch and sell a hundred thousand tickets, or the featherweight Pajarito Moreno, who could punch out a Volkswagen with a right hand and was even the hero of his own comic book, or Toluco López, great macho, wonderful fighter, king of the cantinas.

The orange school bus moved up past the monument honoring the 1938 nationalization of the petroleum industry into Las Lomas de Chapultepec, where the rich people had their great mansions behind stone walls topped with broken glass. That year in Mexico City, there were only three million citizens and the air was clear. On those crisp mornings we could see the snow-topped volcanoes Popocatéptl and Ixtaccíhuatl, the first male, the second a sleeping woman, or so we were told, and so we believed. We came out of the Lomas and turned onto the two-lane Toluca highway, still climbing, with deep gorges falling away on either side, and a vast stone quarry way off to the left; until at the sixteenth kilometer we reached the school.

Mexico City College was a converted country club with the name lettered in deco style over the main archway. I thought, as I stood there on the first day: *I'm here, in Mexico. I did it.* I walked on the irregularly patterned stone path into the campus and found the administration office in a cluster of plain red sandstone buildings. Tim and I completed our forms for the Veterans Administration, then he went off to the general studies office and I went in search of the art department. The studios were on the top floor of an ivy-covered concrete structure that also housed the theater and the cafeteria, and as I climbed the stairs I picked up the fragrance of oil and terps. For a moment, I flashed on Laura. Maybe she was here. Painting. Teaching.

She wasn't, of course, but a pretty Mexican woman took my papers, checked them against her own list, and told me that all I needed for my first classes was charcoal and newsprint paper. My first class was in the morning. I was in. With any luck, I would stay for three years, learn the painter's craft, become the first in my family to earn a degree. Here. In Mexico.

6

IN THOSE FIRST GLORIOUS MONTHS, I gazed in awe at the work of the Mexican muralists. I looked at the dark, brooding drawings and paintings of the new Mexican artists, led by José Luis Cuevas, who were the enemies of the painted oratory of the muralists. I studied Spanish. Money was always short, the checks from the Veterans Administration slow in arriving. But Carta Blanca was one peso a bottle, the equivalent of eight cents in that time when the peso was a solid 12.50 against the dollar. Bohemia and the dark fermented-looking Dos Equis cost more, but another brand, Don Quijote, was only fifty centavos a bottle, or eighty cents for a case of twenty.

There was drinking everywhere, and Tim and I were part of it. We went drinking in the small hut across the highway from the school, in the cantinas near where we lived, at weekend student parties all over the city. Those parties bound us together. In some ways, it was like the navy. Everyone was far from home, far from Ohio and Illinois, from states with age limits on drinking, far from inspection by friends or family, all using drink to deal with strangeness and shyness and a variety of fears. At MCC, there were two American men for every American woman, and the sense of male contest gave the parties a tension that occasionally resembled hysteria. The rule was BYOB, bring your own bottle, and in the doors came cases of beer, bottles of tequila, mezcal, pulque, rum. These were 1950s parties, young men and women packing the chosen apartment, dancing, as we said, teeth to teeth, to the music of Benny More and Los Panchos, drinking with little care about food, faces swirling, ashtrays overflowing with butts, hot eyes falling upon asses and tits, tits and asses, until the midnight hour had long passed, and finally the last of the women were gone, and the remnants of the bleary male squadron kept drinking on until the beer ran out and you could see the worm in the bottom of the mezcal bottle and it was time to face the gray dawn.

I was happier than I'd ever been.

One Saturday night in December, on the eve of the Feast of the Virgin of Guadalupe, there was a big party in an apartment shared by four MCC students. It was more formal than usual, because some Mexican girls had been invited from a commercial school downtown and we'd been told to try to make a good impression. I wore my only suit, dark blue with a thin pinstripe, a shirt and tie. The beer was flowing. As the Orquesta Aragón played a *charanga*, I watched the dancing Mexican women, in their formal dresses, their tapered legs, rustling crinolines, high heels; the American women seemed more formal than usual, even awkward, and the men worked too hard at being cool. I danced a mambo with a girl named Yolanda. Another guy cut in and I moved aside and drank beer. I danced slowly with a girl named Maria to "Sin Ti." She thanked me and hurried away and I drank beer. In the kitchen, I opened another bottle of Bohemia and laughed when some of the louder gringos made bad jokes about La Virgen. Tim Lee was there with me but left early with one of the young Mexican women. I danced a cha-cha with a woman named Lourdes. She left early with two other women. Around midnight, there were about fifteen men still drinking and two American women, neither of whom was free. I was drinking with a Mexican-American friend named Manny when he suggested that we go out on the town.

There's gotta be some women someplace, he said. Let's take a look.

¿Porqué no?

We ended up down on San Juan de Letran, the wide neon main boulevard of *la vida nocturna*, where the dance halls and strip joints and burlesque houses called to the working class and the slumming *ricos*. Down here, you could go in pursuit of the women of *la vida galante*. On this chilly midnight, our goal was as clear as the vision was blurry.

We moved off San Juan de Letran into dark side streets lined with one-story houses, their walls painted, doors and shutters locked against the night, iron grills over the windows. Then we crossed a small cobblestoned plaza and a dry fountain and then up ahead there was a street full of light and noise and people and music. I remember hearing the song of Agustín Lara:

> *Solamente una vez*
> *Amé en la vida,*
> *Solamente una vez —*
> *Y nada mas . . .*

(I loved only one time in this life, only one time, and nothing more.) I was singing the song — or those lines, for I knew no others — as we walked into the Calle de la Esperanza, the Street of Hope, lined on both sides with bordellos. These were the ten-peso whorehouses, the cheapest in the city, and had been here since before the 1910 Revolution. Each had a tall locked door with a window opening into a parlor. Dozens of customers, all of them Mexican, strolled along the street, gazing at the women through those windows, making comparisons, whispering offers or compliments before moving on or choosing admission. I kept humming, *Solamente una vez*, and thinking, in a thrilled, tingling way: Orozco must have come here, and Cuevas, to look at these whores who were old and listless or young and frightened, to see these altars to La Virgen made of cigarette tinfoil and fat candles, to remember the pale harsh light from the ceiling bulbs and the worn furniture and the drinks served on beer trays. From one parlor, glimpsed through the window, a young girl smiled at a visiting gringo, her wide mouth full of gold; another looked up and turned back to a comic book; a third stared at the patterns on the rug as if she would never again have enough sleep.

And then in one of the parlors I saw a frail young woman with cinnamon skin and liquid eyes. She was sitting alone on a flowered chair with worn arms, a Dos Equis calendar of a bare-breasted Indian princess above her on the wall. From a radio, Los Panchos were singing, and I went by, wishing I had a sketchbook, imagining myself sitting in that parlor and drawing that girl, the way Pascin or Toulouse-Lautrec sketched the whores of Paris; imagined then taking her away, to live with me in some other place, where I could draw her and fuck her and sleep with her and then draw her again. She wasn't a beaten hulk, like the whores in Orozco, or a grotesque out of Cuevas. She was beautiful. I was certain of that. In all the other parlors, the women repelled me, and as I moved on down the street, I had a sudden moment of panic; someone else would see her, go in, take her into the back and I would lose her.

Let's go back to that place up the block, I said.

You see one you like?

Yeah.

She was still there. I went up to the door, bent down, and leaned in through the window.

Perdóname, señorita.

She looked at me and smiled.

Uh ¿cómo se llama? What's your name?

She didn't answer. Suddenly, an older woman stepped over and heaved a pan of water at me, drenching me, shouting in Spanish. I didn't know why (and never found out). But I reacted. I lunged forward, like a fullback hitting the line, driving my body half into the window. The door came off its hinges and went straight down, with the older woman under it, screaming. In the same wild action, I stepped on the door, squashing her, and then the young woman, my model, the woman I would take to a more gallant life, attacked, swinging a pocketbook at my head. Other whores came out of the back, belting me with more pocketbooks and ashtrays and a tray of tacos, all shouting and cursing in Spanish, and then Manny grabbed my arm.

Let's get the fuck out of here, man.

We ran out of the Calle de la Esperanza, laughing and still a little drunk. In the cobblestoned plaza, a beat-up rented car pulled over. Inside were three gringos, looking for directions to the whorehouses. They were in their twenties, tourists from Texas, beefy, drinking from a rum bottle. We blurted out what had happened and they opened the back doors and offered to drive us away. We were all laughing now. *Broke down the door of a fuckin' whorehouse! In Mexico! Gah-damn!*

We were laughing right up to the moment a taxi cut us off. Out came the two whores followed by two policemen in blue uniforms. The young whore, *mi vida, mi corazón, amor de mis amores*, was enraged, her body coiled, her nostrils wide, her eyes glazed in fury, with her arm straight out and one painted fingernail pointing at me.

¡Eso es! she screamed. *¡Este cabrón, eso es!* That's him! That son of a bitch, that's him!

And then the cops were aiming guns at us. They ordered us out of the car. The three Texans were jittery. I kept my eyes on the guns while the whores shouted curses. Manny was talking very quickly in Spanish, his manner conciliatory, now smiling, now worried. The policemen were small and mustached, with brown complexions and worn uniforms. They did not look convinced of our good intentions. They ordered us all back into the car, and one of them barked orders at the two women, who hurled a few final curses, entered the taxicab, and were driven away. In our car, Manny sat in the front, between the nervous Texan who was driving and one of the cops. I sat in the back, the other Texans beside me and the second cop planted on my lap. The cop in the front was giving orders to the driver. *Izquierda aquí.* As commanded, the driver took a left. *A la derecha* . . . The Texan dutifully turned right, down empty streets with blind windows.

I was suddenly very sober, struggling to believe that this was happening. Clearly, we were under arrest. All of us. I was the guilty party, but they were taking us all to a police station. Over a broken door! But, hey (I told myself), I didn't do anything so terrible, did I? I asked a whore for her name and another whore threw water on me and then . . . Shit. What a pain in the ass. Still, it wasn't murder. It wasn't some great armed robbery. We'd go to a police station and pay for the broken door and that would be that. And I remembered that I had almost no money. About sixty pesos. Less than five dollars. Maybe Manny had money. Maybe the Texans could loan us whatever we needed and we'd pay them back when we got home. A few bucks. Just for now. *Solamente una vez.*

But then, as the cop ordered an *izquierda*, the driver took a *derecha.* The cop on my lap cursed at him, this *pinche gringo cabrón.* The fucking gringo son of a bitch kept going into the wrong street. And then the Texan beside me changed everything. He threw a punch at the cop in the front seat, hitting him on the side of the jaw. The driver panicked, slammed the brakes, the car skidded, everyone was shouting, and we spun to a halt. The cop on my lap had his gun out. I pushed down on the door handle and he and I rolled out in a tangled heap. I got up and started to run. And then heard shots.

Pap, pap. Pap-pap-pap.

I heard at least three bullets whiz past my head.

I ran. Thinking: They're trying to kill me.

And then, up ahead, I saw a blue wall of police. They were piling out of a police station, alerted by the shots, and I was running right at them. I stopped and one came at me swinging a long club. I bent down and threw a punch and knocked him down. Then all the others were on me, swinging clubs, punching, kicking, screaming *pinche cabrón* and *chingado gringo*, until I was on the ground, pulling myself into a tight ball as they stomped me some more.

They shoved me into the *delegación*, and I saw Manny at the far end of a high-ceilinged greenish room, surrounded by cops. The Texans were nowhere in sight. Obviously, they had chosen a better street, and we never saw them again. But in flight, they'd also taken one of the policemen's pistols. So I found myself charged by a fat lieutenant with *lesiones* (causing cuts with punches), destruction of private property (the whorehouse door), assault, resisting arrest, and *robo*, for stealing the pistol. I didn't have enough Spanish to explain myself. My back and ribs and legs hurt. My nose ached, and when I touched the bridge, blood came off on my fingers. Worse, my teeth felt cracked and sharp to my tongue; one small piece broke off, and when I picked it out with my fingers, one of the cops smiled.

I was in a mess. I asked for *el teléfono* but the lieutenant shook his head and grimaced. *No hay*, he said; there is none. *No hay teléfono público.* I looked out through the dirty window at a car passing on the street and wished I was in it, heading home. The sound of the shots and the whirring of the bullets now seemed louder. And I realized that I could be dead. One bullet in the head and I'd have ended on the sidewalk with my life over before it really started.

The cops shoved me through a door and down a corridor and then opened a blank steel door that led to a cellblock. In some ways, the long night was just beginning.

They put me into a large dark communal cell at the end of the block. One high barred window opened to the night. As the cop locked the cell door behind me, I gazed around. There were about fifteen men in the cell, a few in modified zoots, most in rough clothes; I was the only one in a suit and tie, and I was certainly the only gringo. There were no beds, but some men were sleeping, huddled on the filthy floor against the scabrous walls. The air was a compost of stale beer and rum, sweat and entrapment and shit. The only toilet was an open hole in the floor in the far corner. The men gazed at me. I nodded, shrugged, said *buenas noches*, and smiled. A bone-thin mustached man came over and asked me for a cigarette. I patted my pockets and said, *No fumo*, which was true. He stared at me in a chilly way, his face impassive, his eyes searching for some sign of weakness. I stared back, tense, ready to fight. But he turned and walked away. I felt exhausted and drained and hurting, but I knew that I could not risk sleeping.

I squatted against the bars of the cell, wondering where Manny was, and as my eyes adjusted to the murky light I realized that there were three men in the cell directly across the corridor. There was also a pile of bricks. Some kind of construction must have been interrupted by the holiday weekend. Now more men were being brought into the cellblock, the gatherings of the holiday, and I could hear shouts of recognition from other cells and banging on the steel bars and much drunken laughter. I called Manny's name, yelling in English, Are you there, Manny? But there was no answer. I wondered how I could get word to Tim, to arrange for bail, to get a lawyer, maybe notify the American Embassy. But there was nobody to ask. The guards came in with prisoners, threw them into cells, ignored all pleas or shouts, and disappeared beyond the steel door.

Then they started bringing in the women. Two of them were thrown into the cell across the way, where there were now about eight men. One of them was a worn-out woman, her hair gray and wild. But the other was young. She was wearing a yellow blouse. I could see her white teeth against dark skin. The men in my cell moved toward the bars to examine this new arrival. Suddenly the mood shifted; sexual excitement seemed to thicken the air. Across the way, two men were easing around the young woman. She was terrified, backing away from each of them, screaming in a thin voice, *Ayúdeme, por favor, ayúdeme . . .*

Help me, please, help me.

Nobody came to her aid. One of the men, short, compact, muscular, reached out swiftly and tore open the front of the blouse. She made a yipping birdlike sound, her voice weak and trembling, and then he grabbed the center of her black bra and ripped down, exposing her heavy dark breasts, and now all the men in my cell were shouting encouragement. *¡Vaya, macho! ¡Ándale!* The old woman cringed against a wall, but the rape was delayed. The second man intervened and shoved the short, muscular man, who threw a punch and grabbed at him, the two of them closing violently, throwing punches to do damage, the short man's shirt coming off, the girl retreating in wide-eyed fear, covering her breasts, screaming. And then the combatants found the bricks. Their eyes were wide, faces gleaming with lust and violence, as they circled each other like boxers, each armed with a brick, the men in my cell roaring now as if at a prizefight in the Arena Coliseo, urging them to use the left or throw the right. Every time one of them landed with a brick there was a loud thwacking sound as if something had broken. Sweat glistened on the body of the shirtless man. Blood ran from a gash in the other's cheekbone, and their shoulders and arms were welted and raw.

Finally the young woman was shouting something to them, something about death, and offering her breasts, then placing a hand up under her skirt, as if saying that she didn't want them to kill each other for her. I couldn't make out the pleading words over the roar of the men in my cell. But she seemed to be saying, Stop! Go ahead and rape me if you must, but stop.

They paused.

My cell went silent.

And then the short man lunged at the other, prepared to kill or die, and the roar was immense, the codes of men triumphing over the mercy of women.

Finally, the steel door opened and guards rushed in, hurrying down the corridor. One drew a gun, shouting into the cell. The men stopped, then sullenly dropped the bricks. The girl looked forlorn. The guards opened the cell door, first called out the old woman, then the younger one, while one guard shouted at another about his stupidity. The fighters were locked in with their inexhaustible supply of bricks. The men in my cell were still roaring, calling out to the girl, *Muñeca, eres mi reina,* Hey, doll, you are my queen, and offering to never fight again if only she would take them forever to her bed. But she stared at the floor of the corridor, walking sadly on one high-heeled shoe, the other in her hand, covering her lovely breasts with the shredded blouse. The two women went out through the steel door. I didn't know what had brought her to that cell; I supposed she was a prostitute, perhaps a thief; but I felt certain that she would carry that hour of horror with her for all the years of her life. I knew I would too.

7

IN THE MORNING, they started moving me around. The first stop was another jail, where I was put in solitary confinement. The room was like a closet, no windows, no toilet, no bed, with a thin line of light at the base of an iron door. I ran my fingers over the wall and found letters gouged in the surface. My eyes slowly adjusted. The letters said: *Viva Stalin, el Rey de los Rojos.* Long live Stalin, the King of the Reds. And I thought that maybe Siqueiros had been here, or the leader of the railroad workers, or some amazing guerrilla fighter brought down alive from the Sierras. I wondered too if I was a political prisoner of some crazy kind; maybe they'd separated me because they were afraid the Mexicans would kill me, a gringo, one of the people who stole Texas and California and New Mexico and Arizona and Oklahoma and Utah, one of the people who called them greasers, spics, beaners, and wetbacks on the cold scary other side of the border. Maybe the cop I hit had died. Maybe I fit the description of some other killer. Some fugitive who killed eight people in Nebraska and made it across the border.

And how did I get here? In the black closet, as I gazed at that sliver of light, the night played out in my mind. If I hadn't gone to the party, or if nobody had cut in when I danced with Yolanda, or if I'd said no to Manny, said, Manny, I don't want to go anywhere, if I'd gone home and read a book or made some pictures; if I hadn't seen the young girl in the crib on the Street of Hope, hadn't gone back to see her again; if I'd had some money to bribe the cops; if I'd run down the street behind the Texans; if. If, I said. If. I wondered what time it was too. What day. Where Tim was. Wondered what my mother would think if she heard I was spending my life in a Mexican prison. Wondered if I'd ever read a book again or paint a picture. And fell asleep, wedged against the wall, under the name of Stalin.

That evening, they took me out of solitary, with no explanation, and put me in another large cell with a dozen guys. I was starving now, aching with thirst, my tongue furry with hangover. The mood here was brighter, kinder, the men speaking slowly so that I could understand their Spanish. I quickly learned that nobody was fed in these jails. Food was delivered by wives and girlfriends, and when the other prisoners discovered I had neither, they shared their food with me. They told jokes. They laughed. They explained why they were there. A busdriver was arguing with his girlfriend and ran his bus into a limousine whose owner — a politician — had him arrested. Another man had beaten up his father-in-law at a family party, for coming on to some woman in the kitchen. A third had stolen some shirts from a market and tried to sell them to buy a dress for his *mujer*. When I told my story about the whorehouse, they laughed and slapped each other and handed me some water. I was one of them: another crazy bastard fucked up by women.

They told more stories. They made jokes. They talked about Ratón Macias and Toluco López. They sang mournful ballads. They slept. In the morning, I was moved one final time, outside to have my picture taken on the steps of the jail (it appeared in *El Universal*, where an "l" was dropped off my name and I was described as being of Arabic descent) and then into a van with grilled windows. With four other men I was taken through side streets and across wide gray avenues into the city's penitentiary at Lecumberri, a looming pile called El Palacio Negro. The Black Palace.

I was let out of the van in a courtyard, then taken to a second yard. Dark stone walls climbed above me, topped by barbed wire and guards strolling casually with rifles at the ready. No way out. I remember passing cells that were elaborately decorated with pictures of women and boxers and soccer players; men cooking at stoves; radios playing; and the endless noise of steel upon steel. There seemed to be thousands of men here, some walking independently down aisles, others sleeping, dozens milling around. I knew about this place from our Mexican history classes; Pancho Villa was once a prisoner here; Francisco Madero was murdered beside these walls. But this wasn't a tour; I was a prisoner.

They put me in a single cell and locked me in. There was a scab on my nose now and my ribs hurt and my teeth were a mess. But the fear had gone out of me; I stopped thinking about what had happened and what might happen and focused on what *was* happening. And for the moment I was safe. Even death had lost its scary power. I knew now that if a bullet had slammed into my skull and killed me, I'd have felt nothing. But I was alive. The pain I felt was the proof.

Four days later, when they finally came to take me out, Tim Lee was waiting in an outer office of the prison with a young Mexican lawyer.

They'd been trying for days to find me in the labyrinth of the prison system. Tim saw my picture in *El Universal*, flanked by cops on the steps of the *delegación* as I was being moved to the Black Palace. He got the name of a lawyer from one of the teachers and used his own money for bail. A functionary in the prison office told me to report to the Black Palace once a week to sign in while the judicial process ran its course. The lawyer explained to the official that he was representing me, signed some papers, gave me his card, and left. Then I took a deep breath and walked out into the sunshine. There were groups of shawled women waiting beside the walls to deliver food to their men. They had helped feed me too.

I'm sorry, I said.

Forget it, Tim said. I just wish we'd found you sooner.

I'm glad you found me at all.

We hailed a cab.

Where to?

I laughed.

A bath, I said.

Nothing else? Not even a meal?

No, I said, not even a beer.

I went to bed in a darkened room and tried to pray to the Virgin of Guadalupe. The words would not come. I tossed in the dark for a long time, seeing sweaty men hammering at each other with bricks. Then I turned on the light and slept for eighteen hours.

8

WITH MY FRIENDS, even with Tim, I affected a casual, blasé attitude about what had happened in the night on the Calle de la Esperanza. But for weeks, I woke up sweating, my dreams instantly wiped away, leaving only an ashy residue of dread. The memory of the whistling bullets, the fight with the bricks and the whimpering young woman, the sense of being lost in a system of steel rooms in which strangers spoke a language I did not know: all were woven into me.

I didn't blame the drunken party that had preceded the trip to Calle de la Esperanza; by then, drinking was so natural it would have been like placing blame on the act of breathing. I continued going to the student parties, still got drunk. I didn't blame Mexico either. Too many Mexicans had been kind to me. But *something* had happened. I was trying to discover some deeper principle, some rule of adult life that accounted for accident and choice and human ugliness. Not some divine commandment. Not some vague or blurry generalization. Something that I had learned from experience. After all, an artist should know how to do that; an artist shouldn't just learn what other artists have learned; he should know what *his* life has taught him. But when I made drawings of the events of that evening they all came out looking like comic strips. They were simpleminded and crude, mere diagrams of place and action and consequences. They seemed glimpsed from the outside, instead of felt from the inside.

Because of that failure, and my dissatisfaction, I started to write. I filled pages with accounts of what had happened, telling the story, layering it with dread and fear, trying for what Hemingway called *the real thing, the sequence of motion and fact that made the emotion.* I might get fact into a drawing or painting, but how could I get *motion?* I could get both in writing. And as I wrote more, my passion for painting faded.

There was another reason for this shift: money. Or the lack of it. Drinking at some Saturday-night party, or hanging out between classes at MCC, I could swagger in front of other students about what happened in jail, as proof of a macho ability to survive. I couldn't swagger about money. Like all the other veterans, I was receiving $110 a month. From that I had to pay for tuition, room, board, and expenses. After Christmas, Tim and I moved with two other students into a large apartment off the Avenida Ejército Nacional; that cut the rent to $25 each. But I was also paying back Tim for the money he'd laid out for bail, and I had to make monthly payments to the Mexican lawyer as the case dragged on in legal hearings. I couldn't write home for money. In 1955 my mother had given birth to my brother Joe, and with six kids in the house in Brooklyn, there was no money to spare. Besides, I was a man now (or so I thought), and a man didn't borrow money from his mother. I could borrow books from the Benjamin Franklin Library. I couldn't borrow brushes, paint, or canvas. In the second quarter, I decided not to take an oil painting class and enrolled in a writing class instead.

I did have enough money for a trip to Acapulco, sharing the expenses with four other students to ride down through the wild mountains of Guerrero, where bandits still practiced their craft. After miles of twisting roads through gorges and tropical valleys, we came around a bend and the great curving bay of Acapulco lay before us. Mountains dove sharply to the sea, with tiny white buildings set along their ridges among palms and thick green foliage. The beach looked like a white scythe, touched by the great expanse of cobalt blue water that moved off to touch the darker blue line of the sky. The light was as bright and clear as Matisse.

One of the guys in the car had been there before, and he explained about the morning beach and the afternoon beach, the Caleta and the Caletilla, how one was sunny until noon and then was abruptly plunged into shadow when the sun moved behind the mountains. The white mansion on the edge of the cliff: that was John Wayne's house. He had a Mexican wife and lived here between pictures. And that lavender palace, out beyond the Duke's, out there on the Quebrada, past where the divers plunged into the advancing tides: that belonged to Dolores del Rio.

A beer popped. We were sitting under a straw-roofed *palapa* on the morning beach, the car parked on a cobblestoned street, hawkers selling rum drinks in coconut shells, and an argument briefly raged about which of Mexico's two greatest female stars was more beautiful, Maria Felix or Dolores del Rio. I said there was no contest about pure beauty. Dolores del Rio's perfect oval face, her high cheekbones, the slope of her brow: she was like a Renaissance painting, man. That's the problem, somebody said. She's *too* beautiful. You'd spend your time just *looking* at her; you wouldn't want to fuck her. And someone else said, But you never get to fuck Maria Felix, either; she fucks *you*.

We had no money for the tourist hotels, of course, but we found a place on the beach south of the city where we could rent hammocks tied to palm trees for one peso a night. That beach is gone now, devoured long ago by the Pierre Marqués Hotel, but no place in my memory remains more beautiful. In the evenings, we sat on driftwood and drank beer and laughed and told lies and listened to the fishermen play guitars around an open fire. The Mexicans were friendly, amazed at the crazy gringos who were down there with them on *la playa*. The Mexicans were humble, illiterate, generous, decent; they shared food with us and beer and taught us the words of songs and talked about *las mujeres*, about women gone off and women arriving, about women full of betrayal and women full of trust. I remember gently rocking into sleep under the stars, more stars than I'd seen since Fox Lair Camp, stars forming clouds and clusters, shapes and patterns, dwarfing us all. And then waking in the dawn to the quiet lapping of surf and the arrival of the orange ball of the sun while fishermen dragged dead sharks onto the sand.

On the last day, drinking in the afternoon, I went walking north upon the beach, out beyond the point of the Playa Caletilla. At the foot of a cliff, I lay down on the empty sand and fell asleep. When I woke up, the sky was darkening into dusk. And off to the right a young woman in a one-piece yellow bathing suit was sitting on a towel staring out to sea toward the Isla la Roqueta. Her tightly braided pigtail hung down her back, pointing at the towel. I sat there for a while, brushing the sand off my back, looking at her smooth dark skin. My own skin was reddening from the sun. My mouth felt sour from drinking. She and I were the only people in sight. I stood up and walked slowly toward the surf, angling toward her. She turned to look at me. She was about eighteen, with a long nose and an upper lip dark with down. I saw that she'd been crying.

Are you all right? I said.

She turned away, wiping at her eyes with her forearm.

¿Está bien? I said.

I squatted beside her and touched her hand. She pulled away and then started talking very quickly in sobbing Spanish, something about the *novio* — her boyfriend — and her father, who was so cruel, and how her life was over. I didn't understand the details, but she was full of anger and despair and heartbroken tears. And then she fell against me, her body wracking with sobs, and I put my arm around her and held her tight and whispered to her in English, Don't worry, don't worry, murmured, It'll be all right, murmured, Go ahead and cry, just cry, baby, just cry. Until the sobs ended, and my chest was wet with her tears, and she was still, the warmth of her body entering mine as the sun went down.

We held each other for a long time, whispering, exchanging names, Pedro, Yolanda, the surf growling and pulling and growling, buoys dinging in the dark. I kissed her. She kissed me back. I lifted the pigtail and kissed the nape of her neck. She touched my chest and stomach and discovered my erection. I played with her breasts through the wired bra of the bathing suit and then moved her zipper down and took a lush pliant breast in my hand and a hard nipple in my mouth in the Pacific night, as her hand moved inside my bathing suit. Yolanda. At the foot of the cliff where Dolores del Rio gazed at mirrors. Yolanda, excited and writhing and then suddenly weeping again, withdrawing her hand, pulling away, as I heard what she heard: distant feminine voices calling on the dark beach.

Yo-laaaanda. ¿Dónde estás? Yolandaaaa.

And she was up, panicky, tucking breasts inside the bathing suit, zippering it up in back.

Mañana, I said. *Aquí en la playa. Exactamente aquí.*

Sí, sí, she whispered. *Mañana, en la tarde. Aquí en la playa. . . .* Tomorrow afternoon, here on the beach.

She hurried off in the dark toward the town and the faceless disembodied voices of her keepers, her sisters or aunts or mother. I plunged into the surf. The next day I went back to the spot but she was not there. And that night we all piled into the car to return to Mexico City.

9

MY CASE dragged on, month after month. I would go to a hearing, answer questions, be given another date, then pay the lawyer what I could. I kept taking drawing classes but couldn't afford the painting workshops; I started writing short stories and poetry. In the last week of each month, the VA money virtually all gone, I was eating sandwiches made of hard rolls and slices of raw onion. For the first time, I started smoking cigarettes, dark-papered Negritos, four cents a pack, to help me across the hunger; I became an instant addict. There was one more drunken party and a fight with a young Mexican student. I was in the kitchen when it started, and I hit him hard and he went down in a pile of broken glasses and there was blood everywhere. I thought he was dead. He wasn't, but I hid for a few days, afraid the police would come and get me. And then in May, the school term was over and I knew I had to leave.

I decided to jump bail and try to make it back to New York. Tim stayed behind, to work for a degree, while I shared a ride with a guy from Buffalo who was heading home. As we approached the border, I was certain that my name must be on some list. I would show my visa to the Mexican border guards and they'd see my name and start to arrest me. I rehearsed escapes: sprinting across the bridge, leaping into the shallow waters of the Rio Grande. In my mind, I heard the cracking of shots. I heard bullets whistling. I saw men fighting with bricks to possess the body of a frightened woman.

When we reached the bridge, my heart was pounding, my hands were wet. But there was no list. The guard took my visa and waved us across. The dream of Mexico-as-Paris was over. In Brownsville, we stopped for gas and I had a cold bottle of Lone Star. I looked back at Mexico, relieved and free, but overwhelmed with an almost intolerable sadness.

10

HOME AGAIN in New York, after nine months away, I quickly fell into the earnest rhythms of the 1950s. Necessity was the goad; I needed to eat and get on with my life. I again worked for Ernie Waivada in the advertising agency. I spent a year at Pratt, studying design. I took a small flat on the Lower East Side. After work or school, I went drinking. I wrote a little and painted less.

On one level, the track was clear. *Learn a trade and you'll never go hungry,* my father said. Graphic design was a trade, like plumbing or carpentry. If I mastered it, I would never go hungry. But in truth I was hesitant about moving down the track. In magazines like *Graphis*, I saw the cold elegant layouts of Swiss designers and studied the bolder work of the Americans. Some of them offered more than the example of craft; they promised a vision based on order, the reduction of chaos to a small neat space. But in the art galleries, I finally saw the actual work of Kline and Pollock, de Kooning and Motherwell, stood close to their ferociously confident canvases. There was nothing cold about their disorderly art and nothing small. They had the size and boldness of the Mexican muralists but were free of their preaching. I was drawn to the physicality of their paintings, the almost athletic swagger of the brushwork. But at the same time, their work seemed beyond me, their vision too heroic. After this, where could painting go? Where could *I* go?

Writing remained only a perhaps. In my flat off Second Avenue, or in small dark bars, I filled notebooks with questions about art, politics, my own chaotic ambitions. Sometimes, late at night in the flat, I typed these notes on an old upright Royal I'd bought in a secondhand store and put them in file folders. I tried short stories in the Hemingway manner, more variations on what had happened to me in Mexico, even poems, transcribed from fragments scribbled in bars. But it seemed an arrogant ambition to be a writer, in a world where Hemingway and Faulkner still lived. *Who do you think you are?* some collective voice from the Neighborhood called to me. *Who the hell do you think you are?* Besides, in bars at night, or at Pratt, or at my part-time drawing table at the agency, I could still show off with a drawing. And if there was even small applause, I felt that I never could completely abandon the dream of art; the prospect filled me with dread. For a long time, I'd based my identity on the hope of being an artist; to give up now might cast me into the shapeless fog that had engulfed me after the failure at Regis.

I carried these confusions with me through a New York terrain now permanently changed by the tubular Ben Shahn forests of television antennas and highways leading to the faceless Levittowns of Long Island. The Neighborhood, its streets already emptied at night by television, began to reel from departures to the new suburbs and the arrival of the plague of heroin. When I visited 378, my mother talked for the first time about danger. Standing with my father at the bar in Rattigan's, a full member now of the fraternity, I heard about muggings and overdoses. A few men died of cirrhosis from drinking, but compared to a needle in the arm, that was an honorable death. In tenements where once there was nothing much worth stealing, people now started locking their doors.

The Eisenhower era bragged of the good life for all, a time of abundance and prosperity, but it didn't touch the Neighborhood. The prosperous were gone to the suburbs; among those who stayed, money was still short. Everywhere in the city, factories were closing. Globe Lighting, where my father worked, moved from the Neighborhood to Flushing and then, later, to Georgia. In the daytime, there were more men in the bars, drinking in silence and defeat. The city was changing: gradually, almost imperceptibly in some ways, drastically in others. The world wasn't as solid as it seemed when I was twelve; and that was a confusion. You spent twenty years learning how to live in the world and then it changed on you. I'd wake up some mornings and buy the newspapers and think: What the fuck is going on?

Even in bars, some things were not discussed. McCarthy was gone, but the Great Fear had left its mark. At the agency, I was on the fringe of the world of organization men, men in gray flannel suits, men who talked about the new cult of motivation research, of inner-directed and outer-directed human beings, of lonely crowds and hidden persuaders. They shrugged when you mentioned politics (although Ernie Waivada, from Massachusetts, was a huge fan of Senator Jack Kennedy). Politics was trouble. Get the money. Or get the women. Luscious secretaries from Lynbrook. Sweet fearful file clerks from the Bronx. Noble defenders of the holy hymen. But willing to please at the midnight hour. I knew I couldn't exist for long in that world. Painter or writer, I needed to be free.

In the fall of 1957, Jack Kerouac's *On the Road* was published by Viking Press, with a glowing review by Gilbert Milstein in the *New York Times*. I went out and bought a copy, that first hardcover edition with the famous photograph of Kerouac in rough lumberjack shirt and silver crucifix, his eyes brooding, his square fullback's face unshaven. I read the first sentence on the subway to Brooklyn — *I first met Dean not long after my wife and I split up* — and was carried away. I read in the *Village Voice* (then three years old and full of surprises) that Kerouac was due in town for a Friday-night jazz-poetry reading at the Village Vanguard. I paid the admission, went downstairs, ordered vodka at the bar, and for almost two hours listened to Kerouac, Gregory Corso, and some other poets. I was thrilled with the flow of words and the counterpoint of jazz, and gazed through the cigarette smoke at the remote women, who all seemed dressed in black, cool as ice sculpture. Kerouac was older than I expected (he was then thirty-five) and punched out with his hands to punctuate his lines. At the end, the audience cheered. I wanted to talk to him, about Mexico and Pensacola and jail and women; but I couldn't get close to him when it was over; he was engulfed by reporters and photographers and the cool dark women. That year, Jack Kerouac was a star.

I went back upstairs into Seventh Avenue and wandered east to University Place and eased into the packed bar of the Cedar Street Tavern, where the painters did their drinking. For an hour, I drank beer alone at the bar and listened to an argument over centerfielders. Suddenly Kerouac and his friends came in, shouldering through the door, then merging with the other drinkers, three deep at the bar. Kerouac edged in beside me. He was drunk. He threw some crumpled bills on the bar. I said hello. He looked at me in a suspicious, bleary way and nodded. The others were crowding in, yelling, Jack, Jack, and he was passing beers and whiskeys to them, and Jack, Jack, he bought more, always polite, but his eyes scared, a twitch in his face and a sour smell coming off him in the packed bar that reminded me of the morning odor of my father in the bed at 378. Soon he was ranting about Jesus and nirvana and Moloch and bennies, then lapsing into what sounded like Shakespeare but probably wasn't, because his friends all laughed. Under the combination of Kerouac and beer, my brain was scrambling. The painters gave him a who-the-fuck-is-*this*-guy? look. College girls were coming over. A bearded painter bumped him on the way to the bathroom and Corso let out a wail of protest at the ceiling and the bartender looked nervous and soon I was drunk too.

When I woke up the next day I wrote a poem in Beat cadences, mixing up the Village Vanguard and Brooklyn College and some bad Kenneth Rexroth, and a few days later submitted it (and another) to the Pratt literary magazine. I was astonished when both were accepted. They were my first published writings.

The confusions deepened. After Mexico, I wanted to have enough money to forget about money and chose graphic design as the way to make a living. But the life of a designer demanded steadiness and clarity, qualities in complete opposition to my image of the wild, free-living, hard-drinking bohemian. Design also required submission to the whole buttoned-down gray-flanneled organization-man strictures of the Fifties. I didn't want to do that. I didn't want to accept those tame codes. But in an important way, I used them as a license. Drinking became the medium of my revolt against the era of Eisenhower. Drinking was a refusal to play the conformist game, a denial of the stupid rules of a bloodless national ethos.

I expressed that revolt at huge weekend parties, crowded with students, where cases of beer were jammed into ice-packed bathtubs, and big strapping young women from the Midwest slipped into dark back rooms with various guys, including me. The music pounded, Little Richard meeting Miles Davis, Elvis contending with Coltrane, while the half-digested words of painter-guru Hans Hofmann collided with the lyrics of Lawrence Ferlinghetti. There were wild nights in Manhattan too, stops at The Cedars or the Five Spot, with complete strangers saying, Let's go, man, big party right up the street. And they were right: hard loud whiskey-drinking beer-swilling parties were part of every New York weekend. I remember being at two big parties at The Club on Eighth Street, where I first saw Helen Frankenthaler, beautiful in a camel's-hair coat, de Kooning and Kline cracking wise to each other, women grabbing men by the balls while dancing, men dancing with men and women kissing women. I was at another party in the packed sweaty railroad flat that belonged to the poet LeRoi Jones, who had started publishing a little magazine called *Yugen* and talked to me in a smoky hallway about *Krazy Kat*. I spent one glorious night drinking at The Cedars with Franz Kline, talking about women and cartoonists and London art schools. He took three of us to his studio at four in the morning, where he showed us his big new paintings, which were in color. He looked sad and fatalistic when he told us that the dealers hated them. They wanted him to keep doing "Franz Klines," in his trademarked black and white. I thought: Just like executives at some big company dictating to a man from the advertising agency.

That night, I backed up a few feet from the bohemian ideal. Kline, Pollock, de Kooning all had starved for twenty years before selling any paintings. And here was Kline, at the peak of his fame, worried that the galleries would stop taking the pictures *he* wanted to make. What if I spent twenty years and nobody ever bought a painting? I thought of Laura's bitterness, posing nude to pay rent, then vanishing into obscurity. I knew from Brooklyn that poverty wasn't noble; it was a humiliation. If I chose the freedom of the painter's life, who would pay the bills? I suddenly understood that I wasn't painting because I was afraid to discover that I had no talent. If I had no talent, I would starve.

That was the late 1950s for me. Torn between the desire for personal freedom and the need for a proud security, I postponed the choice. I drank a lot. I got laid a lot. In most of the minor ways, I had a very good time.

11

MUCH OF MY MEMORY of those years is blurred, because drinking was now slicing holes in my consciousness. I never thought of myself as a drunk; I was, I thought, like many others — a *drinker*. I certainly didn't think I was an alcoholic. But I was already having trouble on the morning after remembering the details of the night before. It didn't seem to matter; everybody else was doing the same thing. We made little jokes about having a great time last night — I *think*. And we'd begun to reach for the hair of the dog.

To save money, I began sharing my seventy-five-dollar-a-month apartment with Jake Conaboy and Bill Powers, friends from the Neighborhood. Jake talked about becoming an actor, Billy also wanted to be a painter, and was studying at Pratt. At some point, Richie Kelly came over too, took a flat next door, enrolled at the School of Visual Arts, and began training as an illustrator. Drinking cases of beer, we talked passionately about art, movies, women; we read Pound, Eliot, Camus. We took our own paths through the city but always ended up at the flat on Ninth Street and Second Avenue, in the heart of the Ukrainian blocks of the Lower East Side. And we threw our own parties, mixing together people from the Neighborhood, Pratt, and our jobs. They were noisy, sweating, roaring affairs, full of music, dancing, and booze. In the mornings after, we had to call people to find out what we'd done. For a while, I was going out with a beautiful slender Dominican girl who was saddened in equal proportions by an early divorce and the smallness of her breasts. Jake started going with her sister. We laughed so hard on some nights that my body ached; today I can't remember a single line that was said.

At some point after Tim Lee returned from Mexico, with a degree in philosophy, Billy found his own apartment and Tim took his place in the third bedroom. A few weeks later, Tom McMahon, my English teacher from Pratt, came home from England, where he'd taken a degree at Oxford. He soon had us organized into a weekly study group. Under McMahon's direction, we went through Hemingway's *A Farewell to Arms*; a number of stories in *Understanding Fiction*, an anthology-textbook edited by Cleanth Brooks and Robert Penn Warren, parts of Ezra Pound's *ABC of Reading*; George Orwell's essay "Politics and the English Language." We spent weeks reading and analyzing Aristotle's *Ethics*. All of us joined in, making jokes, sipping beers, smoking too many cigarettes. McMahon had a tough, unsatisfied intelligence; he was brilliant in seeing the stylistic surface of a piece of writing but he also challenged every sentimentality, every glib remark, and insisted that we dig and dig until we'd discovered the moral core of the work. Every session left a permanent mark on my own later writing. McMahon truly taught me how to read. No small thing.

Reading drew me deeper into writing, but I showed almost nobody my own Hemingwayesque short stories, Orwellian essays, Kerouackian poems. Surely they couldn't survive the scrutiny we were applying to Hemingway or Orwell, and McMahon made clear his contempt for the rambling formless style of the Beats. So I practiced writing as a secret vice and kept working as an apprentice designer. I had money now for oil and canvas, but I did no painting at all.

A droll, balding artist's agent named Tom Fortune used to come around to the agency, trying to sell the work of his illustrators. One day he asked me if I did any freelancing. No, I said, but I could use the money. Did I think I could handle the layout and pasteups for a magazine?

What kind of magazine? I asked.

Well, Fortune said, it's a little unusual.

What do you mean, unusual?

It's in Greek.

Within a few weeks I had my first freelance client, a Greek magazine called *Atlantis*. The office was on Twenty-third Street off Tenth Avenue. The editor was an enthusiastic young guy named Jimmy Vlasto, whose father, Solon G. Vlasto, was publisher of the magazine and a daily newspaper of the same name. Obviously, I couldn't read Greek, but neither could Jimmy. We had a great time together, laying out stories about Melina Mercouri or holidays on Mykonos, hoping that the leftover text jumped into the correct place in the back of the book. Sometimes it did. Often it didn't. And at some point I suggested to Jimmy that maybe we should start running some articles in English.

At least *we* can have something to read in the magazine, I said. At least the fucking jumps will be in the right place.

Why not? Jimmy said. The old man'll go nuts but what the hell.

I had been following the career of a sensational young middleweight named Jose Torres. He'd won a silver medal in the 1956 Olympics in Melbourne, had won a number of Golden Gloves, AAU, and All-Army championships, and after seven victories in seven pro fights, he was the new hero of the city's growing Puerto Rican population. He was managed by Cus D'Amato and trained in the Gramercy Gym, five blocks from where I lived on Ninth Street. At a bar near the magazine, I said to Jimmy Vlasto that I'd love to write about Torres. Jimmy was also a fight fan. Go ahead, he said.

A few days later, I found Torres at the gym. Almost immediately, we became friends. He was not only a great boxer but one of the smartest people I'd ever met. I hung around with him, did some interviews, then went home and wrote the article. I needed three days to get it right, and with anxious heart I delivered it the following week to Jimmy Vlasto. I sat in a tattered easy chair while Jimmy read the piece. When he was finished, he smiled.

I love this, he said, his voice surprised. Fuck! Let's run it!
Great.
But listen, he said, I can only pay you twenty-five bucks.
I'll take it, I said.

That was it. I was a professional writer. Billy Powers took some photographs, I laid out the pages, and ten days later my first journalism was in print. I was runny with excitement. But when I went to Twenty-third Street to pick up copies of the issue, a glum Jimmy told me that his father wanted to see both of us in his office. We went upstairs to the wood-paneled room with its muted lamps and photographs of Solon G. Vlasto in the company of presidents and archbishops. The old man stared at the two of us from behind his immense desk.

Let me ask you something, he said, in his thick Greek accent.

Silence. Then his eyes flashed.

How come, he said, in a *Grik* magazine, is a story about a Puerto Rican boxer, written by an *Irish* guy, in *English?*

A pause.

And then Jimmy burst out with an immortal line: *The young Greeks love him!*

Mr. Vlasto looked at us in a deadpan way, thought about this, looked suddenly as if he understood that the world was passing him by, and then sighed.

Next time, he said, find a Grik boxer.

Then, dismissing us, he leaned forward to examine a sheet covered with the logic of numbers.

12

THROUGH ALL OF this time, I was devouring newspapers. There were still seven of them in New York then, and I read them all, like a predator. My favorite was the *Post.* Convinced by my work for *Atlantis* that I had some talent as a writer, I wrote a few letters to the editor, and two of them were printed. One of them took up the entire letters section, a long screed about "my generation," and for a week there were letters of reaction. This got me on some obscure radio show, which led to an invitation to appear on the "Long John Nebel Show," then the biggest thing on all-night radio. Nebel liked me and kept inviting me back to his free-form discussion of Martians, politics, extraterrestrials, comics, and the Beats. I kept writing letters to the editor of the *Post.*

Meanwhile, I was earning more money. I left the agency to open a studio with a partner across the street from the Art Brown art supply store on West Forty-sixth Street. I thought this would give me freedom, the sense of being my own man. But the harder I worked, the more letterheads I designed, the more business cards and employee publications I pasted up, the more I felt trapped. I had an obligation to my partner to pay my share of the studio expenses. My work was getting better, which brought me *more* work, and longer hours. The office building was deserted and foreboding at night, so I pitched a drawing table in the kitchen of the flat on Ninth Street and often worked until dawn, pasting up catalogs and listening to Symphony Sid on the radio, with the volume turned down so the other guys could sleep. On some nights, Coltrane sounded like an accusation: Why are you doing that work when you could be as free as I am?

Those long grinding hours entitled me to a reward. Of course. On weekends, or on nights when I was not making mechanicals for a doll catalog or designing an ad for a machine operator, I went drinking. Sometimes I was with my Dominican *flaquita*. Sometimes with Tim, Jake, and Billy. Sometimes alone. I had money in my pocket, cash I'd earned with hard hours. In the downtown bars, in joints like Birdland, I could afford any drink in the house.

We were in the roaring midst of a New Year's Eve party on Ninth Street when someone arrived with great news.

It's over! Castro wins! Batista left Havana.

You're shitting me, Jake said.

No, man, it's on the radio.

We turned on the radio and the news was true. The bearded young revolutionary had triumphed over the cruel dictator. His army was moving down from the Sierra Maestra in triumph. All night long, we played *charangas* by Orquesta Aragón and listened to bulletins and drank beer and talked bad Spanish and cheered for Fidel. Nobody knew that he was a communist. He was young, from *our* time. He hadn't just talked about change, he'd *done* something. Faced with grinding oppression and a lack of freedom, Fidel had picked up a rifle and gone to the mountains. We cheered because we thought the good guys had won. After a while, I took my Dominican girl next door to a friend's small apartment and fucked her wildly, the two of us yelling together in the revolutionary solidarity of Spanish. Then we went back to the party and danced some more, full of exultation, beer, and joy. Later, when the party was over, Jake went off with one woman and Tim with another. I was alone with La Dominicana again. We made love then in my own bed. The morning arrived, as gray as hangover. I wished we could wake up in Havana.

More than ever, as Jack Kennedy made his great run for the presidency, I was reading the political columns in the newspapers, particularly in the *Post*. Since it had published several of my letters, I thought of the *Post* as *my* newspaper. In the late spring of 1960, Jimmy Wechsler, the paper's editor, published a book called *Reflections of an Angry Middle Aged Editor*. The book was a kind of situation report on American society after the fall of McCarthy; it was sometimes despairing, about race and class, but otherwise full of hope. I read it through in one night and then typed a long letter to Wechsler, agreeing with most of what he'd written, arguing with some of his remarks, singling out a chapter on journalism for my hardest criticism, implying that newspapers had no room for people like me. Working-class people. People who didn't go to Ivy League schools, young men rejected by places like Columbia. Such people, I said, might not have great formal educations but they knew about New York, the world, life. I worked hard on the letter, making three drafts. I didn't think of it as a job application. That's what it turned out to be.

A week later, a brief note arrived from Wechsler. He said he'd enjoyed my letter and agreed with about 90 percent of what I'd said. Why didn't I give him a call sometime and come down to the paper for a chat?

His secretary set up an appointment for a few days later at the *Post*. I told Tim and Jake and tried to be casual about it, but for the next few nights I had trouble sleeping. My mind was full of images from newspaper movies, all those tough fast-talking men in tumultuous city rooms, causing trouble, being brave: Bogart pressing the button to start the presses at the end of *Deadline U.S.A.*, Robert Mitchum moving through fog in a trench coat, Gregory Peck in a glorious apartment in Rome, riding with Eddie Albert to an assignment. Hemingway was there too, of course. He'd started as a reporter in Kansas City, without ever going to college. He'd put a reporter named Jake Barnes into *The Sun Also Rises*, his best novel. I couldn't imagine him writing a novel about a graphic designer.

Finally, on a late afternoon in the last week of May, I took the IRT down to the old *Post* building at 75 West Street, went in through the Washington Street entrance, and rode the elevator to the second floor. I followed a gloomy marbelized corridor around to the back and then, for the first time, stepped into the city room.

Looking for someone? a tall, bespectacled man said.

Yes. Jimmy Wechsler.

All the way in the back.

The room was more exciting to me than any movie: an organized chaos of editors shouting from desks, copyboys dashing through doors into the composing room, men and women typing at big manual typewriters, telephones ringing, the wire service tickers clattering, everyone smoking and putting butts out on the floor. I remembered the day I saw Dan Parker walking out of the *Daily Mirror* building and the newspapermen hurrying to the bars of Third Avenue. They'd all come from a place like this. But this wasn't a rag like the *Mirror*; this was the *Post*, the smartest, bravest tabloid in New York, *my* paper. All these men and women were doing work that was honorable, I thought, work that added to the ideals and intelligence of the world. I wanted desperately to be one of them.

Wechsler was a small man with a large head and thoughtful eyes. He was wearing a bowtie and suspenders. His shirtsleeves were rolled up to his elbows. He took me into his inner office and I sat beside a desk littered with newspaper clippings, magazines, letters from readers, copies of his book. While we talked, he smoked cigarettes and sipped coffee. Near the end of our chat, he leaned back in his chair and put his hands behind his head.

Have you ever thought about becoming a newspaperman? he said.

I mumbled something in reply, but I don't remember what. It must have been something like, Only all my life.

Well, Wechsler said, call me in a couple of days. Maybe I can get you a tryout around here.

At 1 A.M., on June 1, 1960, I was back in the city room, clumsily disguised as a reporter, and my life changed forever.

V

A DRINKING LIFE

Oh, I could drink a case of you, darling
And I would still be on my feet
I would still be on my feet.

   — Joni Mitchell, "A Case of You"

I read the news today oh boy . . .

   — John Lennon and Paul McCartney,
    "A Day in the Life"

1

IN HUMILITY and arrogance, I started to learn the newspaper trade. I was humbled by what I did not know, in the company of so many skilled craftsmen; I was arrogant enough to believe I could learn to do what they did. My teacher wasn't Jimmy Wechsler; for the first eighteen months I worked nights while he worked days and we seldom saw each other. He allowed me in the door, but a man named Paul Sann kept me there.

I saw him for the first time at six o'clock in the morning of my first shift at the *Post*. I had walked in that night full of fear and trembling, not knowing what to expect, carrying a copy of *Under the Volcano* to read on the subway home if they threw me out. The assistant night city editor was Ed Kosner, younger than I was by a few years. He parked me at a typewriter and asked me how much experience I had. When I told him absolutely none, he laughed and without pause explained the fundamentals. I would write on "books," four sheets of coarse copy paper separated by carbons. The carbon copies were called "dupes." In the upper left-hand corner I should type my name in lower case and then create a "slug," a short word that identified the story for editors and typesetters. The slug should reflect the subject; a political story could be slugged POLS. But if it was a story about a murder I should not slug it KILL because the men setting type would kill the story. With that simple lesson, he gave me a press release and told me to rewrite it in two paragraphs, and my career had begun.

All through the night in the sparsely manned city room, I wrote small stories based on press releases or items clipped from the early editions of the morning papers. I noticed that Kosner had Scotch-taped a single word to his own typewriter: *Focus*. I appropriated the word as my motto. My nervousness ebbed as I worked, asking myself: What does this story say? What is new? How would I tell it to someone in a saloon? *Focus*, I said to myself. *Focus*. . . . Near dawn, there was a lull as the editors discussed what they would do with all the material they now had in type. Beyond the high open windows, the sky was turning red. I walked over and gazed out and saw that we were across the street from the piers of United Fruit, whose bananas my grandfather had shipped from faraway Honduras a half-century before. I wondered if he had ever docked at this pier, ever looked up at the building that housed the *New York Post*. When I turned around, Paul Sann was walking into the city room.

He had a great walk, quick, rhythmic, taut with authority, as he moved without hellos across the city room to the fenced-off pen at the far end, where he served as executive editor. He was dressed entirely in black, with black cowboy boots, carrying the morning papers under his arm. From where I sat, I watched him go to his desk, light a Camel, take a cardboard cup of coffee from a copyboy. His face was gray, urban, Bogartian, his mouth pulled tight in a tough guy's mask, his gray hair cut short, and he wore horn-rimmed glasses which he shoved to the top of his head while reading. He immediately began poring over galleys, a thick black ebony pencil in his hand, marking some, discarding others, making a list on a yellow pad. Around seven, the other editors gathered at his desk to discuss the flow of the paper. Sann always wrote the "wood," the page-one headline (so named because for decades it had been set in wood type). Then he moved into the composing room, where the trays of metal type for each page were laid out on stone-topped tables. He was still there when my shift ended at eight and Kosner gave me a goodnight. Sann didn't talk to me that night. He didn't talk to me for weeks.

But in the weeks that followed, as I started going out on fires and murders, knocking on doors in Harlem and the Bronx at three in the morning, I came to understand that Paul Sann was the great piston of the *New York Post*. Wechsler gave the paper its liberal political soul; but Sann made it a tough ballsy tabloid. Wechsler pressed for coverage of civil rights, Cold War sanity, the reform politicians of the Democratic party; Sann was skeptical of all living beings, and leavened the political coverage with murders, fires, disasters, and gangsters. They didn't much like each other, and their conflict was discussed almost every morning after the shift ended, at the bar in the Page One, a block away from the *Post*.

One guy wants a newspaper, said Carl Pelleck, the best police reporter in the city. The other guy wants a pamphlet.

Yeah, someone else said, but without Wechsler, it has no identity, no function, no *soul*. It'll die.

Listen, it's gonna die anyway. It won't last past New Year's.

The uncertainty about the paper's future didn't bother me; I was still working at the studio, and if the newspaper did go down I wouldn't starve. But in the meantime, I'd have had the best time of my life. I just hoped it would last long enough for me to learn the trade. During my three-month tryout, I watched Sann from a distance and got to know other newspapermen up close, in the morning seminars at the Page One. I loved their talk, its cynicism and fatalism, its brilliant wordplay, as we stood at the bar and watched the stockbrokers coming up from the subways to trudge to Wall Street while we waited for the first editions to arrive. When the papers landed on the bar, the seminar would begin. This was an often brutal analysis of stories, headlines, and writing style, presided over by an immense, burly, mustached copy editor named Fred McMorrow, attended by two old pros named Gene Grove and Normand Poirier. They were funny and merciless. About my stories. About others, their works, themselves, and most of the human race.

Then one stormy morning, an hour before deadline, after I'd written a story about the eviction of a family in Brooklyn, Sann called me over. He held the galley in his hands. I was nervous, still on a tryout, still provisional.

Not bad, he said.

Thanks.

I like the part about the rain rolling down his face.

Thanks.

By the way, did this guy speak English?

No.

So how the fuck did you get all these quotes?

I speak a little Spanish, I said.

You do? How come an uneducated Brooklyn Mick like you speaks Spanish?

I went to school in Mexico for a year. On the GI Bill.

No shit?

No shit.

He lit a Camel. Then he pointed at a paragraph near the end.

You see this, he said, where you say this is a tragedy?

Yeah.

I'm taking it out. And don't you ever use the fucking word "tragedy" again. You tell what happened, and let the *reader* say it's a tragedy. If you're crying, the reader won't.

I see what you mean.

You better, he said, taking a drag on the cigarette, then sipping the black coffee. He glanced at the story again.

Maybe in another eight or nine years, you could be pretty good at this miserable trade.

Thanks, I said, and started to leave.

Oh, by the way, Paul Sann said. You're hired.

2

NATURALLY, I got drunk in celebration. The next day, I told my partner I was leaving the studio. He was furious, shouting *You've left me high and dry.* He was right, of course. But there was no going back. I'd found a life I wanted. Every day or night would be different. I would have a ringside seat at the big events of the day. I'd learn about death and life and everything in between. It was honorable work, not putting goods in pretty packages. Somehow the desire for freedom and the need for security had merged. If I worked hard, listened well, studied the masters of the craft, I'd have a trade I could practice anywhere. Even if the *Post* folded. I might never be Franz Kline in his heroic studio. But I wouldn't be a buttoned-down organization man either. I'd be a news-paperman.

After I was hired, after they gave me my first Working Press card, I brought my familiar sense of entitlement to the bar of the Page One every morning. Those mornings were free of the limits of time, and I would drink with McMorrow, Grove, Poirier, and others, while fishmongers made deliveries and the day-shift guys showed up for a morning pop before starting at ten. The Page One was the headquarters of the frater-nity, a place completely devoid of character except for the men at the bar, a way station for all the whiskey-wounded boomers of the business who passed through on their way from one town's paper to another. I loved it. I'd taken a cut in pay to work at the *Post* but I didn't care. I had enough for food, rent, and drink. Each day, after the Page One, I'd take the subway to Astor Place and walk from the station to the flat on Ninth Street, where I'd sleep off the beer, wake up and eat pasta at the Orchidia on the corner of Second Avenue before going off again to the *Post*. My byline was in the paper every day, and I couldn't wait to go to sleep so that I could wake up and do it all again. On days when I did no drinking, I often couldn't sleep, as sentences caromed around my brain and I rewrote myself and others. On such days, I often moved to the refriger-ator and found a beer.

Everybody in the business was drinking then, the lovely older woman on night rewrite, stars and editors, Murray Kempton and the copyboys. Once, when I was working days, Poirier came to me and said, How do you call in sick if you're *in?* We laughed and concocted a ludicrous story of eating a bad clam at lunch, and sure enough, at lunch hour, Poirier called in with his bad clam attack and took the rest of the day off. Another day, working overtime during some disaster in the dead of winter, I finished at noon instead of 8 A.M. and carried my exhaustion directly into the Lexington Avenue IRT, skipping the Page One. Standing in the middle of the subway car, his eyes glassy, a large black Russian-style fur hat making him seem even taller, was McMorrow. He was maintaining his balance with one finger delicately touching the roof of the subway car and he was barking, *Copy! Copyboy!* as strangers edged away from his dangerous presence.

That first newspaper Christmas, there was a staff party in the penthouse office of Dorothy Schiff, the *Post's* owner. The city editor got drunk and fell down the spiral staircase, breaking his arm. He refused to risk the hazards of a city hospital, saying *I'd rather die here at my desk.* He insisted on being taken to his home in Oyster Bay. So Poirier and I helped him to his car, both of us drunk too, and drove through the frozen night to Oyster Bay. When his wife opened the door and saw her wrecked husband and then saw us, she started shouting at us, *You bastards, you bastards, look what you've done to him, you bastards.*

One election night, Kempton was in his third-floor office, sending down his copy one sentence at a time, until it was six-thirty in the morning. The night managing editor, George Trow, asked the copyboy to ask Mr. Kempton a simple, if urgent, question: "How much more?" The copyboy ran up the back stairs to the third floor, burst into the office and said to the paper's greatest columnist: Mr. Trow wants to know, how much more? Kempton lifted his almost-completed bottle of Dewar's and said, Oh, about an inch.

After working a double shift one Friday, reporting three stories, rewriting three others, and doing captions and overlines for about fifteen photographs, I was reading galleys in the city room. At his desk, Sann was typing fast with two fingers on his Saturday page, a potpourri of news items and smart remarks called "It Happened All Over." He finished editing it with a pencil, called for a copyboy, rubbed his eyes, and then walked over to me.

Let's have a drink, you lazy Mick bastard.

We took a cab to midtown and went into a joint called the Spindletop. It was dark and fancy in a sleazy way; if it wasn't mobbed-up then the decorator had been inspired by gangster movies. Sann ordered whiskey, I asked for a beer. We talked for a while about craft and newspapers and the Boston Celtics, whose coach was his friend. Then:

You got a broad?

No.

Good, Sann said. This business is lousy on women.

I had learned that already. My lovely Dominican was gone, defeated by the hours of the newspaper trade.

But you're married, I said.

Yeah, to the greatest woman in America. But it hasn't been easy for her.

I sipped my beer, uneasy about saying anything.

She's sick now, he said.

I'm sorry to hear that.

She's *very* sick, he said, as if speaking to himself.

Then he turned and walked to the pay phone. I heard him placing a bet on the Cincinnati Reds. A few more people came into the bar, and then Ike Gellis arrived. He was the sports editor, short and stocky, Edward G. Robinson to Sann's Bogart.

Where is he? Ike said.

Phone booth.

I bet he's betting baseball. He's a fuckin' degenerate on Fridays.

Sann hung up and came straight to Gellis.

Well, well, the world's shortest Jew.

I hope you didn't bet the Reds game, Gellis said. The Giants'll kill 'em.

Shut up and drink, Sann said.

Two weeks later, early on a Friday morning, Sann's wife died of cancer. We heard the news about six A.M. Around eight, Sann arrived. He walked in his usual hurried way across the city room and went to his desk. He didn't look at galleys or dupes of stories. He started to type. He typed for more than an hour, worked the copy with a pencil, called for a copyboy, and then got up and walked out of the city room without a word.

Someone passed around a carbon of the story. It was a farewell to his wife. Tough, laconic, underwritten. He never used the word "tragedy." My friend Al Aronowitz read it and started to weep.

Oh, man, he said. Oh, man.

Aronowitz was a great reporter, a wonderful writer, and a lovely man. But he didn't drink, so I saw little of him after work. That morning he went to the Page One with me. We drank for a couple of hours in virtual silence. But the booze had no effect.

I don't know if I can work in this business, Aronowitz said. His wife dies and the first thing he does is come in and write about it.

Shut up and drink, I said.

3

 EARLY ON, I learned there were limits to the myth of the hard-drinking reporter. One Saturday night, we threw a big party in the place on Ninth Street. It lasted until dawn. I was due at the *Post* at 1 A.M. Monday. But when we woke up on Sunday afternoon, Jake and Tim and I were still full of the exuberance of the party. We bought a case of beer and started drinking again. Other people dropped in. The day rolled on, full of laughs and drinks. When I arrived at the *Post* that night, I felt sober, seeing things clearly and thinking lucidly. But I was half-drunk. I must have laughed too loud or bumped against a trash barrel too hard, attracting some notice. Then I started to type and my fingers kept hitting between keys. Finally an editor named Al Davis came over and stood above me and said, *I think you better go home.* I was mortified. Davis was part of the saloon fraternity too; he wasn't objecting to the drink but to the obvious fact that I couldn't hold it. I got up and pulled on my coat and he stepped close to me and whispered, *Don't you ever do this again.* And I didn't.

But if it was stupid to come into work carrying a package, as we said, that was no reason to stop drinking. As in most things, you needed rules of conduct. I drank in the mornings when I worked nights and at night when I worked days. When I was sent out to cover some fresh homicide, I usually went into a neighborhood bar to find people who knew the dead man or his murdered girlfriend. I talked to cops and firemen in bars and met with petty gangsters in bars. That wasn't unusual. From Brooklyn to the Bronx, the bars were the clubs of New York's many hamlets, serving as clearinghouses for news, gossip, jobs. If you were a stranger, you went to the bars to interview members of the local club. As a reporter, your duty was to always order beer and sip it very slowly.

On weekends, I went to Brooklyn to visit my father's clubs, and to see my mother, my brothers and sister. My mother was proud of my new career, dutifully buying the *Post* every day and clipping my bylined articles. She reminded me that she had bought the *Wonderland of Knowledge* with coupons from the *Post*, in the days before it became a tabloid.

You look very happy, she said.

I am, I said. I am.

In Rattigan's, there were mixed feelings about what I was doing. In that neighborhood, there were still a lot of people who thought the *Post* was edited by Joe Stalin. Their papers were the *Daily News*, whose editorials kept calling for the nuking of Peking and Moscow, and Hearst's *Daily Mirror* and *Journal-American*. The *Post* was always attacking the people held sacred by the more pious and patriotic: Cardinal Spellman, Francisco Franco, J. Edgar Hoover, and Walter Winchell.

How's it going over there, McGee? my father asked one Saturday at the bar in Rattigan's.

The *Post?* I'm having a great time, Dad.

Good. The checks are clearing, right?

Right.

He sipped his beer and nodded at Dinny Collins, a smart heavy-set man, dying of cirrhosis, who was reading the *Daily News* a few feet away.

What do you think of my stories? I said to my father.

Good, good. Very good. I just . . .

He shrugged and didn't finish the sentence.

You just what? I said.

Goddammit, I just wish you were working for the *Journal-American!*

I laughed out loud, but he didn't see anything funny.

Dad, the *Journal-American* is a rag. They make things up. I *know*. I've covered stories with their reporters, and they make up quotes and details that aren't *true*.

How do *you* know they're not true?

I told you, Dad. I've been there on a story, talking to the same people, seeing the same things. By the time their stories get in the paper they've added stuff. Lies. Bullshit.

Dinny Collins leaned over and said, Listen to the kid, Bill. I always said that *Journal-American* was a load of shit.

Especially, I said, when they interview Franco once a year, or Cardinal Spellman three times a year.

You mean they make up stuff for Spellman?

No, I said. In that case, they just print the bullshit.

Collins laughed. But my father gathered his change.

That does it, he said. I'm going to Farrell's.

Out he went. Collins was still laughing. I ordered a beer.

Don't take him seriously, Collins said. You've made him prouder than hell.

I hope you're right, Dinny, I said, on my way to a long afternoon in the bars of Brooklyn.

At about seven-thirty in the morning of July 2, 1961, in his home in Ketchum, Idaho, Ernest Hemingway put a twelve-gauge shotgun under his jaw and pulled the trigger. The news was smothered for most of the morning. I heard the first bulletin early that afternoon, while watching the Dodgers play the Phillies on television. I was shaken to the core. Hemingway was still the great bronze god of American literature, the epitome of the hard-drinking macho artist. But since the day in the navy when I'd first read Malcolm Cowley's introduction to the Viking collection of Hemingway's work, he had been one of my heroes. No other word could describe him: his writing, his life, his courage, his drinking, were all part of the heroic image. Suicide was not. Suicide, I believed at the time, was the choice of a coward.

But I had little time to mourn Hemingway or even question his motives. The telephone rang. It was Paul Sann.

Get your ass down here, he said. Hemingway knocked himself off, and I want you and Aronowitz to write a series.

The *Post* was famous for its series; one of them — in twenty-three daily installments — had ruined the career of Walter Winchell. The writers were detached from the daily routine and allowed weeks of luxurious reporting and writing on a single subject. I'd never written a series, but Al Aronowitz was a master of the form. He was five years older than I was, heavy, red-bearded, full of sly laughter and dissatisfied melancholy. In his own style, he was struggling as I had struggled over the way to live in the world. He was intoxicated by the careless freedoms of the Beats, about whom he'd written a brilliant series, and pulled in the opposite direction by the demands of a conventional life in the suburbs of New Jersey. For a few years, drinking had helped me postpone a choice; temporarily, at least, newspapers had resolved it. For Aronowitz, newspapers were not enough.

We began working that afternoon in an empty back office. Aronowitz knew almost nothing about Hemingway; I knew almost too much. So we divided the work. I stayed one installment ahead of him, laying out the newspaper clippings, the relevant passages in biographies and monographs, marking passages in Hemingway's own work that were relevant to the installment. We shared the reporting tasks, calling people all over the country who had known Hemingway. Aronowitz did most of the writing. When he finished each installment, I'd go back over the copy, filling in blanks, cutting statements that seemed ludicrous, trying to separate the myth from the facts. We finished some installments near six in the morning, two hours before the deadline.

When it was over, I knew a lot more about writing. Aronowitz was a generous man, showing me what he was doing and why, passing on his hatred of platitude and cliché. And I'd gone more deeply than ever before into Hemingway. I saw his writing mannerisms more clearly, his personal posturing. Some of it was embarrassing. But I had learned that it was possible to be a great writer and an absolute asshole at the same time. None of us then knew how terrible Hemingway's final years had been and the extent to which alcohol had contributed to his anguished decline. It was right there on the pages. I just didn't choose to see it.

There were still parties on the weekend, but the gang that came over from Brooklyn was breaking up. Richie Kelly, who lived next door, found an apartment in another part of Manhattan and started making a living at advertising art. Billy Powers moved with a young actress to an apartment in Chelsea. Tim married a beautiful woman from the Neighborhood. We all got drunk in celebration, and Jake and I decided that the newlyweds should keep the apartment. Jake moved back to Brooklyn while I moved next door. For a while, Jose Torres shared the place with me, then he got married too, and we all danced and drank at his wedding. Even Tom McMahon was leaving, to teach in Puerto Rico. There was a sense of departure and change in the air. It was as if we all had decided it was time to grow up.

At the end of 1961, Jose took me to a Christmas party on Atlantic Avenue in Brooklyn. I saw a small, lovely young Puerto Rican woman there and danced with her and asked for her phone number. Her mother was standing against a wall beside the Christmas tree, looking at me in a suspicious way, like one of the *dueñas* of Mexico. The girl gave me the number. I wrote it on a matchbook and drank some more beer and then moved on to another party. The next day, thick with hangover, I remembered the girl but couldn't find the matchbook. I called Jose, who made some calls and found out who she was. Her name was Ramona Negron. She was seventeen. I was twenty-six. I called her and we started going out. In February 1962, we were married.

4

MARRIAGE didn't end my drinking. Ramona didn't drink, but I did it for both of us. There was a lot of drinking at the wedding reception; drinking in Acapulco, where we went on our honeymoon; drinking to celebrate the birth of our first daughter, Adriene; drinking on weekends; drinking on the way home from work. We moved to an apartment in Brooklyn, and I'd drink beers with dinner and invite friends in to drink with me.

Sometimes I brought home total strangers. One afternoon I found myself drinking in Bowery dives with Richard Harris, the Irish actor, who was in town promoting his first movie, *This Sporting Life*, and researching the world of Eugene O'Neill. In the company of Bowery rummies we talked about O'Neill and *The Iceman Cometh* and about J. P. Donleavy's *The Ginger Man*, a marvelous book about an irresponsible drunk. Harris told me that he'd played the part of Sebastian Dangerfield in a Dublin production based on the Donleavy book and had even tracked down the model for the hero, a man named Gainor Christ. *That book looks like a comedy*, Harris said, *but it's a terrible fuckin' tragedy. . . .* We talked and drank, drank and talked, and I called Ramona and said I'd be home late and home we arrived much later, Harris and I roaring drunk, and I started to make hash in the small low-ceilinged basement, the baby awake now and bawling, Ramona exhausted, hash flying and sticking to the ceiling, until finally Harris wandered into the night. Ramona wept.

Behind all this were some unacceptable facts. At the newspaper, I could write about the problems, doubts, mistakes, and felonies of strangers; I didn't have to deal with myself. I certainly didn't have to look clearly at the girl I'd married.

In the most important ways, we were strangers. I knew facts about her: that she'd been born in Puerto Rico, taken to New York by her mother when she was a year old. She'd grown up in the projects on Grand Street, graduated from Washington Irving High School, spoke perfect English, and could dance the *pachanga*. But I knew nothing of her dreams, her vision of herself, her conception of the future. I never bothered to ask. In some ways, I knew more about the people in my newspaper stories than I knew about my wife.

Neither of us had a useful model for a marriage. Ramona didn't meet her father until she was fourteen; he'd broken with her mother a few months after Ramona was born. He was her mother's second husband. I met him on a trip to Puerto Rico with Ramona; he was white-haired and handsome, charming, a piano player in a nightclub, living with a fat black woman. I got the feeling that he barely remembered Ramona's mother, who was petite, fair-skinned, vain, and given to complaint.

She was a very spoiled woman, he said to me over a beer in the place where he worked. I'm glad Ramona isn't like her.

We spoke with the complicity of men. But when I told Ramona what he'd said, she laughed.

What does he know? she said. As soon as he had to feed a family, he left.

She lived through her teens without a father in the house, and then her mother married a German-American guy who did maintenance in the projects. He brought home a paycheck. He was civil. He watched a lot of television and even read some books. But he offered Ramona no clues about how she should live with the likes of me.

I had no model either. My father went to work, earned his money, found friendship and consolation in saloons. I'm sure he never asked my mother about her dreams either. The principle was clear through all my childhood: men went out and earned the money; women organized the family. Husbands were close-lipped, strong, stoic; wives were conciliatory, open, allowed to show feeling. Without thinking, I assumed the pattern. I didn't work in a factory. But I would do everything that must be done to keep bringing home the paychecks. And I had other goals now: to write novels and short stories, to master the form of magazine articles, to do everything possible within the limitations of my talent. This time I wouldn't walk away, as I had from Regis, as I had from painting. I would go as far as I could go with what I had. Or as Robert Henri had said about an art student, to be "master of such as he has."

In the small flat where we lived in Brooklyn, I didn't talk much about such desires with Ramona. She was too busy trying to become a woman and a mother. In both tasks, she was on her own.

My brother Denis was a wonderfully sweet kid, with big liquid brown eyes, broad shoulders, a wild sense of humor, and an original way of looking at the world. Once, when he was seven and struggling with the mysteries of the Catholic catechism, he was walking with my mother and embarked on a heavy theological discussion.

Mom, he said, is God everywhere?

Yes, Denis, she said. God is everywhere.

Is he in the sky?

Yes, he's in the sky.

Is he in the street?

Yes, Denis, he's in the street.

Is he in the park?

Yes, he's in the park.

Mom?

Yes?

Is he up my ass?

My mother burst into laughter.

By the time he was ten, in 1962, Denis had begun to see me as a kind of father, although I was only the big brother who had lived elsewhere for all of his young life. I didn't mind the role; I was probably a better father to Denis than I was to be a husband to Ramona. Around this time, my father had entered a crabbed, unhappy middle age; there was never enough money and always too much drinking. He beat the kids when they annoyed him or when he thought they weren't doing homework or were talking in too heavy a Brooklyn accent. Tommy was now grown up and gone and Kathleen had a group of girlfriends from school. My father didn't bother either of them. But the smaller boys were always in trouble with him, Denis most of all.

It was no surprise that Denis often turned to me for guidance and male kindness. He was an erratic student, and an unruly street kid, but in his school compositions, he showed hilarious gifts for narrative. His spelling was often atrocious. But he could certainly tell a story. I started helping him, showing him ways to develop stories, correcting his spelling, giving him books to read. When Ramona and I took our first small apartment near Prospect Park, he dropped by all the time, glad to run errands, to read some of my books, to talk about movies or comics. Ramona said she didn't mind his unannounced arrivals; she thought he was cute. I took him with me a few times to the newspaper or to the Gramercy Gym to see the fighters. One of those fighters was now my brother Brian, who at fifteen weighed about ninety pounds and was boxing in amateur tournaments, watched over by Jose and the other professionals. He had a ferocious left hook, a good chin, and a cocky style. Denis would get excited when he saw Brian sparring, upset if Brian got hit, cheering when Brian was punching; he hated to leave the place. My brother John never came to the gym. He was only a year older than Denis, a fine student with a sweet good heart. But he was shy and self-contained where Denis was direct. If Denis wanted to go with me to a gym, he asked. If he wanted to stay at my house, wherever it was at the time, he said so. John never asked.

One summer afternoon, Denis got into a fight outside the YMCA. His opponent whipped out a knife and stabbed him in the stomach. He was rushed to Methodist Hospital, where he almost died. I arrived at the hospital after he came out of the operation. His voice was weak and his lustrous brown eyes were full of fear.

Am I gonna die, Pete?

No, you're gonna be all right. The doctors said so.

I don't wanna die.

You won't.

You won't let me die, will you?

The doctors won't let you die, Denis. You'll have a pretty funny-looking scar, maybe, but you won't die.

I don't want you to die either, he said.

Okay, pal.

Be careful, all right, Pete?

Whatever you say, Denis.

I don't want anyone to die, he said, his voice drowsy.

On December 8, 1962, the printers' union struck the *New York Times*. The Publishers Association, including Dorothy Schiff of the *Post*, immediately locked arms in solidarity against the proletarian rabble and closed the other six papers. We were all locked out of our jobs. The strike and lockout went on and on, past Christmas, past New Year's, past Valentine's Day, 114 days into the spring.

That winter, I learned to write for money instead of sheer love of the trade. I worked for thirty-five dollars a week on a strike paper. I wrote two articles for the *Police Gazette* at fifty dollars each. I borrowed money. I alternated between rage and impotence, furious at the printers, even more furious at the publishers. I had a wife and a baby girl and I couldn't put money on the table. What the hell kind of man was I? What kind of husband? What kind of father? I began to think the *Post* would fold. *My* newspaper. Denis didn't want anyone to die. I didn't want a newspaper to die.

In the evenings, I stayed home more, playing with the baby, cuddling her, cooing to her. In some way, this angered Ramona. She was depressed for a long time after Adriene was born, and I knew so little about the biology and psyche of women that I took this as a personal rejection. It was as if she blamed me for the pain she'd suffered when Adriene entered the world. Her dark angers when I played with the infant infuriated me.

You're jealous of her, aren't you? I shouted one night. She's only a baby and you're jealous!

I'm *not* jealous, she shouted through tears. I just want you to love me the way you love her.

I hugged her, whispered to her, felt her tears on my face. I was ashamed of myself, at my anger, my inability to understand. But I never pushed past the surface, past the things she said to the things she most deeply felt. When she was calm again, I went to the refrigerator and opened a beer.

With the newspaper work gone, I used some of the empty time to read again, everything from Raymond Chandler to Stendhal. They took me out of the intolerable present. They presented challenges too. The weather was gray and cold, and reading novels made me want to go away again. To hole up with Ramona and the baby in some cottage in another country, where I would write stories about the things I knew and discover things I didn't. I wished I were somewhere beyond that small flat.

Because of the lack of money, I didn't see much of Jake or Tim, Bill or Richie; there was no way to meet for a drink without laying bills on the bar. I spoke by phone to Tim every day and checked in every few days with Paul Sann, to hear the latest about the contract negotiations. But I saw nobody from the newspaper; they seemed to have scattered to the winds.

Then, near the end of the strike I sold an article to the *Saturday Evening Post* for $1500, the equivalent of ten weeks' pay at the newspaper. It seemed like all the money in the world. Exuberantly, I paid off my debts and gave the landlord the rent. I brought flowers to Ramona and hugged her and told her I loved her. I bought a bag of toys for the baby. I carried home fat bags of groceries. I lugged home cases of beer and invited Richie, Jake, Billy, and Tim and his wife, Georgie, over for a party. Celebration! Victory! Drink up! A few days later, Dorothy Schiff left the Publishers Association and reopened the newspaper. I went back to work.

Don't get used to being too happy, you Irish bum, Paul Sann said when I took him for a fast drink after work. No matter what happens, he said, newspapers will always break your fucking heart.

5

SOMETHING SHIFTED in me during that strike. I thought I'd work at the newspaper forever. The strike made me understand that in the newspaper trade, there was no such thing as forever. When I went back to work, I kept doing freelance work on the side and found I had some talent for magazine articles. Checks arrived. We moved to a larger apartment in Brooklyn. But Ramona seemed no happier. When I got excited about selling a piece, she seemed uneasy. When the telephone kept ringing, with calls from friends, press agents, editors, she grew annoyed. When I came home drunk, a few days a week, she was disgusted. She was getting to know me better than I knew her.

As spring turned into summer, the old dream of the expatriate life blossomed again, ripening over beers on Saturday afternoons. Who wanted to live here, back in the bourgeois safety of Brooklyn? New York was a great city and I had a job I loved. But there was a world out there. One night, over dinner at home, I started talking to Ramona about going to Spain. Maybe we could live in Barcelona. The city where Orwell once carried a rifle, city of Dalí and Picasso and Gaudi, city that held out to the end in defense of the Spanish Republic. Barcelona! I'd write articles for the *Saturday Evening Post* and we'd live well on the money and to hell with newspapers. She looked at me as if I were drunk.

What's the matter with New York? she said.

It's not Spain, I said.

But you've never been to Spain.

I know, I said. But I don't want to see it when I'm sixty.

She shook her head in a dubious way, tempering my enthusiasm. For weeks, I avoided any more discussion. I worked hard at the paper. I won some awards. But the notion of another escape wouldn't go away. Over beers one night, I talked about Spain to Tim, suggesting that he could go too and work with me on the research while mastering the magazine form himself. He was very smart and a good clean writer; if I could do it, he could do it. At first, Tim was skeptical. But we looked in the *New York Times* at the rate of the peseta against the dollar, bought Spanish newspapers in Times Square, and saw that we could live more cheaply than in New York. We were young, we could afford it; when would we have such a chance again? A strange, inevitable momentum took over. It was like going to Mexico again. There was nothing complicated about it. We'd just go, live in a foreign land, walk where Hemingway walked, speak Spanish and eat olives and brown ourselves on the Costa Brava. We'd support ourselves with writing.

Ramona and Tim's wife, Georgie, were at first skeptical. We addressed every argument, speaking with the authority of men who had lived in at least one foreign land. I showed Ramona travel articles from magazines, picture books from the library. I sold some more articles to magazines and built up a small bank account. Slowly it must have seemed like a great romantic adventure to the women too. By July we were ready to leave.

You're going *where?* Paul Sann said, when I came to his desk to give him the news.

To Spain.

He chuckled in a sardonic way.

Vaya con Dios, pal, he said. I wish I'd done that when I was your age. I wish I'd done it last fucking month.

For me, Sann's words were the only blessing I needed. It was settled. We were going to Spain.

The night before we left, Tim and I went to a farewell dinner with the other guys who'd made the journey with us across the river from Brooklyn: Bill Powers, Richie Kelly, Jake Conaboy. After the delicious beer-swilling years on Ninth Street, we'd gone our own ways. Billy had become an excellent photographer and layout man, Richie an illustrator and designer, while Jake returned to Brooklyn and the safety of the Transit Authority. But I wanted to believe it didn't matter where we'd gone or where we were going; we came from a common place, had shared a glorious time, and we'd be friends for life.

The five of us took a table in the back room of a bar on the corner of Twenty-third Street and Second Avenue. Jake had been drinking before we arrived; whiskey always broke him out of his shyness, and he was hilarious and profane. We ate hamburgers and drank a lot of beer and whiskey. I talked about the glories of the Spain I'd never seen, urging the others to come and join us. I must have made it seem like another subway ride from Brooklyn. We made jokes. We talked about politics. Billy and I argued the comparative merits of Matisse and Bonnard with the passion once reserved for centerfielders. Around midnight, Jake's chin was resting on his chest. We talked on, drinking more, laughing louder. Richie's eyes were glassy, a thin smile on his lips. Then it was time to go. Tim called for a check. Richie stared hard at me, the smile gone, his eyes suddenly deeper under his brows.

You're really an arrogant bastard, you know, he said.

I laughed, thinking he was joking.

I know, I know, I said. Worse than Charles de Gaulle.

Richie didn't smile. The muscles in his jaw tensed.

Nobody wants to tell you this, he said. But it's true. You treat the rest of us like inferiors. You think if you say it should be done, then we should do it.

You're serious, aren't you?

Tim said, Hey, Richie, cool it.

Yeah, Billy said. This is a good-bye dinner, not a grand jury.

Richie ignored them.

All this shit about Spain, this Hemingway crap, Richie said. You're saying you can do things and we don't have the balls to do them. You think you're hot shit. You pose like a good guy but you always think of yourself first. You always did. Even back in Brooklyn.

It was as if he wanted to start a fight. But we were leaving the following day for Spain. I didn't want to arrive in Barcelona with a split lip or a broken hand. I backed up.

Richie, I said, all I ever tried to be with you was a friend. If I got lucky, I wanted you and the others to share it.

Yeah, so you could feel like you were better than us.

Fuck it, I said, standing up abruptly. Come on, Tim. Let's go to Spain.

I threw some money on the table and turned for the door.

Look at the truth, Richie said. Look at the truth . . .

Tim and I took a cab back to Brooklyn. We were staying at our parents' places for this final night, because Ramona, Adriene, and Georgie had gone on ahead to Barcelona to find an apartment. Tim and I had closed our apartments, stored or sold our possessions, settled most of our accounts. All the way to Brooklyn, I was furious with Richie. Some things I had taken for granted: he was my friend, he shared the sentimental solidarity of the group, he cheered for my small successes as I would cheer for his. Tonight, he had pissed all over those assumptions. It was as if he wanted me to feel his accusations all the way to Spain. And though I was hurt and wounded, another thought slid through my mind: Maybe he was right.

There was one final wrenching scene. A few weeks before the date we chose to leave for Barcelona, I had told my brother Denis that I was moving to Europe. He was twelve, reading newspapers every day, but this news item hadn't seemed to register. I didn't press it. But I worried about him all the time. I had no idea how long we'd be gone. I might make a career as a writer in Europe and stay forever. I could be back in six months. I was sure Brian and John would be all right, but Denis had a fragility that made him seem more vulnerable. I hoped the Neighborhood wouldn't trap him.

On that last morning at 378, Denis and the other kids hung around the kitchen while I washed and ate breakfast. My father was there, dim and silent. My mother busied herself with dishes and tea. Fragments of Richie's indictment kept drilling into me, combining with hangover to make me feel disconnected from the others. Finally, I packed my last small bag, said my good-byes, and went downstairs.

Suddenly, Denis came running after me, in tears.

Please don't go, Pete, please don't go, he kept saying. Please, please . . .

Denis, I have to go. My wife is there. My baby . . .

Please, he said, please stay.

Tim was waiting with a cab in front of Rattigan's and came over to help me with my bags. But Denis was bawling now, holding on to my arm with both hands, saying *Don't go, Pete, don't go, don't go, don't go, pleaaaase* . . .

Until I had to shake him off.

Send me some stories, Denis . . .

And he ran off then, his face a blur of tears, swinging his hands wildly in the air. He was the last person I saw on Seventh Avenue as the cab pulled away to take us to the airport.

6

THUS BEGAN too many years of wandering, of arrivals and departures, sitting in airport waiting rooms, packing and unpacking books, smoking strange brands of cigarettes, speaking badly the languages of strangers, and drinking their beer and whiskey. Ramona and I exhausted the dream of Spain in six months. We lived in Dublin then, and later in Rome and San Juan and Mexico City, Laguna Beach and Washington, D.C., and saw a lot of other places in between. Each time, we made the long circle home, back to New York.

The moves had a pattern, of course. I would return to New York, settle in, start working at my trade. Then routine would assert itself. The routine of work. The routine of family. The multiple routines of the drinking life. These couldn't be separated. If I wrote a good column for the newspaper, I'd go to a bar and celebrate; if I wrote a poor column, I would drink away my regret. Then I'd go home, another dinner missed, another chance to play with the children gone, and in the morning, hung over, thick-tongued, and thick-fingered, I'd attempt through my disgust to make amends. That was a routine too.

Self-disgust would spread its stain to everything: my work, the apartment, New York itself, until I felt I had to get out of there or die trying. Then I'd grant myself the vision of the Great Good Place. Most of the time, it was a place where I heard more vowels than consonants, with bougainvillea spilling down whitewashed walls, fountains playing in the blaze of noon. In the Great Good Place I would work like a monk on my writing. I would be a good husband and father. I would be far from the tumult of saloons, their giddy excitements and sly flatteries. Once the vision took hold, we were soon packing the books. I never did find the Great Good Place.

During this long odyssey, there were some wonderful times. There were long sunny afternoons reading Lorca and drinking beer in huge one-quart glasses in the Plaza Real in Barcelona. There was one glorious evening in Rome with the raffish producer Joe Levine at the Hotel Excelsior, the two of us drinking brandy, with women all around us, musicians playing violins, Joe's wife pleading with him to go to bed. I spent hours drinking rum with John Wayne during an interview on his converted navy minesweeper in Barcelona bay; I hated his politics and liked him. In Brussels, I wandered into some huge beerhall with a reporter from UPI and got hilariously drunk with some touring American paratroopers. There were good beery times in pubs in Dublin and England, the barmaids flirting, the regulars grumpy at this Yank invasion, then offering the pack of Senior Service and buying a round in the fraternity of drink. I drank beer with the mariachis in the Plaza Garibaldi. I got loaded in a place on the Calle Cristo in Old San Juan, singing along with Los Panchos on the jukebox. I got pleasantly smashed watching the sun crash into the Pacific in Laguna. Sometimes Ramona came with me; most of the time she stayed home.

She was with me in Belfast when my father came home in the late fall of 1963. She was a background figure, her dark skin exotic to the pale Irish, but existing only as an appendage to the visiting Yank. On that trip, my father held center stage.

He had been away since the early 1930s. I paid for his ticket because I wanted to see him there in the home place, on the streets that had shaped him. For a week, we wandered those streets on foot or by cab, stopping at the Rock Bar, the Beehive, the Long Bar, snug dark wool-smelling refuges from the gray hard drizzle of the North. He found old friends among the living and heard reports about the dead. He sang his songs, making the young Irish laugh with "Paddy McGinty's Goat." A few times, confronted with some old photograph of soccer teams, he turned away in grief. He had less tolerance now for drink; he got drunk quicker. But he was back where he'd started from and he was happy to be there.

One evening, all of us were in my cousin Frankie Bennett's house, sipping warm lager, dressing to go out for dinner. My father was at his brother Frank's house and we were to meet him later. The television was on in the small living room. The Bennett kids were leaping over couches and rolling around on chairs. A coal fire glowed in the hearth. I was full of a buzzing warmth, part beer, part Ireland.

And then the first bulletin broke.

. . . President Kennedy has been shot in Dallas.

What? I turned to the black-and-white screen of the television set. What did he say? *What the fuck did he just say?* And he said it again, grave, British, restrained: Shots had been fired at the presidential motorcade in Dallas. *No.* The president was being rushed to Parkland Hospital. *No. No.* The room hushed, Frankie moved in from the kitchen, Ramona came downstairs, holding Adriene in her arms, Frankie's wife stood by the set. *No.* I popped open a can of warm lager. A sitcom was playing. Then the announcer was back.

John Fitzgerald Kennedy, the president of the United States, is dead.

I let out a wail, a deep scary banshee wail, primitive and wounded, mariachi wail, Hank Williams wail, full of fury and pain. *Nonono-nononononononononoNo.* Ramona hugged me, weeping, and kids were wailing now, and Frankie was there beside me, but I turned, ashamed of my pain and my weeping, and rushed into the night. All through the Catholic neighborhood called Andersonstown, doors were opening and slamming and more wails came roaring at the sky, wails without words, full of pagan furies as old as bogs. I wanted to find my father, wanted to hug him and have him hug me.

But I careened around dark streets, in the midst of the wailing. I saw a man punch at a tree. I saw a stout woman fall down in a sitting position on a doorstep, bawling. I ran and ran, trying to burn out my grief, my anger, my consciousness. I found myself on the Shankill Road, main avenue of the Protestant district. It was no different there. Kennedy wasn't a mere Catholic, he was *Irish*, Kennedy was *ours*, he was one of our sons, our Jack, and they have killed him. Along the Shankill, I saw a man kicking a garbage can over and over again in primitive rage. I saw three young women heading somewhere, dissolved in tears. I saw another man sitting on a curb, his body heaving in gigantic sobs.

Somehow, I found my way back to Falls Road in the Catholic area. My head was full of imagined demons, the gunmen of Dallas: Cuban exiles and right-wing bastards, Klansmen and Mob guys. But when I finally reached the Rock Bar I only wanted to find my father. He was upstairs where the television set was, sitting at a table beside a retired IRA man with three fingers missing from his right hand. I went to the table and the old IRA man said, *It's a terrible bloody thing, lad, terrible, terrible . . .* My father stood up, his face a ruin. We held each other tight, saying nothing, and then the bar was packed and we drank whiskey and there was a documentary playing about Kennedy's trip to Ireland in May, smiling and laughing and amused, promising at the airport to come back in the springtime and I thought of the line from Yeats, *What made us think that he could comb gray hair?*

After that, there was almost nothing left except whiskey. Until the screen filled with Kennedy's face, superimposed on the American flag, while "The Star-Spangled Banner" played on the sound track. And then the whole bar crowd was standing, old men and young, men with hard whiskey-raw Belfast faces, and all of them were saluting and so was my father and so was I. That night in Belfast, we both discovered how much we were Americans.

7

THE PRICE I was paying was very large, but for a long time, nobody presented me with the check. Our daughter, Deirdre, was conceived in Spain and born in St. Vincent's Hospital in Manhattan while I was thick with hangover at the 1964 Democratic Convention in Atlantic City. Norman Mailer drove me to the hospital. I was full of joy when I saw her. But Ramona never forgave my absence.

When Deirdre was less than a year old, we moved to Mexico. That was always the basic model for the Great Good Place, and going back was like an act of contrition. I was heartily sorry for the way I'd messed up in 1956. But now a decade had gone by. I thought I could repair the great rupture by going back. A Mexican friend confirmed what I suspected: the Mexican police were not looking for me, my name was on no list, my offenses were lost in the human avalanche of newer felonies. I signed a small contract to write my first book and we left New York. We sublet a friend's apartment a block from the Pasco de la Reforma in the Colonia Roma. For a week, I had dreams about men bashing each other with bricks. But then Carta Blanca gave me dreamless sleep. I talked to Ramona about staying this time for good.

During the summer of 1965, Deirdre got sick with salmonella, probably from unpasteurized milk. She had begun talking before the infection; then all her talking stopped. Most of the time she looked stunned. I was heartsick, blaming myself for taking a child to Mexico, risking her life in my own self-absorbed quest for the Great Good Place. Work stopped; I never did write the book I'd gone there to write. One night I sat in the dark, listening to Cuco Sánchez, and got drunk alone, while Ramona and the children slept. A few days later, a letter arrived from Paul Sann. He wanted to know if I had any interest in going back to work at the *Post*. If so, he was looking for a columnist.

Once more, we packed up and went home.

We took an apartment in a new building off Union Square. Before we could furnish the place, I announced to Ramona that we'd have a house-warming party. The place was jammed. Tim, Billy, and Jake came from the Neighborhood; dozens arrived from the *Post*, including Sann, who looked around at his stumbling wards and left early. Among the late arrivals were Mick Jagger and Keith Richards, friends of Al Aronowitz, in town for their first appearances in America. They were full of charm, smoking joints and drinking vodka, but they too left around the midnight hour. At some point, huge Fred McMorrow lurched into the bedroom where Deirdre was sleeping, fell across a glass-topped table, and smashed it. He didn't even scratch himself. But Deirdre woke up screaming and Ramona was again in tears.

That poor little girl, Ramona said, over and over again. That poor little girl . . .

Deirdre was still not talking. One Saturday afternoon, she was walking with me on Fourteenth Street and suddenly fell on her bottom. I picked her up, and she looked at me with those brown eyes but didn't cry. I stood her up and she walked a few more feet and plopped down again. Ramona told me she'd been doing the same thing in the apartment.

I was alarmed. The next day, while I went to work at the newspaper, Ramona took Deirdre to St. Vincent's.

She called me at the paper, her voice trembling.

They're trying to tell me that she's retarded, Ramona said.

What?

Retarded! It must be from that milk in Mexico! From the goddamned salmonella.

I rushed to the hospital and looked at our little girl. I didn't believe the analysis. Her eyes were bright. She recognized me. She laughed when I played with her. Ramona and I found another doctor and insisted that more tests be made. That girl, we told each other, is not retarded.

We were right. There was a chemical imbalance in her brain, possibly brought on by the salmonella. But it could be cured with medication. There was no permanent damage. She was definitely not retarded. It was my time to cry, in thanks, in remorse. When Deirdre did resume talking, it was in complete sentences.

Through all this time, I managed to do a lot of work: newspaper columns, magazine articles, a first novel. The novel was a thriller. I learned the form without risking an examination of myself. If I was able to function, to get the work done, there was no reason to worry about drinking. It was part of living, one of the rewards.

But many things were being lost on the erratic journey. A shipment to some foreign place would never arrive, and notebooks, drawings, precious books, would vanish forever. I lost all my apprentice work. I lost my collection of original cartoons. A book of childhood photographs disappeared. I still didn't realize that I was also losing my way.

8

I STARTED writing a column for the *Post* in October 1965. On the day after Christmas Paul Sann sent me to Vietnam, where in the first week I got drunk with some Marine Corps officers in Da Nang and heard them predict a dirty, bloody, perhaps endless war.

What can be done to pacify Vietnam? I asked one of them, late at night, with the artillery rumbling in the distance.

Pave it, he said, and stared at his drink.

In Vietnam, I discovered that I wasn't afraid of death. The stoic codes of Hemingway served me better at thirty than they did at eighteen. Maybe Hemingway was an asshole, but he knew something about war and fear. In Vietnam, my only worry was about my daughters: If something happened to me, who would bring them up? Who would get them through school? Ramona would survive, but I fretted about the girls. Sometimes I worried in the same way about Denis. I got rid of these imaginings by drinking on the roof of the Caravelle with the other correspondents, watching the distant orange flashes of the artillery, or by inspecting the pain and fear of uniformed strangers. I wrote often to Ramona, and I had the city desk call her each time a dispatch arrived, to tell her I was all right. I did not mention the bars of Tu Do Street or the long afternoon when I wandered drunkenly into Cholon and two boys bumped me and slipped my watch off my wrist. I did not mention the anxious turmoil in my stomach, the product of the conflict between my aching desire to stay for the duration of the war and my responsibilities as husband and father. I wanted to stay, to make this my war. I did not say this to Ramona.

Every few days I went out to the killing fields, saw boys dying, heard the anguished screams of the wounded. A tourist at the war. Then I came back to Saigon and wrote my pieces in the room at the hotel and took them down to the post office for shipment to the *Post*. Afterward, wanting to stay and needing to go, wishing I were single and missing my children, I wandered through the bars of Tu Do Street, listening to Aretha and the Stones, talking to the perfumed women in their tight *ao dais*. They were all very young, but their faces were hardening and they had no stories they were proud to tell. The sensuality of the war, its *erotic* demands, urged me toward sex with them; but I was afraid of disease, of having my money stolen, of ending up in some humiliating public mess. I got drunk instead.

When I came home, there was a new outpost in my personal geography. Normand Poirier had discovered a saloon on Christopher Street called the Lion's Head. In the beginning, the Head had a square three-sided bar, with dart boards on several walls and no jukebox. The location, a few steps from the Sheridan Square station of the Seventh Avenue IRT, was perfect for newspapermen from the *Post*, the *Times*, and the *Herald Tribune;* the *Village Voice* was then cramped into a few tight rooms upstairs; and within a few weeks of its opening, the joint was a roaring success.

I don't think many New York bars ever had such a glorious mixture of newspapermen, painters, musicians, seamen, ex-communists, priests and nuns, athletes, stockbrokers, politicians, and folksingers, bound together in the leveling democracy of drink. On any given night, the Clancy Brothers would take over the large round table in the back room and the place would be loud with "The Leaving of Liverpool" and "Eileen Aroon" and "The West's Awake." Everybody joined in the singing, drinking waterfalls of beer, emptying bottles of whiskey, full of laughter and noise and a sense that I can only describe as joy.

It was as if we'd all been looking for the same Great Good Place and created it here. Not in some foreign land but in the West Village. I was soon one of the regulars, there every night, and sometimes every day. In the growing chaos of the Sixties, the Head became one of the metronomes of my life, as regulating as the deadlines for my column. It was also the place in which everything was forgiven. Lose your job? Betrayed by your wife? Throw up on your shoes? Great: have a drink on us.

In addition, the Head provided a refuge from the more self-righteous fashions of the Sixties. Few of us did drugs. Not many were true fans of rock and roll. Almost all of us hated the war and despised Lyndon Johnson, but we did not slide off stools to join protest marches. We honored those who did. I covered all the great antiwar demonstrations in Washington and New York; but marching just wasn't our style. In my columns, I defended "the kids" from the onslaught of cops and FBI men; but nobody from the Head was likely to join SDS or send money to the Black Panthers. I felt I was part of the Sixties and separate from them, sometimes a participant, more often a mere witness. My writing was altered by the fury and despair I saw in the ghetto riots. But it was Vietnam that inflamed the deepest emotions in my work and in the lives of millions. Vietnam was the focus for all public passion, the one great binder of generations. I don't think any of us hated America; we wanted the war to end because we loved America. We wanted justice and baseball too.

As the Sixties moved on, as the Head became my local Great Good Place, my marriage to Ramona was disintegrating. Once, in Rome, where I went off each day to try writing in the cafés of the Via Veneto, Ramona had asked me for a divorce. I was, in my invincible stupidity, stunned.

What do you mean, a *divorce?*

I mean I can't live like this anymore, she said.

How do you want to live?

In a house. With a room for each of the girls, with a backyard, with a husband who comes home every night and has dinner.

I can't promise you that kind of life, I said.

I know, she said, and started weeping. I know, I know, I know.

That small crisis was healed with sweet talk and promises. But I began to imagine a life without her. I didn't want that; I still believed that we would be together for the rest of our lives. After all, my mother had gone through much worse with my father, and *they* were still together all these years later. In my erratic way, I tried to be better. I'd come home three evenings in a row, find a baby-sitter, take Ramona to a movie. Then I would miss dinner, call with some excuse about meeting a source or doing an interview, and try to remember the excuse in the morning. By 1967, Ramona was immune to my words.

You say things, she said one Sunday morning. You don't mean them. They're just words.

I make a living with words, I said. We eat because of my words. My words pay the rent.

I mean the words you say to me. Not the words you say in the newspaper.

Her disdain was clear. As I did after Richie cut into me on the night before I left for Barcelona, I saw the possibility that she was speaking the truth. Instead of accepting that possibility and bringing my life into line with my words, I turned her complaint around. I convinced myself that the problem wasn't my neglect of her; it was her neglect of me. I would drop into the Head and have strangers praise some column I'd written. Letters about my columns poured into the newspaper. Most days, Paul Sann thought I was doing swell. But when I reached home for dinner, Ramona never said a word. She had stopped reading the *Post*. Instead of trying to earn her respect, I luxuriated in the delicious emotional state of feeling hurt.

If my work was ignored at home (I reasoned), then I had a license to go where it was appreciated: the Lion's Head. Sometimes we hired a baby-sitter and I took Ramona with me; but the combination of drinking, machismo, intellectual bullshitting, and flattery seemed to repel her. She was sober and, after a while, I wasn't. I remember some very good times; her memories are surely different.

9

THERE WAS ONE final move, one last attempt at repair. I heard about an apartment in Brooklyn, a few doors down from 471 Fourteenth Street, the lost sunny paradise of the first six years of my life. Maybe the girls could play under the elm trees as I did so long ago. Maybe we could go on long green summer walks in Prospect Park and in winter I could stand with them in a bright white meadow and together we would eat snow, as I had that time when I was a child. Maybe I could leave behind the life of the Head, the slippery delusions of Manhattan, and begin to make something more solid, back here where I'd begun my life. In our marriage now, we were living on maybe.

So we moved to Brooklyn, into what was called a parlor floor and basement. On the first day, I led the girls through the iron gate under the stoop and showed them their room to the left and the kitchen beyond it and then took them into the yard. A few doors away was the yard of 471, but when I looked for the great tree of my childhood, it was gone.

For a while, we were happy. I cut down on drinking, stayed away from the Head, worked hard. The children asked me to tell them stories or draw pictures of alligators and elephants. People came to visit. Jose Torres stopped by once a week to talk about his own writing, which he was doing now for *El Diario* and then for the *Post*. My brothers came around, sometimes alone, sometimes with friends. We had barbecues in the yard. We drank beer. My father rang the bell on his way to Farrell's and occasionally I went with him. He didn't care for Ramona, but he liked the children. They loved him to sing "Paddy McGinty's Goat." So did the younger crowd at Farrell's, the fans of Mick Jagger and John Lennon.

But the Sixties were remorseless in their power. There were drugs everywhere, and my brothers were not immune. When he was sixteen, Denis came by one night and he was stoned. In tears and remorse, he explained that he'd been doing pills and reefer. I arranged for him to go to Ireland and work for a while on a farm owned by Patty Clancy of the Clancy Brothers. Driving him to the airport, I remembered his brown

wounded eyes on the day I went to Spain; now those same shy eyes
looked at me as he went off to a kind of exile of his own.

I'll be good, he said. I'll make you proud of me.

I know you will.

I'll write you letters.

Write stories too.

Off he went. But if Denis saved his life in Ireland, when he returned,
his friends were already dying, some in Vietnam, too many from drugs.
In 1969, Denis, along with Brian and John, put together a group that was
going to the great rock festival in Woodstock. Ramona asked me if she
could go with them.

I need to have some fun, too, she said. You've had plenty of fun.

Where will you stay? Are there hotels or inns?

I don't know, she said. I'll stay where they stay.

And I stay home with the kids?

Well, yeah . . .

Okay, I said. Go ahead. You need some fun too.

So they all moved off to one of the great hedonistic festivals of the
Sixties and I stayed home to mind the girls. They liked this, because I
cooked each meal following recipes from a cookbook. I told them stories.
I drew a lot of pictures. But while Ramona moved through the rains,
drugs, and music of Woodstock, I was thinking about the grieving drizzle
at the heart of our marriage. In a way, Ramona was now having the years
that she'd lost when she married me at eighteen and had two children
very quickly. At night, with the children asleep, I watched the television
coverage of Woodstock and imagined her lost in the vast rain-drowned
crowd.

After Woodstock, the sense of unravelment returned to our marriage,
more powerfully than ever. She seemed to be moving through a different
landscape than the one I inhabited. There were visible signs of it: the
music playing steadily, *her* music, not mine; no answers to my calls from
the newspaper; eyes that made no contact. More and more, I cooked
dinner while the laundry piled up and beds went unmade. There was an
arctic chill in the marriage bed.

I found consolation once more in the Head. The pattern resumed,
the phone calls with excuses, the amiable lies. At the bar, I could believe
that my life was a delight. When the talk turned to women, I assumed
the mask of the stoic. Sometimes, hurting from hangover, I wondered
whether my Lion's Head friends were really my friends, whether they
put up with me because of my personal qualities or because I wrote a

newspaper column. The unspoken question was usually dissolved in vodka and laughter. I often got very drunk and then lurched into Sheridan Square to find a taxi that would bring me to Brooklyn, to the street where I was a boy with yellow hair. One time I came home drunk at three in the morning, made a mistake, went up the stoop of the house next door and climbed in the window. Two men were in bed together and started screaming in terror. I thought this was hilarious when I was told about it the next day. But the actual incident doesn't exist in my memory; all I have is the version of the story told by others. That and the sense of shame that morning after when I tried to imagine what I looked like to those frightened men.

Ramona and I now had only the common ground of the children. One night, drunk again, I came home, opened the outer gate beneath the stoop and lurched into the inner door, smashing the window. In my hand I had two roses I'd bought from a flower seller in the Lion's Head, one for Adriene, the other for Deirdre. I stepped over the broken glass and turned left into their bedroom. They'd awakened with the crash and there, suddenly, was their father. Their eyes were wide in fright or apprehension. I handed each of them a rose and told them I loved them. I did — but I'd broken too many things. It was time for me to go.

When we separated at last, I rented a basement apartment in a friend's brownstone at the far end of Park Slope. The children could walk along the parkside to visit me; I could easily visit them. We went to Coney Island together, to block parties, to museums, as I played the new role of the Sunday father. The girls were delighted with the attention. They were baffled and confused about the fact that I was no longer living with them.

When are you coming home, Daddy? Adriene asked one day.

I don't know, baby.

I want you to come home, Daddy.

We'll see.

Almost all our talks ended this way. Deirdre was too young to understand; but Adriene understood very well that something terrible had happened to her life. After dropping them at home, I would walk slowly back to my place, loaded with misery. Sometimes, I walked it off. Other times, I reached for the easy solace of a bar.

In most ways, I felt an immense relief. It was no longer necessary to concoct lies if I wanted to stay up all night drinking. There were fewer evasions. The strained tension of life with Ramona was replaced with a correct civility. I realized finally that I could no longer escape to that elusive Great Good Place; it didn't exist. I did more drinking than ever, sometimes alone, but I felt better about myself in the morning. I started reading fiction again and writing more carefully. At the Lion's Head now, I even had the freedom to go home with women.

Then I started an affair with precisely the wrong woman for me. She was lovely, kind, smart, sensual, and rich. She was also a drinker. Soon we were parked together at the bar of the Lion's Head. We were drinking at a table in Elaine's (for she was an Uptown Girl). We were drinking at parties or traveling south to drink at some friend's plantation. We got drunk a lot. And the drinking led to scenes, jealousies, anguished telephone calls, a variety of stupidities, not all of them mine. Doors were slammed. In the purple spirit of melodrama, all sudden departures were made in the dead of night.

This went on for almost a year. That year, I wrote a movie script that was filmed in Spain. We got drunk a lot in Almería, where all the spaghetti westerns were staged, and one night, coming to the defense of one drunken actor, I knocked out another actor and thought I'd killed him. My Uptown Girl had already gone home. I soon followed her, moved in for a few days, then fled to Brooklyn. There was one final angry night, both of us sodden after two days of drinking. The details are lost. But words were hurled in cruelty. There were curses and tears. And I was gone for good.

The next afternoon, I was alone in the Lion's Head, reading the *New York Times* and sipping beer. I had no column to write and that was usually the best of days. Don Schlenck, the day bartender, was down at the far end, reading the *Post* and eating lunch. I looked up in the gloomy silence and peered out through the barred windows that opened at ground level to Christopher Street. I could see human legs going by. Two pairs of women's legs. A man in jeans. A man in a gray suit. A man with a woman. Faceless. Without histories. Hurrying along. And then snow began to fall.

I guess God doesn't want me to go home today, I said.

Didn't you hear? God is dead. It says so in your own paper.

Don't believe everything you read in a paper, Schlenck, I said.

I picked up my change and walked out into the storm. I walked downtown, block after block, as the swirling snow obliterated the edges of buildings. The snow-bright streets looked as innocent as childhood, and I wanted to walk somewhere with my girls. But I couldn't even do that. A few months earlier, Ramona had made her own trip to Mexico, to work for a degree at the University of the Americas, and she had taken the children with her. I was in New York, alone in the snow; they were in Puebla. And I was sick of myself. Sick of drinking. Sick of the routines of my life. At City Hall, my hair and coat fat with snow, I hurried down into the subway and went home. In the basement apartment in Park Slope, I took the telephone off the hook and slept.

10

I MET Shirley MacLaine in Rome in 1966 at a party thrown by the producer Joe Levine. We talked and had a few laughs before she went off to another table. I saw her again during Bobby Kennedy's last campaign in California. She was with her husband, Steve Parker, who lived in Tokyo. That night I ended up at her house in Encino, drinking whiskey at the bar in the living room with Steve and Shirley, talking politics until three in the morning. She was funny. She was intelligent. She was passionate about the problems of the world. She never talked about movies. I liked her very much.

A year after I separated from Ramona, Shirley published her first book, a charming memoir called *Don't Fall Off the Mountain*. Reading it, I discovered that we shared one common childhood passion: Bomba the Jungle Boy. One night she came into Elaine's with some friends and stopped at my table to say hello. I mentioned Bomba. She sat down.

The only book I could never find, I said, was *Bomba at the Giant Cataract*.

He had eye trouble too? she said.

I laughed.

Do you want a drink? I said.

I'm not here to ride horses, she said.

A month later, we went to England together, where she was working on a television series, and moved into a large rented house near Windsor Castle. I kept writing my newspaper column, shipping it from various places in Europe. Before we met, I'd started writing movie scripts to supplement my newspaper habit; with her, I learned much about the craft, about putting people on stage, establishing conflict, using action to show character. But I was still drinking. I didn't often get drunk. In her world, most people simply didn't drink the way I'd learned to drink; they would soon be out of the business. But I did drink steadily, easing the tension created by meeting so many new people, adjusting to a relationship in which I was not the principal.

Shirley never mentioned the drinking to me. Her father was a hard drinker too, and like me she'd grown up in the hard-drinking Fifties. But there was an indirect scrutiny. Sometimes in conversation she'd dismiss an actor or director as a drunk. If she saw a scene in a movie, or read a script where a character succumbs to another because of drunkenness, she'd shake her head. *It's a cheat*, she'd say. *It's using the drink instead of forcing the painful choice.* As an actress she was relentless in trying to get to the core of human character and discovering human weakness. *Why does he do these things?* she'd say about a character in a script. *What hurt him? What warped him? What does he want, and what's preventing him from getting it?*

When she was off at work one morning, I was sitting at my typewriter, gazing at the gardens of England, and began applying those questions to myself. I couldn't accept my own answers.

Back in New York, I started to work harder than ever before on movie scripts and magazine articles and columns. Necessity drove me: I needed the money. After they returned from Mexico; Ramona and I had agreed to place the girls in a boarding school, to give them some steadiness and structure while she tried to sort out her life. This arrangement wasn't intended to be permanent; I bought a big house in Park Slope in Brooklyn, full of vague plans about getting custody of the children and having them live there with me and Shirley. This was absurd, of course; Shirley was an old Broadway gypsy, an itinerant who lived where the work was. She did help me set up the house. But she kept her apartment in Manhattan. She was never going to live among the burghers of Brooklyn.

A year went by, then another. Ramona and I were divorced in an amicable way. She found another man to live with and tried for a while to be a photographer. But the children remained in boarding school in Switzerland. Sometimes I paid for Ramona to visit them. I visited them myself three or four times during the school year, laden down with gifts, wrote them long letters, spoke to them by telephone. They came home to stay with me at Christmas and Easter and across the summers. But then it would be time for them to leave and I'd be full of sorrow and grieving guilt. I wanted them with me all the time, but Shirley made clear to me that she wasn't going to be part of a household that included Adriene and Deirdre.

I have no talent for that, she said. I would be terrible at it. It would be a mess.

The girls resented her, blaming her for the breakup with Ramona, which wasn't her fault at all, seeing her as the person who was keeping them from her father, which was true.

I want to come home to stay for good, Adriene said to me one evening in the big house in Brooklyn. I want to live in my own room. I want to be with you, Daddy. Please. Please.

Her words drilled into me. But I felt paralyzed. Instead of making a decision, choosing my children over a woman, I postponed the choice. Off they went again to the airport, Adriene in tears, Deirdre sullen. I went back to the empty house, choked with remorse, and drank until I slept. There were too many versions of this same scene.

In addition to vodka, I used movement and traveling to prevent too much brooding. When good parts for women began drying up in the movies, Shirley created a nightclub act, singing and dancing and cracking wise. I admired the power of her will, her refusal to simply end her career that early, the way in which she whipped herself into physical shape, driving herself harder than any athlete. I traveled a lot with the show, back and forth to California, to Las Vegas and Canada and Florida. In 1972, Shirley got involved in the presidential campaign of George McGovern, which I covered; that also put us on the road, checking in and out of hotel rooms, making long-distance calls to friends and children and family. Sometimes I would stay behind in New York and return to the Head and get drunk in the old style. Sometimes I would retreat to the Brooklyn house and get drunk in its empty rooms. Then I'd be gone again, following my star. Most of the time, when I was away, my brothers Denis and John lived in the house, watering the plants, reading the books, throwing parties. They loved the place. But it never felt like a home to me. I didn't want to look at the rooms where the girls stayed on their holidays. I didn't want to imagine domestic scenes that could not become real.

As the months passed, I began to notice odd little signs of deterioration. Typing a column or a script, I would misspell simple words, not just once, but eight or nine times. Sometimes my fingers felt like gloves filled with water and typing was a plodding effort of physical labor. My hands trembled too, and there were odd twitches in my legs, little spasms of protest, or I'd wake up with no feeling in my legs. I shook off most of these signals. I was just getting older, I told myself. I'm thirty-seven, and that makes me older than most of the ballplayers and all of the prize-fighters. Hell, even the police lieutenants are younger than I am. But on a few clear-eyed mornings I knew that my body was sending me a message. I just wasn't ready to hear it.

Besides, I was also having a good time. There were parties to attend, political fund-raisers, movie premieres. Shirley sampled my world too. One St. Patrick's night, we piled into a car with five uniformed firemen, all of us drinking, and went over the bridge to Brooklyn. That night, Shirley became the first woman ever served at the bar at Farrell's, a personal triumph that was discussed for months in the Neighborhood. She sampled hot dogs at Coney Island and clams at Sheep's Head Bay. She came with me on some nights to the Lion's Head, to stand at the bar, talking politics, or to listen to the singing in the big table in the back room. But these were usually mere excursions. We ended up at Elaine's or at her apartment. She never got drunk. But now she was drinking even less, watching her weight to stay in dancing trim. I was drinking more.

11

IN THE POLITICAL YEAR of 1972, I'd begun to hang out in a new saloon on Fifty-second Street. It was called Jimmy's and was located in the building a few doors from 21 that had once been occupied by Toots Shor's famous joint. Shor's old circular bar was still there, and for a while the place had a kind of forced magic. Two of Mayor John Lindsay's former aides — Sid Davidoff and Dick Aurelio — owned the place, and they helped attract a core crowd of newspapermen and politicians. A wonderful guy named Doug Ireland was a regular, a pilgrim from the Lion's Head; he was a political operator who wanted to write. Some other members of the downtown crowd found their way to the circular bar, but the place was no substitute for the Head. There were no Clancy Brothers singing at tables, no old communists, nobody from the Lincoln Brigade, no seamen or poets. That was the year of George McGovern and the Watergate burglary; Nixon was triumphant; human beings were still dying in Vietnam. The binding element of the regular Jimmy's crowd was politics.

As I stood at the bar of Jimmy's one December night, while Shirley was playing in Vegas, I talked with passion about Nixon and the Watergate burglary, making epigrams, telling jokes, repeating lines that had gotten laughs from others. Suddenly, hearing myself repeat lines I'd used in other places, I began to feel oddly detached. I was *there;* but I was also looking at myself being there. Part of this eerie feeling came from living with Shirley. From her, I had learned much about the way actors worked, the mechanisms they used to become other people, the small signs and tags that they offered to display emotions they might not feel. That night, for the first time, I began to feel that I was performing my life instead of living it.

The feeling haunted me for days. The girls were home for Christmas and I brought them to see my mother and father, who had moved from 378 to a new flat in Bay Ridge. But as Adriene and Deirdre ate dinner and accepted presents that were not to be opened until Christmas, I wondered if I was *being* their father or *playing* their father. Was I truly being the thoughtful son with my mother, the loving admirer of my father, or was I just playing a role? I wanted all four of them, children and parents, to love me. But I felt as if my lines were calculated, not spontaneous. They might love the person I was presenting to them. But that person might not be me.

A few nights later, Denis came to visit me in the Brooklyn house. He was in college now. We sat in the living room, drinking beer from cans, while the lights of the Christmas tree bubbled and danced. The children were asleep in their rooms on the top floor.

I'm gonna try and do it, he said. I mean, really become a writer.

I waved at the bookshelves.

You have to read all of them, I said. They'll teach you everything. The more you read, the more you'll know about writing. Look at the way a guy writes a paragraph and try to break it down. If the guy makes you cry or laugh, analyze how he did it. . . .

I stopped. Was I speaking genuinely, or was this some unwritten script I was performing? Was I being generous to this good, talented kid or playing the wise older brother? In some peculiar way, did I need him to need me? Was I being real or playing a role? I didn't know. I drank some more beer and talked about Nixon.

On New Year's Eve, Jimmy's tossed a party. Shirley was back from Vegas, and we went early in the evening and sat at the crowded bar with Doug Ireland. Everybody was drinking. Doug was witty. We exchanged lines. But once more, I felt as if I were shooting the scene with a camera from across the bar. At one point, as I lit a cigarette, I noticed that my hand was trembling and wondered if that was in the camera shot. Other people came in and I saw myself embracing them, heard my voice wishing them well. I saw Doug's head fall forward, then jerk up. He recovered with a funny line. It was New Year's Eve. We were supposed to be having a good time. Look: There were balloons. There were funny hats. There were noisemakers. Charlie? Bring me a vodka and tonic, will you please?

I was in the men's room when I thought about Adriene and Deirdre. I wanted to be with them in the house in Brooklyn. I wanted to sit in the living room with them and hug them and tell them stories. I wanted to heal some of the wounds I'd cut into them. If this was a play, I wanted a better script.

Back at the bar, I sipped my drink and held Shirley's hand. Then the band started playing. A group of gangsters came in with a group of women in beehive hairdos. The gangsters smoked cigars, the women chewed gum. They sat down front, with waiters bowing to them. All played their parts to perfection. Then the star of the evening came on. *Ladies and gennnulman, the one and only . . . Buddy Greco!* The singer was perfectly groomed and perfectly dressed and he began to sing in still another of the endless varieties of the Sinatra style his version of "Lulu's Back in Town." The gangsters followed their scripts, nudging each other in approval, their knees bobbing to the rhythm. A few celebrants snapped their fingers. Doug nodded. I stared into my glass, at the melting ice and vodka-logged lime.

And I said to myself, *I'm never going to do this again.*

I finished my drink. It was the last one I ever had.

VI

DRY

One night I did hear a material car there, and saw its lights stop at his front steps. But I didn't investigate. Probably it was some final guest who had been away at the ends of the earth and didn't know that the party was over.

— F. Scott Fitzgerald, *The Great Gatsby*

1

I DIDN'T JOIN join Alcoholics Anonymous. I didn't seek out other help. I just stopped. My goal was provisional and modest: one month without drinking. For the first few weeks, this wasn't easy. I had to break the habits of a lifetime. But I did some mechanical things. I created a mantra for myself, saying over and over again, *I will live my life from now on, I will not perform it*. I began to type pages of private notes, reminding myself that writers were rememberers and I had already forgotten material for twenty novels. I urged myself to live in a state of complete consciousness, even when that meant pain or boredom.

The first weeks stretched into a month, and after thirty days, I already felt better physically. My hands stopped trembling. There were no more twitches in my legs or numbness in the morning. And the strange misspellings disappeared from my copy. I had a tremendous craving for sugar and began to eat more ice cream and candy than I had since moving away from Sanew's. In the mornings, I felt clear and fresh.

When the month was up, I set a deadline for a second month. I sat down and wrote my novella, *The Gift*, in one miraculous spurt, working day and night, removed from the world. The book was full of drinking and love for my father and the sweat poured out of me while I wrote. I thought of the book as my own gift to him, a declaration of his value that he could read while he was alive, and an explanation of myself to him and to me. Jason Epstein bought it for Random House. Another dry month went by, and now my mind was teeming with ideas and projects. I realized that for years I'd been squeezing my talent out of a toothpaste tube. I'd misused it and abused it and failed to replenish it with deep reading and full consciousness. I began to listen to music again. To Erroll Garner and Ben Webster. To Ray Charles and rock and roll. I was greedy for what I had missed.

Finally I tested myself at the Lion's Head, standing at the bar with the regulars. I didn't want to come among them with the zeal of a new convert. They knew I was off the sauce and smiled in a knowing way when I ordered a ginger ale. The smiles were understandable; a lot of people we knew had quit drinking before, and some of them were right there at the bar, belting down whiskey. But I had one major ally among the regulars: the bearded poet Joel Oppenheimer. A few months earlier, the doctors had ordered him to stop drinking and he'd followed their orders. He still smoked his Gauloises, still arrived each day in the afternoon, still looked lecherously at the young women. But he did it all on Coca-Cola. *You won't have as much fun*, Joel cautioned me. *But the fun will really be fun.*

The sensation of performance ebbed. I cared less about the way I appeared to others, prepared to be dismissed as a bore, no longer as quick, silly, or entertaining as I'd been in the past. But Joel laughed at my remarks; I laughed at his. It was the drunks who were the problem. I started hearing stories I'd heard many times before, or relatively new ones repeated four times in an evening. I was polite. I listened. I laughed at the punch lines. But I didn't drink.

Shirley was on the road, and I enjoyed staying in the house in Brooklyn, leaving the Lion's Head in the cold evenings, my eyes blurring from the wind, my lungs swelling with the fresh air. I liked reading myself to sleep a lot more than falling into a swollen stupor. When I was with my children at Easter — the months piling up now — they seemed to notice a difference. I took them to restaurants and they exchanged glances when I ordered ginger ale or club soda. They began asking me endless questions about American sports, American music, and American history. Adriene reminded me of the night I broke the door on Fourteenth Street and then gave them each a rose. She laughed. I felt a stab of pain. I never wanted to be drunk in their presence again.

There were some crucial tests. The first took place at the end of January, when Frank Crowther from the Lion's Head organized a huge party at the Four Seasons to celebrate Norman Mailer's fiftieth birthday. It was like a rush hour crowd in the A train, except that everybody was drinking or smoking joints or both. I put my back against a pole and watched the crowd eddy around me. Joe Flaherty. Jules Feiffer. Jack Lemmon. Hello. How are ya? What's doing? Editors, photographers, politicians. Whatta you hear? Need a drink? No, I'm on the wagon.

And then Mailer stood up in a spotlight to make a speech, squinting into the light, adopting his most belligerent stance. He was very drunk, holding a glass in his hand. He told a pointless joke about an Oriental cunt and then moved into some heavy metaphysical description of an organization or movement or cult that he was founding, called the Fifth Estate. He said it would monitor the multiple paranoid operations of the CIA. I remembered the way he drove me all the way to Manhattan from the 1964 convention in Atlantic City when Deirdre was born. And how kind he'd always been to me at prizefights and parties. Up there in the light, did Mailer feel that he was performing his life too? From the safe darkness of the crowd, people started shouting insults; others laughed; Mailer looked confused, exactly like an actor who was being hooted for a performance he thought was brilliant. Suddenly I wanted a drink. This was like bearbaiting. A friend was in trouble and there was nothing I could do about it except join him. I turned toward the bar and saw more laughing idiot faces. And said: No. Fuck it all, *no*. Not a drop. Not here. Not with these people. Never. I pushed my way through the crowd, found my coat, and went out to the street.

I walked for blocks, suddenly understanding clearly that another of the many reasons I drank was to blur the embarrassment I felt for my friends. If a friend was drunk and making an ass of himself, then I'd get drunk and make an ass of myself too. And there was some residue in me of the old codes of the Neighborhood, some deep adherence to the rules about never, ever rising above your station. Getting drunk was a way of saying I would never act uppity, never forget where I came from. No drunk, after all, could look down on others. Being drunk was the great leveler, a kind of Christian act of communion. Who could ever point the finger of harsh judgment at a drunk if we *all* were drunk? I'd do the same thing in the company of friends who thought they were failures and I was a success. Who could accuse me of snobbery, a big head, deserting my friends, if I was just another bum in the men's room throwing up on his shoes?

The second test was more dangerous. On May first, my father celebrated his seventieth birthday and we threw him a party. There were hams and pasta and chicken and cold cuts; cases of beer; bottles of whiskey and bowls of ice. With all the kids and cousins and the singing of songs, I was back in the dense sweet closed grip of family. And history. Irish history and my father's history. And mine. The party rolled on. The music played. I was laughing, singing, making plump sandwiches, and then, suddenly, I wanted a drink. My father was being urged into "My Auld Scalera Hat." Someone found a hat and he took it as his prop and his face was transformed, he was beaming and happy, his jet-black hair still as shining and young as it was back when I first saw him perform. I loved him; Jesus Christ, I loved him. But then I backed up, quiet, allowing him his moment on the stage. I was myself now, for better or worse. I was forever Billy Hamill's son, but I did not want to be the next edition of Billy Hamill. He had his life and I had mine. And if there were patterns, endless repetitions, cycles of family history, if my father was the result of his father and his father's father, on back through the generations into the Irish fogs, I could no longer accept any notion of predestination. Someone among the males of this family had to break the pattern. It might as well be me. I didn't have a drink.

Across those first months, I began to think that I only had to give up one drink: the next one. If I didn't have *that* drink, I'd never have another. If that was a trick, then the trick worked, most of the time. The rest of the time, I needed words. For years, I had interviewed politicians in bars. Now I suggested we go for a cup of coffee. Dinner parties were problems because I was always explaining myself.

No, I don't drink, thank you.

Not even *wine?*

Nothing, thanks.

But *why?*

I have no talent for it, I said.

Now I saw more clearly what drinking did to people. In Hollywood, I met old directors and forgotten screenwriters and unemployed actors: all broken by booze. I heard jokes about the Malibu AA, where there were eleven actors in one group and one driver's license. But I didn't laugh, felt no comfort in their humiliation. I remembered some of the final tortured stories by Scott Fitzgerald and felt surges of pity, for Fitzgerald, for the people I met, for my friends. I resisted pitying myself. I have stopped, I said to myself. If I begin again, I don't even deserve pity.

The temptation to begin again grew weaker and then, before the year was finished, disappeared. Somehow, I'd replaced the habit of drinking with the habit of nondrinking. I still visited bars, listened to the stories, remembered the few memorable remarks, but even the bartenders now began to pour a soda when I walked in. My own imagination helped me. I couldn't imagine enduring again the physical horrors of hangover. And I didn't ever want to spend a day lacerating myself over the social or personal crimes and misdemeanors I'd committed while drinking. No more apologies for stupid phone calls, asinine remarks, lapses in grace. I might still do such things, but I would do them with an unimpaired mind.

Now I had more time than I'd ever had as an adult. I had gained the time I once spent drinking and the time I needed for recovery. And I began writing as never before, studying the craft with a professional's forever unsatisfied standards. I had lived past the first rush of arrival, when raw talent can carry you across most barriers. Now I had to learn enough to last a lifetime. I'm still learning.

2

ONE JANUARY afternoon, after five sober years, I went for another walk in the snow. The children were home in the big house on Prospect Park West, and if I had not yet repaired some of the damage I'd inflicted on them and others, I was trying, I was trying. I wandered into the park, which was whitening under the heavy snowfall. And stood under a dense pine tree and then imagined figures coming down hills and across snowy meadows. Down there by the lake, Maureen Crowley was waiting for me on a bench. Over in the boathouse, Burne Hogarth was explaining trapezoids and Laura was in a blue smock, pulling heavy drags on a cigarette, while snow skirled like fog. In the snow, my mother was calling us home to dinner. Tim was there and Billy and Jake, all of us laughing, bellywhopping on Suicide Hill before heading for Boop's, and Jose was jogging down snowy roads, and Joel Oppenheimer was defiantly smoking his black tobacco cigarettes while snow gathered on his Mets cap. Beside the Swan Lake, the Tigers and the South Brooklyn Boys were gathering in some violent ritual of the tribe. Up on the hill beside the Quaker Cemetery, Bomba the Jungle Boy was waiting out the winter beside a fire in a cave.

Then I heard my father singing.

> *On the west coast of Ireland*
> *One morning there was seen . . .*

And I loved my life, with all its hurts and injuries and failures, and the things I now saw clearly, and the things I only remembered through the golden blur of drink. I reached down and took a great mound of fresh snow in my hands and began to eat. I was home. I was free. I'd leave the rest to Providence and Paddy McGinty's goat.